SCIENCE FICTION WRITING SERIES

Aliens and Alien Societies

Science Fiction **EDITED BY Ben Bova** Writing Series

Aliens AND Alien Societies

Stanley Schmidt

WRITER'S DIGEST BOOKS
Cincinnati, Ohio

This hardcover edition of *Aliens and Alien Societies* features a "self-jacket" that eliminates the need for a separate dust jacket. It provides sturdy protection for your book while it saves paper, trees and energy.

Other fine Writer's Digest Books are available from your local bookstore or direct from the publisher.

00 99 98 97 96   5 4 3 2 1

Library of Congress Cataloging-in-Publication Data

Schmidt, Stanley.
    Aliens and alien societies / Stanley Schmidt.
        p.   cm.—(Science fiction writing series)
    Includes bibliographical references and index.
    ISBN 0-89879-706-3 (alk. paper)
    1. Science fiction—Authorship. I. Title. II. Series.
PN3377.5.S3S24   1995
808.3'8762—dc20   95-25813
                                                                            CIP

Designed by Angela Lennert Wilcox
Cover illustration by Bob Eggleton

Ben Bova, the author of more than ninety futuristic novels and nonfiction books about science and high technology, is the six-time winner of the coveted Hugo Award for Best Professional Editor in the science fiction field. He has been editor of *Analog Science Fiction* and *Omni* magazines, and is the author of *The Craft of Writing Science Fiction That Sells*, published by Writer's Digest Books. Bova is President Emeritus of the National Space Society and a past president of Science Fiction and Fantasy Writers of America.

Dedication

To my mother,

who introduced me to the magic of storytelling.

ACKNOWLEDGMENTS

I have often thought that a book like this should exist, and I am grateful to Ben Bova and the folks at Writer's Digest Books for making it possible. Several people provided helpful input, including but not restricted to W.R. Thompson, G. David Nordley, Joan Slonczewski, Daniel Hatch and Robert R. Chase. I especially thank my wife, Joyce, for reading the manuscript and making valuable suggestions—and for her patience and support as the deadline drew nigh.

TABLE OF CONTENTS

CHAPTER 1

Why Write About Aliens?

A liens—nonhuman beings, usually intelligent and sentient, usually from places other than Earth—are one of the most familiar elements of science fiction. Even people who don't read science fiction have, in recent years, become well acquainted with quite a few of them through television shows and movies. "E.T." was the title character of one of the highest-grossing movies ever made; the *Star Wars* movies popularized wookies, Yoda and Jabba the Hut; *Star Trek* offered a steady parade of nonhuman life-forms, some of them as regular members of the cast.

Movies have been dealing with aliens for much longer, of course. Invasions of giant spiders and such have long been a staple of low-budget horror films, while occasionally a film would try something a bit more sophisticated, like the Martian invasion based on H.G. Wells's *War of the Worlds*. The same novel also inspired Orson Welles's 1938 radio broadcast that literally terrified thousands of listeners.

Printed science fiction has also featured a great many aliens, often with more care and finesse than they've usually received in the visual and broadcast media. Wells I've already mentioned; many others spring readily to mind—Stanley G. Weinbaum's Tweel (in "A Martian Odyssey"), for example, and the several varieties of Venusian who inhabited what Isaac Asimov called "the most perfect example of an alien ecology ever constructed" (in "Parasite Planet" and "The Lotus Eaters"), back in the early 1930s. The shape-changer in A.E. van Vogt's "Vault of the Beast" came along a few years later.

Some writers have made a specialty of creating fascinating, believable aliens, along with their cultures and the worlds that produced them. Hal Clement is famous for beings as diverse as the one in *Needle*, who takes up residence inside a human being, and the Mesklinites, adapted to a rapidly spinning world with extremely high gravity. Poul Anderson has created a wealth of worlds peopled with beings who clearly belong there. Some recent aliens hail from still more exotic locales, such as the neutron star in Robert L. Forward's *Dragon's Egg*.

Intelligent, sentient nonhumans have been an important element in human literature much longer than what we now know as science fiction. Gods, demons and talking animals appear in the most ancient mythologies. The folklores of many lands have produced elves, dragons and trolls that have persisted in some form into the written fantasy of today.

These beings clearly have a certain kinship to the aliens of science fiction, yet there are important differences as well. Those differences will constitute much of the subject of this book.

BASIC QUESTIONS

To get things started, let's consider these two questions:

1. What are "aliens"?
2. Why would anyone want to write about them?

For the moment, I will define aliens simply as nonhuman beings who can, to one degree or another, think, feel and act. You will immediately note a couple of things about that definition that will make us both want to put some additional limitations on it as we get deeper into the subject. First, it's awfully broad; second, its boundaries are rather fuzzy. As it stands, it could apply to virtually any nonhuman animal on Earth, as well as any that might exist elsewhere.

This is not necessarily a bad thing. When I was growing up, a book that exerted considerable influence on my later thinking was *Masked Prowler*, the biography of a raccoon, told from the raccoon's viewpoint. The world a raccoon lives in is sufficiently different from yours or mine to illustrate much of what I'll say about imagining and writing about aliens. So could many other Earthly species—especially if they turn out to be different from the way we've traditionally pictured them.

Quite a few animals have been doing just that in recent years, and at least one of the "aliens" I'll discuss later *is* something that we've long known lives right here on our own planet. For that matter, some "aliens" can be offshoots of humanity itself—isolated populations of human beings molded by alien circumstances into something quite different from what we're used to (such as the culture that *must* practice cannibalism in Donald Kingsbury's novel *Courtship Rite*). Contrary to the old saying, you *can* change human nature. If you change it enough, doubt can arise as to whether human or alien is the more apt term.

For the moment, let's allow the vagueness to stand and acknowledge that aliens could include raccoons and robots, gods and devils and humanity's own descendants, as easily as space travelers from other solar systems. Why would you want to write about any of these nonhuman beings, particularly if you believe, as William Faulkner once claimed, that, "The human heart in conflict with itself is the only subject worth writing about"?

As it happens, I don't agree with Faulkner. I'd modify his statement to say that the human heart in conflict with itself is one of many things worth writing about. But even writers who might agree completely with Faulkner have often written about nonhuman beings. One obvious reason for doing so is that such beings can act as a mirror for human foibles. In Aesop's fables, talking animals serve as stand-ins to model common human traits, implicitly inviting human readers to think about them without taking them personally.

In more modern, complex and sophisticated stories, such an approach might be useful if a writer wishes to get his readers to think about a theme so controversial in his own society that setting his story there would either get it banned or generate too much emotion to allow rational thought. As I write this, abortion is a good example of such a topic. It's being so hotly debated in real life that a contemporary novel about it is likely to make one set of readers applaud it (for echoing their own views) and another condemn it, while neither group does any real *thinking* about it. But if you create a believable alien society in which parallel problems arise naturally, a reader might think about them from a new perspective—and then recognize how his thoughts might apply to his own society's problems. Similarly, the relationships between the sexes are a highly charged area, so you might hold a mirror up to them by writing about beings whose relationships work differently, as Ursula K. Le Guin did in *The Left Hand of Darkness*. (The Gethenians have much in common with humans, but have a sexual cycle in which any individual may become sometimes male, sometimes female.)

One of the earliest reasons for telling stories about nonhuman beings was the widespread urge to explain natural phenomena. Peoples all over the world developed myths to explain things like storms and droughts and the very existence of the world and its peoples. Obviously somebody had to do these things that were beyond human capabilities, so they postulated gods and demons.

Many people today no longer feel the need for such anthropomorphic explanations. Science has provided a new set, based on the operations of natural laws that simply *are*, whether or not one believes in animate beings which are in some sense responsible for them. But far from destroying the urge to speculate about nonhuman and extraterrestrial beings, science has provided a new and powerful motivation. As we shall see later, those natural laws provide a new and uniquely compelling basis for suspecting that nonhuman intelligences and civilizations actually exist, and may even be common, elsewhere in the universe.

Human imaginations are mightily tickled by actual evidence that we are not alone in the universe. If there are other civilizations out there, what are they like? Are they a threat to us? Could they talk to us, or even visit? Why haven't they visited us already—or have they? Science fiction, aided by science, tries to imagine possible answers to such questions.

If they are out there, and if understanding natural law enables us to make educated guesses about what they may be like, aliens are no longer just a convenient literary device for holding a mirror to humanity. They are a real possibility, interesting in their own right. Some writers are drawn to aliens because they have glimpsed some of the possibilities and find it a fascinating intellectual and emotional exercise to try to imagine some of the kinds of aliens that might exist—and how they might someday interact with us.

Those same natural laws also suggest that *that* is a real possibility, and could happen at any time. If so, it would be a good idea to have thought about the possible ramifications before we are faced with the urgent need to minimize the dangers and maximize the opportunities in such a contact.

POTENTIAL STARTING POINTS

The relatively recent desire to speculate scientifically on the possible nature of aliens and alien worlds is a new reason for writing about them, but it does not replace the older reasons. A writer may still wish to set up a "thought experiment" to model some problem of human relationships—but now he may simultaneously seek to make those aliens believable and intrinsically interesting. His primary interest and emphasis may be on either aspect, or he may strive to give equal attention to both. And either may come first in the development of the story.

Sometimes, as in the case of Hal Clement's Mesklinites or Robert L. Forward's neutron star dwellers, the germ of the story lies in an author's recognition that a certain type of world can exist. Thinking about its physical characteristics suggests things about how life might develop there, for the kinds of life that can evolve in a place are strongly shaped by the conditions that prevail there. The way life develops in turn shapes the way civilization develops—and the kinds of stories that can take place there. A writer with a strong interest in world-building may start by creating an interesting world, letting life and civilization develop there, and letting its natural beings generate a plot.

Another writer might start instead with a general idea of a story line that requires aliens with certain general characteristics, and fill in the outline enough to make the story "feel real." Sometimes, if that's what you're doing, you can get by with relatively little attention to the scientific background—but the result will probably feel less real. The writing is, at least in my opinion, also more fun that way. The factors that shape ecologies and civilizations are fascinating, and one of the pleasures of writing science fiction is that it gives you a good excuse to dabble in a wide range of fields.

But there's one more compelling reason to take a close look at how your aliens work and how they got that way. The better you understand them, the more likely it is that the things you learn in working out their background will suggest aspects of your plot that you wouldn't have thought of otherwise—and that are better than you would have thought of otherwise.

I might humbly offer an example from my own experience. (Author's note: I will sometimes use my own stories as examples of how a story developed. It's not that I have any specially high regard for my own stories, but simply that I can speak with much more

authority about how they were created than about anybody else's!)
My first novel, *The Sins of the Fathers*, grew out of two main ideas:

1. Entire galactic cores sometimes explode in a way that would
   make planets uninhabitable throughout the galaxy. Our galaxy could have suffered such a catastrophe at any time in
   the last 30,000 years, and we wouldn't know it until the first
   radiation reached us.
2. If the Earth were about to become uninhabitable and aliens
   offered to rescue us, should we accept their offer?

Ben Bova, the first editor I approached with the idea (and who
eventually bought it), pointed out in our first meeting that a key
question was going to be, "Why are they making this offer?" To
answer that, I had to come up with believable motivations—believable, that is, in terms of the aliens' psychology. That required me
to get to know how their psychology worked, and since their psychology was shaped by their evolution and history, I had to think
about those. Furthermore, since the galactic core is a long way
from Earth, I needed to know what kind of technology they were
using that could let them get here in time to give us advance warning. Then I had to work out the detailed chronology of the events
leading up to that story. At one point in that process I was horrified
to discover a 30,000-year discrepancy in the chronology—so I invented some new physics to account for it. The implications of that
new physics wound up generating some of the best parts of the
story.

Every time I figured out an answer to a background question
that had to be this way or that, it forced the story in directions that
I could never have anticipated otherwise. And the end result was a
far stronger story than I had originally expected to write.

GOALS OF THIS BOOK

If you're reading this book, I assume that you are interested in
writing science fiction and would sometimes like to use aliens in
your stories, for one or more of the reasons I've mentioned (or
perhaps others that I haven't). I further assume that you don't want
to write about just any aliens, but would like yours to be believable
and memorable. This book is intended as a guide to help you do
that.

It is *not* intended to be a comprehensive compilation of everything you might ever need to know to create and write well about aliens. I've already hinted that writing science fiction will likely lead you into corners of the library you never expected to visit. (In one morning of editing, I once found myself writing to authors about mountain climbing techniques, the physics of atmospheres, grammatical details in Jamaican dialect and the construction and playing of tubas!) What I *will* try to provide is a good guide to the principles involved—the kinds of things that you will have to think about as a matter of course when creating *any* aliens. Once you have created your aliens, some special problems may arise in telling their story, and I will also try to provide some assistance with those. In connection with both creating and writing, I will direct you to some good examples of what has worked for other writers and reference sources to which you might go when you need more help or more detail on a particular subject. (The "Xenologist's Bookshelf" at the end of the book provides bibliographic information to help you locate all references cited.)

Finally, I should emphasize right up front that this book will, for the most part, limit itself to more or less plausible aliens. Or, to put it another way, I am addressing my comments to readers who are interested in writing science fiction rather than fantasy. You may think that science fiction and fantasy are more or less equivalent—for which you can hardly be blamed, since in recent years there has been a sneaky movement afoot to treat them as interchangeable. There is, in fact, a somewhat fuzzy boundary between them with some room for debate about where the boundary lies and on which side of it some works fall. But, as an astute observer of human foibles once observed, "The fact that there's twilight doesn't mean you can't tell the difference between night and day."

In this book, a fundamental assumption will be that there *is* an important difference between stories that are clearly science fiction and those that are clearly fantasy. We will be primarily concerned with the former. Science fiction writers try to deal with things that are, or can be made to seem, plausible. For the particular purposes of this book, that means one of our first concerns will be to make our aliens and their societies plausible.

And that, of course, leads us directly to that big, fundamental, and somewhat thorny question: What *is* plausible?

CHAPTER 2

What Is Plausible?

The Difference Between SF and Fantasy

What does it mean to say that science fiction tries to make its speculations plausible while fantasy does not? Basically, fantasy writers don't expect you to believe that the things they're describing could actually happen, but only to *pretend* that they could for the duration of a story. Fantasy readers understand that and willingly play along. Science fiction writers, on the other hand, try to create worlds and futures (and aliens) that really *could* exist and do the things they describe. Their readers expect that of them, and write critical letters to editors and authors when they find holes in the logic (or the assumptions) that would make a science fiction story impossible.

This may sound like a rather snooty claim of superiority for science fiction and a denigration of fantasy, but it isn't. They are simply two different games. I enjoy both, when they're well played—but I think it's important to understand the difference between them and keep in mind which game is being played in any particular story. My objection to seeing science fiction awards given to fantasy stories, or vice versa, is much like the objection a sports fan might have to seeing a major baseball award given to a football player.

Often the same basic story material can be treated as *either* science fiction or fantasy, depending on how the writer approaches it. For example, the old fable of "The Goose That Laid the Golden Eggs" is fantasy because real geese don't lay golden eggs and the story makes no attempt to convince you they could. It merely asks you to consider what might happen *if* one did. Isaac Asimov's short story "Pâté de Foie Gras" takes this basic idea and turns it into science fiction by postulating a biochemical mechanism by which it could happen. He tells enough about that mechanism so that readers can judge for themselves whether it might actually work.

Both science fiction and fantasy commonly deal with things that would seem, at first glance, to be impossible. The difference is that science fiction attempts to imagine ways they could actually happen. Fantasy is fun; but for some readers, at least, there's something extra special about a story that not only stretches the imagination, but just might be a real possibility.

How science fiction creates this additional level of "suspension of disbelief" depends on the nature of the speculation. Sometimes it uses ideas that may seem far-out to a layman who doesn't follow developments in science and technology, but are clearly based on well-established principles easily recognizable to someone who does follow such developments. An example would be almost any story written in the forties about space travel. Even in the fifties, when I was growing up and Sputnik I was on the verge of departure, many adults of my acquaintance considered spaceflight impossible. But readers of science magazines like *Astounding* and novels like those of Robert A. Heinlein and Arthur C. Clarke had long known that the possibility was clear, and only engineering problems stood in the way.

A science fiction writer will often work into the story enough explanation (an art in itself!) so the reader can see why he should see something as a real possibility, however remote, rather than a blatant impossibility. Sometimes, of course, she can only hint at it. Anne McCaffrey's *Dragonflight* is often mistaken for fantasy in part because there is very little explanation of what the Threads (an infestation that periodically falls from the sky) are, where they come from and how. None of the characters in the story are in a position to know these things, so most of what they say, think and do about the Threads sounds more like folklore than science. However, they stumble onto just enough hints, in the form of fragmentary old records, to show that the author did her homework—and to enable a moderately knowledgeable reader to figure out the broad outlines of the explanation: The Threads are organisms whose spores periodically cross space from another planet of the system.

Some phenomena postulated in science fiction may appear particularly impossible to a reader who *is* familiar with current science and technology. Examples include faster-than-light travel, time travel, telepathy and the telekinesis of Anne McCaffrey's dragons. Physics as we now know it provides no clear mechanism for such things, and in fact provides some reason to doubt they can happen. But our knowledge of real science is not fixed and immutable. We now do things in everyday life (such as writing this book on a powerful computer that sits on an old typewriter table in my home office) that would have seemed at best highly unlikely just a few decades ago. Some physicists have lately even begun speculating on ways that things like faster-than-light travel and time machines *might* be possible! (See, for example, the Cramer and Donaldson articles in the References.)

If you do use things that appear to be forbidden by the scientific principles accepted at the time you're writing, you need to be aware that you're doing it. If you want your reader to accept it as a real possibility, you have to assume (and implicitly invite him or her to assume) that some new scientific principles have been discovered between now and the time your story takes place. This might very well happen; scientific worldviews have been revolutionized several times in this century alone, by such concepts as relativity, quantum mechanics, the double helix of DNA and plate tectonics. But if you make such an assumption and you want to be convincing about it, you need to formulate your new principles in such a way that they don't contradict the old ones *in the areas for which we already have data.* And you need to work out the logical implications of your new assumptions—which quite often, as in *The Sins of the Fathers*, will turn out to generate important parts of your story.

That may sound a bit intimidating if you don't think your grasp of science is up to doing such things. It isn't really as fearsome as it sounds; you don't necessarily have to be a professional scientist to do a good job on the scientific aspects of science fiction. First, many forms of space travel, time travel, etc., have become so familiar that science fiction readers no longer need to be convinced of their basic possibility. Many writers who aren't that interested in the mechanisms *per se* merely adopt one of the general forms that have become widely accepted, and use it as needed to tell their story. Second, there are ways to learn what you need for a story (and doing so is an important part of the job).

I'll say more about these matters in the last chapter. For now, let's just say that anything that can't be rigorously proved *impossible* with current knowledge is fair game for science fiction. In general, if it *appears* to be impossible, you'll strengthen your credibility by providing some sort of explanation. Whether you're dealing with the clearly possible as already foreseen by present science, or the farther-out that goes beyond present science, you need to know at least the basics of what present science says. So we'll concentrate on that for the next several chapters.

KNOWING YOUR SCIENCES

There's a great deal of evidence that the laws of nature are the same throughout the universe. This fact enables us to make reasonable guesses about what sorts of things might exist in other parts of it. We would not expect, for example, to find civilizations growing in atmospheres consisting principally of hydrogen and oxygen. The laws of chemistry make such an atmosphere too unstable to exist, on Earth or anywhere else. Nor would we expect to find real counterparts of that hoary old cliché of monster movies, giant spiders exactly like Earthly tarantulas but a hundred times larger. A really determined science fiction writer could concoct plausible aliens that superficially looked somewhat like big spiders, but inside, they would have to be very different.

Later in this book we shall look in more detail at why such statements can be made. To be able to do that, we'll have to survey some of the basic principles of several sciences. In doing that, you may be surprised and impressed to discover just how interrelated all the sciences are.

In school, you may have gotten the impression, since chemistry class was in one room and physics in another and biology in still another, that each science is a separate little box of knowledge having little connection to the others. Nothing could be further from the truth, and nowhere is this more apparent than in trying to imagine what kinds of worlds and life-forms might exist.

Physics is the foundation; a few brief principles govern everything that happens in the physical universe. (This doesn't mean it's trivial, of course; understanding just what those few principles mean and working out all their implications is far more than the work of a single lifetime! On the other hand, adults who claim to know nothing of physics are magnificently mistaken. They may not know the academic formalisms of physics, but organisms who don't understand many of the principles don't survive to adulthood!)

Some of the implications of physics are astronomy and chemistry. Given the fundamental nature of matter, energy and how they interact, it becomes inevitable that elementary particles will form into atoms that behave in certain ways, including combining into molecules and crystals with the qualities we call chemical properties. It is similarly inevitable that large aggregates of matter will collect and turn into things like stars, planets and galaxies, which show certain kinds of behavior both individually and collectively.

In some of those concentrations of matter, chemical reactions may become very complex, leading to the special kinds of things we call life. Exactly how that happens is shaped by the laws of chemistry, which are in turn shaped by those of physics. Once life is established on a planet, it is very much shaped by astronomy. The kinds of life that *can* evolve on a planet like Earth are very different from those that might be found, say, on Jupiter.

As a simple but dramatic example of how true this is—how completely our astronomical background shapes and permeates every aspect of our lives—consider the Earth's axial tilt. Earth is, of course, the only planet whose life-forms most readers of this book have any firsthand knowledge of. An astronomer might describe the general nature of the Earth by specifying such numbers as its mass, its average radius, how far it is from what kind of a Sun, and so on. One of those numbers is the axial tilt. That's the angle by which the planet's axis of rotation is tilted from the perpendicular to the plane of its orbit. (If that sounds frighteningly technical, don't worry about it. I'll explain in more detail, with pictures, in the next chapter.)

Stated in such dry terms, axial tilt may sound like a very academic concept of concern only to astronomers. In fact, it's of fundamental importance to everyone and everything that lives on this planet. If you changed it from its real value of 23.5° to, say, 0.2°, *virtually the entire body of human literature would have to be rewritten*—not trivially, but radically. Why? Because seasons—winter, spring, summer and fall in temperate zones; wet and dry seasons in the tropics—pervade virtually everything about human life. And that 23.5° axial tilt is the main reason for the existence and nature of seasons, and for the existence of tropical, temperate and arctic regions.

With other things being equal and axial tilt reduced to essentially nothing, seasonal variations and everything that depends on them are also reduced to essentially nothing. "The winter of our discontent ...," "The flowers that bloom in the spring ...," and "The good old summertime ..." are all meaningless phrases to beings who *have* no winter, spring or summer. Plots that depend on enduring a hard winter, or hoping the rains come in time to save the crops, would neither happen nor be intelligible on a world that has no seasons because it has no axial tilt. Human literature is just full of things that are shaped, explicitly or implicitly, by the fact that Earth has seasons. If you make the axial tilt appreciably less (or more) than it is, *all* those things will be very different.

It is possible to imagine alien life-forms and intelligences that don't evolve or live on planets at all. Such things could conceivably arise on neutron stars or in interstellar space itself, though they would necessarily be very different from us. We will look a little closer at such possibilities in a later chapter; but for most of this book we will be most interested in intelligences that arose more or less as we did, on planets.

HUMOR: A SPECIAL CASE?

You can't judge a caricature by the same standards as a photograph. A caricature deliberately distorts and exaggerates reality, sometimes just to be funny and sometimes to make a point about reality by calling attention to a particular aspect of it.

A similar relationship exists between humor—especially farce and satire—and "serious" writing. In a predominantly serious story, you will want to create a convincing illusion of reality—the feeling that what the reader is reading could really happen. If one of your main goals is to be funny, you may not want to do that. Funny things happen in real life, but seldom in such concentrated sequences as in a good piece of comedy. Humor usually depends on exaggerating or distorting reality to some extent. Does that mean that the usual requirements for plausibility don't apply to humorous science fiction, and anything goes?

Not exactly. It doesn't mean you can get away with *anything*, but it does mean you can get away with more than in a straight story. The aliens in Poul Anderson's "Peek! I See You" or Grey Rollins's "Victor" stories are pretty unlikely sorts. Victor resembles an upright three-foot sausage with stubby legs, a single eye, a "voice" system operating like a loudspeaker and capable of imitating any sound from a mouse to a symphony orchestra, a *long* prehensile tongue, and a taste for well-aged garbage. If you met him in a story of solemn tone, you might wonder how such an improbable critter could have evolved. But when the author is obviously not taking himself too seriously, you might go along with him and enjoy the ride. Victor isn't *impossible*, just unlikely. If you find the story amusing enough, you may be willing to accept his existence and not press the question of how he got that way.

In other words, readers are more tolerant of the improbable in humorous stories than in serious ones—but they'll still balk at the impossible. And the more improbable it is, the funnier it had better be. Just plain wrong science, especially if it doesn't have to be wrong for the sake of the story or the joke, simply turns readers off. Sound simply doesn't travel in a vacuum, and science fiction readers won't go along with a joke that requires them to believe that it does. If you're telling a funny story of aliens that doesn't depend crucially on where they're from, don't say they came from a planet or star system that is not likely to produce life. Use one that could, or simply make up a name.

In general, the less stretching or distorting you have to do the better. Stretch only the points that directly contribute to the humorous effect. You'll probably find that you actually enhance that if you make the rest of the background as solid as you can, and avoid including a lot of unnecessary detail.

CHAPTER 3

Astronomical Basics

To speculate intelligently about what kinds of life can arise on planets, you must first understand something about what kinds of planets can exist. Since we have firsthand knowledge of very few of them, and all of those are "siblings," our speculations must be guided by what we think we understand about how planets form.

Planets, like people, are born, develop and die. So do stars, galaxies and the universe as a whole. In fact, all kinds of natural evolution can be considered stages of a single process on a grand scale. The primordial universe evolved into the one we know. As part of that process, galaxies were produced. Galaxy formation leads to the formation of stars. Stars (at least sometimes) produce planets as a by-product. As planets evolve, the process can sometimes go as far as the creation of life. And so on.

All this takes place on such a time scale that no human being has had a chance to observe it directly. So how do we know it happens? Well, we don't absolutely know exactly how it happens. What we have is a set of models—theoretical pictures of what seem the most likely mechanisms by which the universe we see could arise from the action of known physical laws. That picture has been built up over many years by many scientists collecting detailed observations of What's Out There and deducing from those observations and physical laws How It Probably Got That Way.

I.S. Shklovskii and Carl Sagan drew a delightful analogy (in *Intelligent Life in the Universe*) to show the task astronomers face. Imagine an alien making a brief visit to Earth, looking around at all the various shapes and sizes of human beings. He doesn't have time to see any human being change appreciably, but he wants to figure out how the various types are related, how they're produced, how they change with time (do big ones turn into little ones, or vice versa?) and what ultimately becomes of them. In other words, he wants to figure out the human life cycle, with no data except a quick look at a bunch of specimens in various stages of that cycle.

That's what astronomers, astrophysicists and cosmologists are up against. They get essentially static glimpses of a whole lot of stars, usually clumped into galaxies and sometimes accompanied by planets, and they would like to figure out how all those things evolve. They know that they *must* evolve, because every star is full of violent physical processes that cannot leave it unchanged. But how do they change? And how do we know?

In this book I will not have room to explain in detail how our current picture of the universe was built up. As a science fiction writer, you might not want to wade through that much background anyway. What you will need is a summary of what that current picture is—the current consensus of scientists about what principles govern the universe, and about how those principles operate to form the stellar menagerie we see (and inhabit). That is what I shall attempt to give.

However, even as a science fiction writer, you may find it worthwhile to explore the methodology of science in more detail, if only because you may find good story ideas there. Contrary to popular belief, science is *not* cut and dried, fixed and immutable. Our picture of the universe has been built up, however meticulously, by human beings with imperfect data that they've had to interpret. Sometimes that picture must be changed, because somebody finds a new datum that doesn't fit, or a new interpretation that works better than one that has become generally accepted. So it may pay you, as a science fiction writer, to know where and how these interpretive jumps have been made. You just might be able to think of an alternative that could be possible, and that could be the foundation of a good story.

TOOLS OF THE TRADE

You will need to know at least the basics of how astronomers collect data about stars and planets—partly because some of the descriptive picture is only understandable in terms of the observational methods used to assemble it, and partly because some of your characters may have to use those same methods in your stories. If you have a shipful of human explorers debating whether to try to land on a particular planet, they'll have to learn as much as they can about it from a distance. And you'll have to talk, at least superficially, about how they do it.

Telescopes

Until recently, essentially everything we knew about stars and planets was obtained by looking at them through *telescopes* on the surface of the Earth. Basically, a telescope is some combination of lenses and/or mirrors that forms an image of what it's pointed at. Sometimes that image is observed directly, but for serious astronomy it's more often recorded on a photographic plate. A popular misconception about telescopes is that their main purpose is to *magnify* the image. They do that, and it's important for close-up subjects like the Moon and the planets in our own Solar System; but their most important purpose in astronomy is to gather as much light as possible. Astronomers have been known to refer irreverently to a particularly large and expensive telescope as "a good light bucket."

With the exception of our own Sun, or Sol (I will often use lower-case "sun" to mean the star around which *any* planet revolves), all the stars are so far away that their images remain mere pinpoints, not visible disks, even under the highest magnification we can muster with Earthly telescopes. Any planets that might accompany them would be completely invisible. What a telescope can do for a star is make its image much brighter. That's important because those great distances also mean most starlight is very faint. The vast majority of stars in the sky are invisible to the naked eye—even out in the country where on a clear night you might see a couple of thousand instead of two or three, which might be all you can manage in a big city.

The stars we can see with the naked eye are a very small sample of the ones that are out there, and not a truly representative sampling. To be visible from here, they must be relatively close or unusually bright. Most of the ones that look brightest—the ones with well-known names like Sirius, Betelgeuse or Antares—are both intrinsically bright and close. For reasons that you'll soon see, intrinsically bright stars are among the least likely prospects to have life-bearing planets, so "aliens from Antares" are another

SCIENTIFIC NOTATION AND UNITS

Scientists, especially physicists and astronomers, often need to deal with quantities so large or small that ordinary numbers are impractical for writing them. To avoid the awkwardness of writing things like 3,121,000,000,000,000 or 0.0000000000096, they use *scientific notation*, in which any number is written as the product of an "ordinary" number, usually between 1 and 10, and 10 raised to some power. "10 to the nth power" means "10 multiplied by itself n times" and is usually written "10^n." For example $100 = 10^2$; $10,000 = 10^4$, and so on. 10 itself is 10^1.

Multiplication of different powers of the same number (or *base*) is easy: You just add exponents. Thus, $10^2 \times 10^4 = 10^6$. To divide, you subtract exponents: $10^6 \div 10^4 = 10^2$. Those rules show you the meaning of negative exponents: $10^4 \div 10^6 = 10^{-2} = 0.01$. Thus the long, hard-to-read numbers in the previous paragraph are written more compactly and clearly as 3.121×10^{15} and 9.6×10^{-12}.

For measurement, scientists generally use metric units—either mks (meters, kilograms and seconds) or cgs (centimeters, grams and seconds). In this book, I will usually follow that practice and assume that you learned the metric system in school; if not, look it up! However, since many of my readers are Americans and are not as comfortable with metric measurement as they should be, I will also occasionally use English units, particularly if I'm trying to convey a vivid mental picture of something.

There are also a few special units in common use among astronomers and spectroscopists. Wavelengths (see figure 3-1), especially those in the parts of the spectrum containing infrared, visible light, ultraviolet and X-rays, are often expressed in *Angström units* (1 Å $= 10^{-8}$ cm $= 10^{-10}$ m).

Distances within the Solar System are sometimes expressed in *astronomical units* (1 AU = the mean radius of the Earth's orbit). By extension, in talking about other planetary systems, we will often take many quantities associated with the Earth and Sun and their relationship (such as mass, orbital radius and year length) to be numerically equal to 1. As you'll see in the section "A World-Building Primer," this has the advantage of easily giving direct comparisons of other planets to ours.

Larger distances, such as those between stars, are often measured with one of two special units. A *light-year* is the distance light travels in one of Earth's years. Since the speed of light (often called *c*) is very close to 3×10^8 m/sec, or 186,000 mi/sec, a light-year is about 9.46×10^{15} meters, or 5.87×10^{12} miles.

Parsec (abbreviated "pc") is shorthand for *parallax second*. It's based on the simplest method for measuring distances, namely looking at it from two viewpoints and measuring the angle between the two lines of sight. That's the method you use all the time when you're awake: Your brain measures the angle between the lines of sight as your two eyes look at the same object. The principle of astronomical parallax measurements is the same, but the two viewpoints, instead of two eyes, are different points in the Earth's orbit around the Sun. A parsec is equivalent to 3.26 light-years. (Note carefully: light-years and parsecs are *always* measures of *distance*. They are *never* units of time, and using them as if they were is a sure sign of an unprepared or careless science fiction writer!)

Temperatures are measured in degrees *Celsius* (C) or degrees *Kelvin* (K). Both scales use the same size degree (1.8 degrees Fahrenheit), but the zero points are different. 0 C is the freezing point of water, and absolute zero (the lowest possible [or almost-possible] temperature) is -273 C. 0 K is absolute zero and water freezes at +273 K. The difference between the two scales is obviously important when talking about planetary surfaces, but is often of little consequence for stars, where temperatures are at least 3000 on either scale.

almost-sure giveaway for a writer who hasn't done his homework.

Since light gets "less bright" with distance by spreading its energy over a larger area, the easiest way to get a bright image of a very distant object like a star is to gather as much of its light as you can and focus it all into the image. That is the main function of a telescope, and the reason why, other things being equal, bigger is better in the telescope business. Light from, say, Deneb, arrives

STAR BRIGHTNESSES AND MAGNITUDES

Brightnesses of stars are expressed as *magnitudes*. Historically, the brightest stars in the sky were described as being of "first magnitude." Somewhat less bright stars were called "second magnitude," and so on. When it became feasible to measure the brightness of stars quantitatively, those terms became associated with precise numerical brightnesses, and it also became possible to have fractional magnitudes like 1.6.

Technically, the magnitude scale is logarithmic, but you usually won't need to be concerned about that. The essential points are that 1. the smaller the magnitude, the brighter the star; and 2. a *difference* of one magnitude is equivalent to a brightness *ratio* of 2.512 (the fifth root of 100). Thus a star of magnitude 1.3 is 2.512 times as bright (i.e., it gives us 2.512 times as much light) as one of magnitude 2.3, and 100 times as bright as one of magnitude 6.3. You can also have negative magnitudes. A star 100 times as bright as that 1.3 would have magnitude $1.3 - 5 = -3.7$. (An ironic side effect of making the scale quantitative is that the brightest star in our sky, Sirius, is no longer magnitude 1, but magnitude -1.6.)

Under good conditions, our unaided eyes can see stars from negative magnitudes down to about $+6$. These are *apparent magnitudes*, measuring brightness as seen by us, and depend on both the star's intrinsic brightness and its distance from us. Light follows an "inverse square law": its intensity (amount of energy delivered to a standard area in a standard time) is inversely proportional to the distance from the source. For example, if you point a light meter at a candle in an otherwise dark room from one foot away, and then from ten feet away, the amount of light you measure at ten feet will be $\frac{1}{100}$ of what it was at one foot. The explanation is simple. A candle (or star) emits a certain amount of light energy every second, and as it travels outward from the source that amount of energy is spread out over an evergrowing spherical surface, whose area is proportional to the square of its radius.

To compare the *intrinsic* brightnesses of stars, they are expressed as *absolute magnitudes*. The absolute magnitude is the apparent magnitude the star would have if viewed at a standard distance. That distance is chosen to be ten parsecs.

with equal intensity (energy per unit area per unit time) all over the Earth. The brightness of the image formed by a telescope is determined by the total energy brought to focus, and that is simply the intensity times the area of the main lens or mirror (the objective) of a telescope. A fully open human eye typically gathers light from a circular area about 6 mm in diameter, so a 50 mm binocular or telescope objective (as on 7 × 50 binoculars) gives you an image about 70 times as bright as you can see without it. The two-hundred-inch telescope at Mt. Palomar gives you a brightness advantage of more than 700,000 times—or about fourteen magnitudes. In other words, it lets you see stars down to magnitude twenty or so, instead of six. (That's assuming direct visual observation, which professional astronomers seldom use. They actually get an even bigger advantage, and see even more otherwise invisible stars, by recording their images with long exposures on sensitive photographic plates or films.)

Spectroscopes

Just as important as the telescope is another instrument often used in conjunction with it: the *spectroscope*. Light is a form of electromagnetic radiation, a kind of wave produced whenever electrical charges vibrate (see figure 3-1). The light from a real source, such as a hot campfire or a distant star, usually contains a mixture of wavelengths (or, equivalently, frequencies). The job of the spectroscope is to tell you how much light the source is producing at each wavelength.

Why is that important? Since we can't form an image big enough to show pictorial detail for most stars, spectroscopy is the source of most of the detailed information we have about them—and that turns out to be quite a lot. First, hot bodies radiate their energy with a characteristic distribution over wavelengths (a "continuous spectrum" including some energy at all wavelengths over a broad range) whose detailed shape depends on temperature. (See figure 3-2.) In general, a hot body radiates at all wavelengths, but not equally. The hotter the radiator, the shorter the wavelength of maximum intensity. Since the longest visible waves are red and the shortest are violet, this means that as you heat an object, at first it doesn't glow at all, because all the waves it emits are longer than we can see. When it gets hot enough, it begins to glow red, at first dimly, then more brightly. As you continue to heat it, the glow

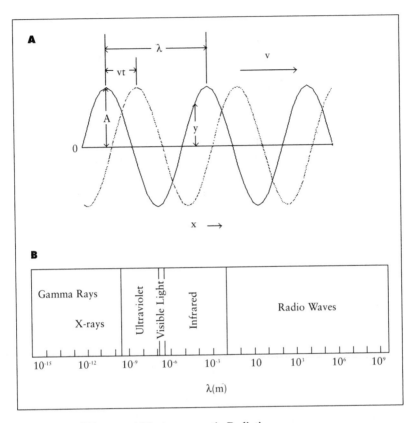

FIGURE 3-1 Waves and Electromagnetic Radiation.

A Any wave can be thought of as a pattern of disturbance traveling through a medium. This sketch could be an instantaneous side view of a wave traveling through water whose undisturbed surface is the horizontal line labeled 0. At any position x, the surface is displaced up or down by a distance y; the maximum displacement is the *amplitude*, A. The entire wave is traveling to the right at speed v, so if the solid curve shows the surface at one instant, a time t later it looks like the dotted curve—that is, the entire pattern has moved to the right a distance v. The distance between successive crests (high points) or low points (troughs) is the *wavelength*, λ. If you watch any point on the surface, it oscillates up and down between y = A and y = -A; the number of oscillations per second is the *frequency* (f). (Oscillations per second used to be sensibly called "cycles/second"; now, for reasons that baffle the author, it's usually called by the far less informative name "hertz.") The velocity of propagation of a wave is related to its frequency and wavelength by v = fλ.

B In an electromagnetic wave, the kind of most interest to astronomers, the "medium" can be empty space and the "disturbance" is an electric or magnetic field at right angles to the direction the wave is traveling. In empty space, v for electromagnetic waves (or radiation) is c $= 3 \times 10^8$ m/sec. Their wavelengths and frequencies cover an extremely wide range, commonly divided into several regions called by different names and studied with different kinds of instruments. The diagram shows the approximate ranges of wavelength designated by each of the common names. Note that visible light, as defined by humans, is a very small part of the total. Note also that gamma rays and X-rays overlap in wavelength; the terms refer less to wavelength than to how they're produced. In general, X-rays are produced in atomic (electron) transitions and gammas in nuclear or subnuclear.

becomes more yellowish, then white as the broad peak of the spectrum moves across the middle of the visible range, and finally bluish as the peak moves left of the visible range and the visible intensities in the spectrum decrease from the violet end toward the red. This observation applies directly to stars: The hottest stars look bluish and the coolest reddish.

A second important application of spectroscopy comes from the fact that when light passes through matter, some of it is absorbed. The absorption spectrum is discrete rather than continuous—that is, light is strongly absorbed only at certain sharply defined wavelengths. Which wavelengths are absorbed depends on the material doing the absorbing. Each element or compound has an absorption spectrum determined by its atomic or molecular structure, and therefore is as distinctive as a fingerprint. This is our main way of learning about the chemical composition of stars and planetary atmospheres. Most of the light we see from a star is produced by the hottest layers, and as it passes through cooler layers farther out, absorption lines are superimposed on the continuous hot-body spectrum. By comparing the absorption wavelengths with those characteristic of various substances, astronomers can identify chemical constituents of the cooler layers.

Sometimes the absorption lines in a star's spectrum don't exactly match those of known chemicals—unless you correct them for *Doppler effect*. That leads to a third important use of spectroscopy. Doppler effect is an apparent change in frequency and wavelength caused by motion of the source toward or away from the observer. You can get a cheap, easy demonstration by standing near a railroad crossing as a train approaches and passes while blowing its whistle.

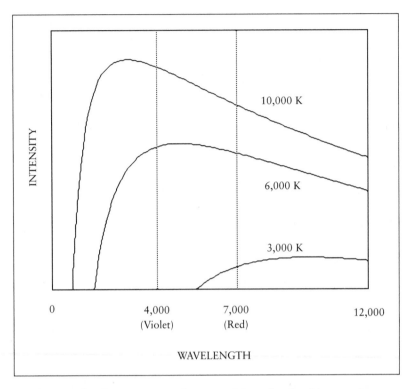

FIGURE 3-2 Continuous spectra for stars of three "surface" temperatures: 3,000 K, 6,000 K and 10,000 K.

Since the train is initially moving toward you, the sound waves are "squeezed together" in front of it so that you perceive them as closer together (shorter wavelength) and arriving more often (higher frequency) than if the train were stationary. When the train is moving away from you, the opposite happens. So as the engineer sounds what *he* hears as a steady pitch, *you* hear it start out high and then drop as the train approaches and passes.

A stellar spectrum will often match a set of known chemical spectra *if* you assume that all the lines have been Doppler-shifted up or down because the star is moving toward or away from you at a certain speed. Such observations indicate that most galaxies are moving *away* from us (their light is shifted toward longer wavelengths, or "red-shifted"); and the farther away they are, the faster they're moving (and vice versa). This observation, known as Hubble's law, is one of the foundations of any cosmology (theory of the universe). At the other extreme, the Doppler effect can provide information at a much finer level of detail. If a star is rotating around an axis perpendicular to your line of sight, one side of it is moving toward you, one side away from you, and the middle part simply moves across your line of sight. Thus some of its light shows no Doppler shift, some is red-shifted by various amounts, and some is blue-shifted. The net result is that all its spectral lines are broadened, and the amount of broadening can be used to estimate how fast the star is rotating.

Other Sources of Data

The last few decades, and especially the last few years, have brought some dramatic additions to the astronomers' bag of tricks. First, visible light is not the only kind of radiation stars emit. Electromagnetic radiation ranges from gamma rays with wavelengths as short as 10^{-15} m, through X-rays, ultraviolet, visible light, infrared and radio waves, some with wavelengths of many kilometers. Out of that entire range, equivalent to many octaves of musical pitch, the unaided eye can see less than one octave. (For comparison, we hear about ten.)

Astronomical observations are now made in all parts of the electromagnetic spectrum, and each tells astronomers things that the other parts can't. The equipment for observations in different parts of the spectrum looks very different. One of the best-known radio telescopes, for example, is the "dish" at Arecibo, which is built into a bowl-like valley in the mountains of Puerto Rico.

Second (and third, and well beyond), our newfound capability for traveling or sending instruments into space has completely revolutionized astronomical fact-finding. As somebody said at least a decade ago, "Astronomy has changed more in the last ten years than in the previous four hundred."

Telescopes and spectroscopes on Earth have always been plagued by clouds, haze, atmospheric turbulence, dust, industrial pollution and stray light from cities and towns. All of those problems can be eliminated if you put your instruments outside the atmosphere. Thus, despite its early problems, the Hubble telescope has already been able to do many things that no telescope before it could—including the first direct observation of numerous planetary systems in the process of formation. Many astronomers are eager to get still more instruments "out there," whether in Earth orbit, on the Moon or still farther out.

Finally, space travel has made it possible to get, literally, a much closer look at other bodies in our own Solar System than we ever had before. We have now seen most of the major and a good many of the minor bodies "close-up," in television pictures and instrument readings sent back by robotic spacecraft flying by or even landing there.

Is this important for science fiction writers? Profoundly! When we first started getting telemetry from other planets, instantly revolutionizing our pictures of them, it seemed to me that one of the first effects on science fiction writers was to make them a little afraid to set stories on "local" planets. If you wrote a story about Mars while a probe was on its way there, whatever you said might be hopelessly obsolete by the time the story was published.

But that phase soon passed. Soon so much brand-new information about the planets was in hand that fiction writers could no longer resist the temptation to start weaving it into stories. It's an exciting thing to be able to speculate about Mercury or Jupiter using knowledge that nobody on Earth had even six months ago. Of course, it can also keep the writing process a bit tense. One of the first novels I serialized in *Analog Science Fiction and Fact* was Bob Buckley's *World in the Clouds*, which dealt with humans colonizing the atmosphere of Venus. Bob was writing this, and I was editing it, at a time when American and Soviet probes were descending into the atmosphere of Venus and sending back packet after packet of firsthand information about what was actually down there. Bob, like any good science fiction writer, wanted to get it as right as he could. So every time a new burst of data came back, I'd get a big brown envelope containing several replacement pages to stick into his manuscript.

FROM BIG BANG TO GALAXIES

Fascinating as our local planets are, their potential as homes for aliens is rather limited. In any case, they are simply special cases of the general principles describing stars and planets everywhere. So I'm not going into a detailed discussion of conditions on each of the planets and moons of our Solar System. Instead I'm going right to the description of how stars and planets form, and what forms they can take as a result.

In the beginning, according to the best guesses of most contemporary astronomers, all the matter in the universe was concentrated in an extremely small space, and in one very brief period it started expanding—in other words, it exploded. This explosion, popularly known as the Big Bang, is the starting point for most current models of cosmology—the history of the universe. A number of problems in the details have led to variations on the theme, such as inflationary models, but since this book is about aliens and few of their personal problems are likely to be on such a scale, I won't elaborate on them here. (Of course, some science fiction writers will rise to almost any challenge! For an example of some aliens who *do* have such problems, see Marianne Dyson's "The Critical Factor.") If you want to go deeper into the fascinating enigmas of cosmology, you might start with the Rothman and Ellis article in the References.

For most alien-creating purposes, you'll need only the basic outline of how the universe is believed to have developed. With all that matter suddenly expanding outward from the Big Bang, structure begins to develop. Some pieces are moving faster than others, so after a given time, the faster pieces have moved farther than the slower ones, thus accounting for Hubble's Law. (No, this does not imply that we are at the center of the universe or the original site of the Big Bang. If you look a little closer at the dynamics of such a system, it turns out that *every* fragment sees all the others receding from itself at speeds proportional to their distances.)

Initially, there are no stars or galaxies; all the matter in the universe started out in a space small compared to such things. Initially the matter itself is not in familiar forms like atoms and molecules. We'll skip over the brief initial period when things were still striving toward even that degree of familiarity, and rejoin the story when we have an expanding cloud consisting principally of hydrogen. The initial explosion is so violent that soon this material is spread quite thinly, by our standards—and not uniformly.

Gravity, the weak but ubiquitous attraction of all matter for all other matter, tends to increase the "lumpiness" in the primitive universe. The gravitational force between two bodies is proportional to the product of their masses, and inversely proportional to the square of the distance between them. ($F = GMm/r^2$, where G is the universal gravitational constant [values are listed in various unit systems in standard tables of physical constants], M and m are the two masses, and r is the distance between their centers.)

Thus bodies that are already close together attract each other more strongly than those that are far apart. So if you look at a region in which the thin primordial gas is a bit denser than in surrounding regions, the dense "clump" will tend to get even denser as its constituent particles draw each other even closer.

So the general trend is for the universe to get lumpier. Initially we're talking about very large "lumps"—clumps of gas that we would still consider a pretty good vacuum, spread over volumes millions of light-years across, but still enough denser than their surroundings to begin acting like fairly well-defined lumps, that continue drawing still closer together.

Quite likely any such lump you look at will be spinning—a very slow spin, in everyday terms, but still representing quite a lot of *angular momentum*. Angular momentum is easily defined for something simple like a small but heavy mass (such as a fishing sinker) being swung around in a circle on a string. You simply multiply the mass by its speed, and multiply that by the radius of the circle. ($L = mvr$, where L is the angular momentum, v is the tangential velocity, and r is the radius of the circle.)

For a more complicated object, like a galaxy or a stuffed giraffe being spun on an axis through its shoulders, angular momentum is more complicated in practice, but not much more so in essence. The trick is to regard the more complicated system as made up of a lot of small masses revolving about an axis, calculate the angular momentum for each, and add them all up. (Which is a little more complicated than it sounds, since it's a *vector*—that is, it has both a magnitude [size] and a direction. In the unlikely event that you need the details, they're readily available in standard physics texts.)

The important thing about angular momentum is that it, like energy, is *conserved*. That is, if changes happen within a system (without forces being imposed from outside), the angular momentum stays the same. A familiar example of conservation of angular momentum is an ice skater performing a spin. If she starts the spin with arms and a leg outstretched, and slowly draws them in, she spins faster and faster. Since each of her parts still has the same mass, but its distance from the spin axis is decreasing, its speed has to increase to keep the product constant.

The same thing happens with astronomically large masses of gas that are gravitationally contracting. As matter gets closer to the axis of spin, the rate of spin must increase. Then something else comes into play: the effect commonly described as "centrifugal force," even though in strict physical terms it isn't really a force at all, but simply the tendency (Newton's First Law) for anything in motion to continue in motion at the same speed and in the same direction unless acted upon by an external force. That fishing sinker being swung on a string would prefer to fly in a straight line (and it will, if the line breaks). To make it go in a circle, the string must provide a *centripetal* (toward-the-center) force. The person holding the other end of the string feels an *away*-from-center force, and therefore is likely to say, if the string breaks and the sinker flies off, that it was made to do so by a centrifugal force.

If the string is slowly pulled in, forcing the sinker to travel in a smaller but faster circle, more and more force is needed to make the circle still smaller. Extending the principle to big globs of gas in space, you can see why they tend to flatten: The same amount of gravitational attraction will pull matter in more effectively *along* the axis of rotation than perpendicular to it, since the latter has to work against the "centrifugal" tendency of off-axis matter to fly off on a tangent. The net result is that if you start with a roughly spherical glob of galactic size, it contracts faster along the polar axis than at the equator. First it develops an equatorial bulge, and eventually looks more like a spinning disk than a ball. For more complicated reasons, galaxies that form into disks often develop pinwheel-like spiral arms, and so are called spiral galaxies. Different initial conditions and different stages of evolution also lead to other types of galaxies, such as elliptical (really ellipsoidal) and irregular.

Our Solar System is located in one arm of a spiral galaxy often called the Milky Way (figure 3-3). Our Galaxy will serve as a good illustration of the kinds of sizes and distances involved in galaxies. It contains something like 100 billion (10^{11}) stars, most lying in a disk approximately 100,000 light-years in diameter and averaging some 1,500 light-years thick. There's also a central bulge, and the whole thing is surrounded by a roughly spherical cloud of hot gas with a few scattered stars, mostly in dense globular clusters.

The Solar System (of which Earth is a small part) lies about 30,000 light-years out from the galactic center. (For comparison, the Earth is only eight light-*minutes* from Sol.) That's why we see our galaxy, when we see it at all, as a "Milky Way." In that band of directions, we're looking along the galactic plane, with dense stars extending thousands of light-years out. In other directions, we're

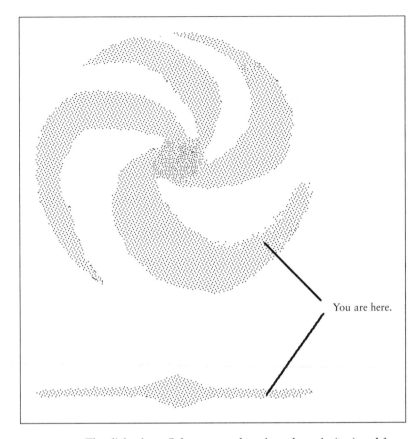

You are here.

FIGURE 3-3 The disk of our Galaxy, seen along its polar axis (top) and from the edge. The roughly spherical halo surrounding the disk is not shown.

looking more or less directly out through the nearest part of the disk, with a relatively thin layer of stars before we come to "empty" intergalactic space.

"Intergalactic" means many orders of magnitude more distant than merely "interstellar." As a science fiction writer, you must be well aware of the difference. You cannot talk casually about "aliens from another galaxy" coming to Earth with spaceflight technology not very different from ours. Our nearest "neighbor" galaxies are the Magellanic Clouds, two irregular galaxies a couple of hundred thousand light-years from ours, while the nearest galaxies very similar to our own are a couple of *million* light-years away. Anyone traveling from one to another must use *very* advanced technology, and quite possibly some science beyond any we know.

You might think this would mean that galaxies as such would seldom be of more than background interest to science fiction writers, but in fact they can play a very central role. My novel *The Sins of the Fathers* grew directly out of the fact that galaxies sometimes suffer enormous explosions involving their entire cores. The radiation from such an explosion could render planets uninhabitable throughout the affected galaxy—and we wouldn't know if our Galaxy had become uninhabitable until the deadly radiation started arriving. But suppose we were given a little bit of advanced warning, and an offer of help, by some aliens who already knew, could travel faster than the radiation, and could move entire planetary populations to *another* galaxy for safety.

Yes, those aliens—the Kyyra—were *very* advanced. But they've given me two novels so far, and I had a lot of fun (and learned a lot) working with them.

A MENAGERIE OF STARS, AND HOW IT GREW

Meanwhile, back at our forming galaxy, we still have to account for the existence of stars. By the time the collapsing cloud is down to something like galactic size, matter has become dense enough for atoms to collide and form molecules, and for molecules to collide and build up dust particles. We're still talking about very sparse matter—a better vacuum than you'd find on the Moon, for example—but we're also talking about time scales of billions of years. So after a while the incipient galaxy contains not only hydrogen and a smattering of slightly heavier atoms, but some simple molecules and dust.

For the same reasons that the original cosmic cloud got lumpy, and the lumps started turning into galaxies, the protogalactic cloud also gets lumpy, and the lumps, if they're in the right mass range, turn into stars. Star formation is most likely to occur in nebulae, clouds of relatively dense gas and dust (such as the well-known "stellar nursery" in the constellation Orion). If a piece of protostellar size separates out, it, just like the bigger one that formed a galaxy, contracts under the gravitational attraction of its parts toward each other. If it has any spin, it will tend to accelerate, for the same reasons as a figure skater or an incipient galaxy.

But a couple of additional things happen as a protostar collapses and spins faster. The average density in such a cloud is much higher than in a whole galaxy, and so atoms collide more often. They also collide at higher speeds: Like any falling objects, the atoms in a protostellar nebula speed up. Since energy is conserved, all that gravitational potential energy is converted first into kinetic energy of infalling objects and then spread around to other atoms by high-speed collisions. In other words, the interior gets both denser and hotter.

A *lot* hotter. The collisions become so violent that the electrons are stripped off many of the atoms, converting the gas to a plasma (a gas consisting not of electrically neutral atoms, but electrically charged particles including bare nuclei and loose electrons). When the core gets hot enough, some of those colliding nuclei can stick together to form larger and more complex nuclei—the process called thermonuclear fusion. The first fusion reaction to ignite in a new star is actually a sequence of reactions, but their net effect is the jamming together of four hydrogen nuclei (protons) to form one helium nucleus, with the release of a huge amount of energy. This reaction is now Sol's source of energy, and is expected to remain so, at roughly its present level of output, for maybe eight billion more years.

How long a star can sustain itself by hydrogen fusion depends primarily on its initial mass. In general, the more massive a star is, the more fuel it has, but the faster it burns it. Thus, the most massive stars burn hottest and brightest and exhaust themselves most quickly.

Stars are commonly classified according to their continuous spectra, or, equivalently, their temperatures (more precisely, the temperatures of the layers from which most light is emitted). The classes (or types), in order of decreasing temperature and increasing redness, are called O, B, A, F, G, K and M. (The time-honored mnemonic is "Oh, Be A Fine Girl, Kiss Me.") Table 3-1 summarizes the essential properties of each class. Each class subdivides into ten subclasses, each identified by a number after the letter, such as G0, G1, . . . G9. (Sol is usually considered a G2.)

One of the columns in table 3-1 is "Time on Main Sequence." If you plot the luminosities (or absolute magnitudes) of the stars in a region of space against their temperatures (or spectral classes), you get something like figure 3-4, often called a Hertzsprung-Russell (H-R) diagram. (For more detailed versions, see astronomy texts such as Smith and Jacobs.) The main sequence is the diagonal

Class	Temperature	Color	Luminosity	Time on main sequence
O	25,000 & up	Blue	>30,000	$<8 \times 10^6$
B	10,000-25,000	Blue	100-30,000	$8 \times 10^6 - 4 \times 10^8$
A	8,000-10,000	Blue	5-100	$4 \times 10^8 - 4 \times 10^9$
F	6,000-8,000	Blue-white	1.2-4.8	$4 \times 10^9 - 1 \times 10^{10}$
G	5,000-6,000	Yellow-white	0.4-1.2	$1.1 \times 10^{10} - 42.7 \times 10^{10}$
K	3,700-5,000	Orange-red	<0.1-0.35	$2.8 \times 10^{10} - 410^{11}$
M	$<3,700$	Red	<0.1	$>10^{11}$

Table 3-1 Spectral Classes of Stars.
(Temperatures are in degrees Kelvin (K), luminosity in solar units [i.e., the Sun's luminosity = 1], and time on main sequence in Earth years. Ranges given are approximate; values quoted in different sources vary slightly.)

band running from upper left to lower right, which is where most stars spend most of their lives.

A protostar first enters the H-R diagram near the upper right, that is, as a red giant. It is still contracting from a large protostellar nebula, and when it finally gets hot enough to emit any visible light, that light barely touches the red end of the visible spectrum. Its luminosity is high, not because each square centimeter of it is very bright, but because there are a great many square centimeters. As it continues to contract, the luminosity decreases—that is, the star moves downward on the right side of the H-R diagram—rather quickly, in astronomical terms. When hydrogen fusion begins, the star moves onto the main sequence at a point determined by its mass. The blue giants of class O, perhaps 20 or 30 times as massive as Sol, burn tens of thousands of times as brightly as the Sun, but only last a few million years. Sol should last at least ten *billion* years (and probably still has more than half its lifetime to go). The orange and red dwarfs of types K and M are expected to stay on the main sequence for tens of billions of years—much longer than the estimated age of our Galaxy, so presumably none of these stars have yet left the main sequence.

Why should a star ever leave the main sequence? Eventually all the hydrogen "fuel" is used up, and the thermonuclear reactions that have maintained a sort of equilibrium for so long must stop. No longer "inflated" by those reactions, the core again begins to contract under the influence of gravity. Again gravitational energy

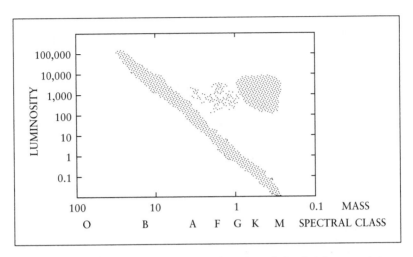

FIGURE 3-4 Hertzsprung-Russell (H-R) diagram relating brightness of stars to their mass and spectral class.

is converted to thermal, so the core temperature rises—enough to overcome the effect of gravity on the cooler outer layers and begin pushing them out. As they expand, they cool; but their surface area increases even faster, with the net result that the star gets bigger, redder and brighter. In other words, it moves up and to the right off the main sequence, becoming (again) a red giant. (From here, that means "a whitish star with an excess of red." Close-up, it's probably a good deal more complex and interesting. See Poul Anderson's story "Starfog," Chesley Bonestell's cover painting, and John W. Campbell's editorial in the same issue of *Analog* [August 1967], for a discussion of why a close-up view of such a star might look more like a brilliant white dwarf surrounded by a thin reddish cloud.)

Yes, this will happen to Sol eventually, as to all other main-sequence stars. (There's plenty of story potential in that simple observation, by the way. If humankind aspires to lasting more than a few billion years [which, admittedly, would break all previous records for longevity of a species], it will *have* to spread beyond this Solar System, since the Sun's expansion to red giant status will incinerate any nearby planets.) But the end of hydrogen fusion and expansion to red giantdom is not the end of a star's story. Remember that the core is still getting smaller and hotter. When it gets hot enough (on the order of one hundred million Kelvin), a new fusion reaction can begin, converting helium to carbon and moving the star back to the left (toward the main sequence) on the Hertz-sprung-Russell diagram. When the helium is exhausted, the outer layers again expand while the core resumes contracting. When the core gets hot enough, yet another fusion reaction begins, "burning" carbon to produce oxygen, neon and magnesium.

You see the pattern: An old star goes through a succession of stages using the elements produced by previous fusion reactions to build heavier and heavier elements. How do they get to places like the Amazon rain forest or your pantry? Stay tuned. . . .

This process of building higher and higher elements can only go so far; elements heavier than iron don't lend themselves to being built by fusion. Eventually a star runs out of nuclear energy sources, and the core resumes contracting—and still further heating—while the outer layers expand. Typically, the outer layers are lost altogether, either gradually or by more or less violent events such as the explosions called *novas* (or novae), while the core is left behind as a very small, hot, dense, white star called a white dwarf. For a star of relatively little mass (like Sol), things are pretty much downhill from there. Eventually the star (which used to be the core of a bigger star) can be compressed no further; its gravitational attraction cannot overcome the mutual repulsion of atoms. So the size stabilizes and the star is no longer producing new thermal energy to replace what it radiates. So, very slowly, it cools and dims, eventually fading away as a black dwarf.

A somewhat more massive star (above 1.4 solar masses) can meet a more dramatic end. Its gravitational attraction is strong enough to, in effect, squash the electrons into the nuclei of its atoms, converting the entire star to "neutronium," a form of matter consisting of densely packed neutrons. Such matter is far denser than anything in our everyday experience; the mass of the Sun might be squeezed into a sphere only ten or twenty kilometers in diameter. Furthermore, the spin acceleration that occurs with contraction has been carried to extremes. A neutron star makes a complete rotation in a time on the order of a second, producing the rapidly periodic bursts of radiation that we know as a *pulsar*.

A still more massive star can meet the most dramatic of all ends. It can collapse to such a high density that even light can no longer escape it, leaving a *black hole*.

Neutron stars and black holes have a host of extraordinary

properties, which have too little to do with "routine" alien-building to warrant my spending much time on them here. I will, however, say a bit more about them in the last chapter. Such exotic possibilities do offer exceptional story potential (see, for example, Robert L. Forward's novel *Dragon's Egg*, about life on a neutron star), but developing that potential poses challenges that go well beyond most writers' needs.

Meanwhile, there's a bit more that we need to say about stellar evolution. The fusion reactions I've described can't account for all the elements and isotopes we observe. Where do the others come from? Remember that old stars tend to eject their outer layers into space. That matter gets mixed back into the interstellar medium, portions of which may gather and form new stars. These "second (or later) generation" stars, containing material from earlier stars, have an important difference from "first-generation" stars. First generation stars had only hydrogen and a little helium to use as raw materials when they got hot enough to support thermonuclear reactions, which limited what reactions could take place. Later-generation stars already contain bits of heavier elements that were produced in earlier generations, and these can participate in new kinds of reactions to produce nuclei not possible in first-generation stars. Such reactions "fill in the gaps"; furthermore, some of those reactions produce neutrons that can cause still other reactions producing still other isotopes—including elements heavier than iron.

Making the very heaviest elements requires quantities of neutrons that are probably produced only in *supernovas* (or supernovae). A supernova is an *extremely* violent explosion that ends the life of some very massive stars. This is one of the few incidents in stellar evolution that happens fast enough for humans to observe directly (the time scale is on the order of days); however, such events are extremely rare. They average maybe one per galaxy per century—which is probably fortunate, since a supernova can temporarily become brighter than the entire galaxy that contains it, and produce radiation that could drastically affect life on planets of even moderately nearby stars. There is obvious story potential in that (see, for example, Poul Anderson's "Supernova" and my "The Prophet"). There is also less obvious relevance for stories that might seem to have no connection with such things. As we shall see in the next section, planets are a by-product of star formation, and therefore must be made of materials present in the nebula from which their sun formed. Since so many elements can only be produced in late-generation stars, and some of them only in supernovas, a solar system like ours, with a rich variety of even heavy elements, must have had earlier ancestors, almost certainly including at least one supernova. A planet forming around a first generation star, or from a nebula containing only a little input from earlier generations, would be poor in metals and other heavy elements. Any civilization that developed there would necessarily be different from ours. (See, for example, Jack Vance's *Big Planet*.)

A MOST IMPORTANT SPINOFF: PLANETS AND MOONS

The second important thing that happens as a protostar contracts and spins faster and faster is that it flattens into a disk—and pieces of material break off at the equator. Those can then condense into planets, and angular momentum can be transferred to them from the central star, causing the planets to follow stable orbits around the central star. A similar process on a still smaller scale can cause the planets themselves to be circled by still smaller satellites.

The details are much more complicated, of course, and still not completely understood. Until very recently, the only example of such a "solar system" we had ever seen was the one we live in. One of the long-standing central controversies in astronomy has concerned the frequency of planet formation: Are the Earth and its siblings unique, or are this galaxy and others full of such things? Science fiction writers would usually prefer the latter, for the obvious reason that it suggests a much wider range of story possibilities. (If we knew that we *were* unique, there wouldn't be much point in my writing this book!)

Most astronomical thought in recent years has been on the science fiction writers' side, suggesting that planets were relatively common, but that suspicion remained a conjecture founded on theory and unsupported by direct observation. Lately that has been changing—in fact, while I was working on this chapter, a report came out that the Hubble telescope had detected disks like those expected in emerging solar systems around many of the young stars in the Orion Nebula.

Since planets are expected to condense from a disk spun out from the equator of a spinning protostar, you would expect their orbits to lie at least approximately in the same plane. They can be perturbed by gravitational interaction with passing bodies from outside, but when the orbit of one planet in a system is significantly skewed from that of the others (like that of Pluto in our system) you might suspect that that planet itself is a former outsider that has been gravitationally captured.

The characteristics of planets, like those of stars, are largely determined by their masses. In the case of planets, there is another major determining factor as well: the nature of the primary, or "sun," and the distance at which the planet orbits. Moreover, these factors interact.

In our Solar System, the planets (with the possible exception of Pluto, which may be an adopted outsider) seem to fall naturally into two broad categories. The innermost planets—Mercury, Venus, Earth and Mars—can be lumped together as "terrestrials": Relatively small, rocky bodies whose atmospheres, if any, are heavy in such gases as nitrogen, water, carbon dioxide and oxygen. The outer planets—Jupiter, Saturn, Uranus and Neptune—are "jovians" (i.e., like Jupiter): gas giants, much larger than the terrestrials, with thick atmospheres (at least some of them may not even have solid cores) consisting largely of the same sorts of light gases that are common in the interstellar medium (lots of hydrogen and helium, with smaller amounts of methane and ammonia).

It's no coincidence that the terrestrials lie close to the Sun and the jovians farther out. Originally, *all* the planets must have had the same general composition as the protostellar nebula from which they formed. The jovians, far from the primary star, still have something close to that composition, and most of their original mass. The terrestrials have lost much of their original mass, and in particular the lightest gases, because their proximity to the primary heated those light gases enough to escape their gravity.

For a science fiction writer, "terrestrials and jovians" is probably too simple and limited a classification for all the kinds of planets that might exist. The variations within each class are fairly large—Mercury, for example, is much smaller and hotter than Earth, with little or no atmosphere, while Venus is about the same size as Earth but has a much denser atmosphere and a much hotter surface. If the universe is as full of planets as it seems, it's unlikely that our small local collection contains samples of all possible types. Other planetary systems may, for example, contain planets intermediate between Earth and Neptune, or more massive than Jupiter.

Since the nature of planets must be determined by the laws of physics and chemistry, we can make some educated guesses about the types that might exist. As a science fiction writer, I've found it useful to think of them in terms of an expanded classification system described by science fiction writer Poul Anderson (in *Is There Life on Other Worlds?*): superjovians, jovians, subjovians, superterrestrials, terrestrials and subterrestrials.

Superjovians

These planets would have masses several times that of Jupiter. Really large ones, with masses ten or fifteen times Jupiter's, might represent the borderline between stars (which shine by their own light) and planets (which don't). They may have quite hot cores, and if they were just a little more massive, might be able to start their own fusion reactions. (Such objects are sometimes called "brown dwarfs.") The compositions of superjovians should be quite starlike, with hydrogen overwhelmingly predominant, helium abundant and everything else "mere traces" (which may still mean quite large tonnages, by our reckoning, but very spread out).

More mass does not necessarily mean larger diameter. It may lead to greater compression, so Jupiter itself may be close to the maximum possible diameter for a planet. Such compression implies that superjovians hold their atmospheres more tightly, and therefore could keep them (and remain superjovians) even in orbits too close to the primary for planets like our jovians. It also implies that they would be spinning very rapidly and might therefore be very flattened along the polar axis, with much stronger "effective gravity" at the poles than at the equator.

Hal Clement has described such a world, Mesklin, in his novel *Mission of Gravity*. Mesklin's day—that is, the time it takes to spin once on its axis—is about eighteen minutes. Standing on its equator, you would feel about three times as heavy as on Earth; on a pole, about *seven hundred* times. Needless to say, such a world would impose very special requirements on anything that lived there. We're not in a position to say much about those yet, but we shall surely return to Mesklin later.

Meanwhile, I'll mention another option for somewhat less exotic life in connection with a superjovian. Such a planet could have a more or less terrestrial planet as a satellite, and since a superjovian can be stable relatively close to its star, its moon could be relatively

Earthlike and harbor life. It would, of course, have some unusual characteristics. Because of tidal forces (about which we shall say more later), it would probably be locked into synchronous rotation, always keeping the same face toward the superjovian, just as our Moon is locked into facing Earth. Inhabitants of the "near" side would, unless the satellite's orbit was very tilted, have what we would consider quite unusual cycles of light and darkness, with eclipses every day and nights dominated by a huge, bright "moon." Residents of the "far" side might have more "normal" days and nights, but never suspect that the superjovian primary existed— until their first explorers to circumnavigate their globe got a big surprise!

Jovians

These planets, comparable in mass and size to our Jupiter and Saturn, must lie relatively far from their sun, for the reasons already mentioned. They can lie closer to a cooler star than to a hotter one. A few decades ago, the possibility of life on such worlds used to be shrugged off on the grounds that they would be too cold. Now we recognize that it's not necessarily so. For one thing, those thick atmospheres have powerful greenhouse effects, and their deeper layers may be quite balmy. For another, we're not really very sure what *is* too cold for life. In any case, before we can say much about the possibility of life on these or other kinds of planets, we'll have to take a closer look at how life works—first in the few cases that we know about, and second, in the many that we can at least dimly imagine. That will be the business of the next chapter.

Subjovians

These planets, like Uranus or Neptune, are more like jovians than terrestrials, but with appreciable differences in composition and related characteristics. The smaller masses and higher densities of our known specimens, compared to Jupiter and Saturn, suggest that they have lost more of their hydrogen and helium, and therefore have higher concentrations of heavier elements.

Why did they lose more of the lightest elements? Since Uranus and Neptune are farther from the Sun than Jupiter and Saturn, the explanation in their case is presumably that they started off with less mass, and didn't have enough gravity to keep the light atoms from leaving. In other places, a similar effect might be obtained by starting with a larger mass closer to its star. Increased gravity would make it harder for light atoms to leave, but more solar energy would help them overcome the larger barrier. If you made the starting mass smaller still, or put it closer to the primary, these changes would go still further, leading to . . .

Superterrestrials

This type is somewhat more Earthlike than Uranus or Neptune, but still sufficiently different to seem quite exotic. A planet with eight times the Earth's mass, and the same density, would have twice the diameter and twice the surface gravity. Without observational data, it's hard to say how close the densities of such planets might actually be to that of Earth. On one hand, the greater mass might lead to greater compression and higher densities. On the other hand, that tendency might be offset by an ability to retain more of the planet's original supply of light elements. Other things being equal, a higher surface gravity might lead to a denser atmosphere and stronger greenhouse effect, though the atmospheric density and pressure would fall off more quickly with altitude. Too close to its star, such a planet might cook like Venus; or it might maintain something like temperatures we like around a cooler star.

Terrestrials

This class, now more narrowly defined to mean planets with masses quite close to that of Earth, can still be wildly different— as our two known examples dramatically demonstrate. Venus, with a mass very nearly the same as Earth's, has an atmosphere whose surface pressure is some hundred times that on Earth, whose temperature is high enough to melt lead, and whose composition would be extremely toxic to us.

Subterrestrials

These planets include bodies like Mercury, Mars and the Moon: Appreciably smaller than Earth, rocky, and commonly with little or no atmosphere—though I say that more cautiously than I would have a few years ago. As my choice of examples indicates, such bodies can occur either as "independent" planets or as satellites of larger ones, and their atmosphere or lack of it depends very much on where they are. Mercury has little, if any, atmosphere, because of its proximity to the Sun; but some of the satellites of Jupiter and

Saturn are of quite similar size and now appear to be some of the more promising abodes for native life in our Solar System. (For details, see the latest results from space probes to the outer Solar System!)

A WORLD-BUILDING PRIMER

There is a great deal more that I could have said about the topics in this chapter, but space does not permit. Any galaxy, star or planet is a far more complex thing than I've made it sound; I've had to summarize and hit the highlights because our main interest in this book is aliens—the things that might live on these worlds. How deeply you get into the details of world-building depends both on your interest in such things and on the nature of your story.

You will obviously need to get more detailed about your aliens' world of origin if your story's action takes place on that world than if your aliens merely visit humans on their own turf. In *The Sins of the Fathers*, I said very little about the original form of the Kyyra's home world (though I knew quite a bit about the history that led from it to their present situation). We only saw them thousands of light-years from where they started, and even before they left, their technology had changed their home world into something very different. In *Mission of Gravity* or Poul Anderson's *The People of the Wind*, on the other hand, the nature of the world and the beings it produced were central to the story. (Chapter ten gives more details about these stories.) Hal Clement imagined an exotic world that could exist and tried to figure out what kind of life and civilization might develop in such a place. Poul Anderson imagined a kind of being and tried to figure out how it could exist—and what kind of world could make it so.

If you want to try either of those things—creating fully fleshed beings and a world that could make them, or vice versa—you must expect to put considerable care and effort into your world-building. You will need more detailed information than I can give you here. On the other hand, if you start with a general idea of your plot and merely need aliens who can fill a particular kind of role in it, you may only need a general idea of the bounds of plausibility. (However, I have never known a story to suffer from its author's knowing its background too well, as long as he knew when to stop talking about it. In general, the more vividly you have visualized the scenes and actors, the richer your tale will be.)

No matter where on that spectrum your ambitions lie, you will likely want to think your aliens' home world out in at least broad outline. So let's talk through the basic sequence of steps that such thinking is likely to follow, and then I'll direct you to some additional sources where you can go for more detail or concrete examples.

The Importance of Your Star

You start with a star, since everything else is shaped by that. As I've already hinted, you'll seldom, if ever, want to use a "big-name" star like Deneb or Sirius. Such stars are usually giants. The blue and white ones lie high on the left end of the main sequence, and the time they spend there is likely too short for them to evolve advanced life even if they form planets—and there is some evidence (albeit controversial) that they usually don't. The red giants are either in a brief formational stage, or one of the later episodes of swelling after finishing one nuclear fuel—a process that probably destroys any life-bearing planets they might have had.

At the other extreme, red dwarfs, at least those at the extreme lower right, are likely too feeble to develop life on any planets they might have. So you'll most likely want a star somewhere fairly far to the right on the main sequence, but not *too* far. Several writers have estimated that for a planet to be habitable by us or reasonably similar beings, the star's spectral class should probably lie between classes F5 and K5. Within that range, you can start with Earthlike conditions and life-forms and imagine how they might be modified by somewhat different conditions. More dissimilar beings may evolve around more dissimilar stars, but developing them will require more than elementary world-building.

If you can't use "big-name" stars, what can you use? The stars we can see are identified and catalogued in some way. One of the most common methods is to use a Greek letter, in order of decreasing brightness, followed by the genitive case of the Latin name of the constellation in which the star appears from Earth. (A constellation is not a cluster of stars, close together, but merely a group that is in nearly the same *direction* from Earth. From a planet of another star the constellations would be different—the farther from Earth, the more different.) Thus the brightest star in the constellation Centaurus is Alpha Centauri, the next brightest is Beta Centauri, and so on. In general, you'll need to use a real star only if it's important that your aliens hail from somewhere fairly close—say, a couple of dozen light-years—of Sol. If you do, you'll have to consult a table of nearby stars (the ones in the Dole and Kepner books in the References are particularly useful) and make sure that the properties you describe are consistent with the ones your chosen star actually has. If your star doesn't have to be so close, you're usually better off inventing a possible one and letting your characters name it.

A large percentage (say, a third to a half) of the "stars" we see are actually double or multiple star systems—two or more stars orbiting each other (more precisely, their common center of mass), probably having formed in a way similar to star-and-planet systems. Alpha Centauri, for example, is really a triple star, which, for many purposes, can be treated as a double—but *never* as a single like Sol. Alpha Centauri A is a class G star similar to Sol; Alpha Centauri is a smaller star (class K) in an eccentric orbit with a period of about eighty years. A and B are sometimes as close as 11.2 AU apart and sometimes as far as 35.2 AU. Component C, sometimes called Proxima Centauri (because it's presently the closest to us), is so small and orbits the A-B combination at such a great distance that you can usually ignore it in considering A or B. But if you want your aliens to come from Alpha Centauri A, you will surely have to consider the complications B causes in such matters as climate and evolution.

Those complications, and still more dramatic ones such as the interactions that can occur when the components of a binary get very close, can certainly provide good story material. In Jerry Oltion and Lee Goodloe's story "Contact," a human-alien cultural contact coincides with an astronomical contact that will doom a native civilization. If you use a double star, you must expect those complications to play an important role in shaping your story, and you must be prepared to work out the details and their consequences. Unless you're prepared to do those things, you'll be better off putting your aliens' planet around a single star.

Once you have your star, you can start putting planets around it. Where you put them, and what you've chosen for a sun, will immediately determine some of the fundamental characteristics of your planet. One of the first considerations will be the amount of light reaching the planet's surface. From the H-R diagram, and equations and/or diagrams in the references, you can determine the mass (M) and brightness or luminosity (L) of your sun.

You'll probably find it most convenient to measure these and other parameters in terms of the corresponding values for Sol and Earth. For example, the irradiation or insolation (amount of energy per unit time) reaching a planet at distance r is

$$i = L/r^2.$$

For Earth, we take L (for Sol) to be 1, and r (the Sun-to-Earth distance) as 1, and find $i = 1$—i.e., unit insolation means the amount of energy we on Earth get from the Sun. A planet 2 AU from Sol would have $i = \frac{1}{4}$; getting one-fourth as much solar energy (per area) as Earth does.

If you choose an F6 star for a story, you'll find it has about 1.25 times the mass of Sol, and 2.2 times the luminosity. (For main sequence stars, to good approximation, $L = M^{3.5}$.) To give your planet the same *insolation*, or rate of receiving solar radiation, you'll have to put it about 1.5 times as far from this hotter sun as Earth is from Sol. Of course, it still won't get *exactly* the same kind of radiation that we do. Since its star is hotter, its light will be whiter, richer in ultraviolet, more likely to show erratic flare-ups, and so forth.

Once you know the mass of your system's sun, and your planet's distance from it, the planet's period of revolution (P), or year length, is determined. For any planet in a circular (or nearly circular) orbit around a much more massive sun,

$$P^2 = r^3/M.$$

Again taking "our" values of all the parameters as units, the period for our sample planet in a 1.5 AU orbit about a 1.3 solar mass F7 star is

$$P = \sqrt{(1.5)^3/1.25} = 1.6 \text{ year.}$$

A longer year will affect conditions on the surface and the nature of things that evolve there. For example, if this planet has an atmosphere and axial tilt similar to those of Earth, it will show similar seasonal variations—except that all the seasons will be longer than ours. Temperate zones will have more time to heat up in the summer and cool down in the winter, so everything that lives there will have to be adapted to more extreme seasonal variations of temperature and precipitation.

Day Length and Axial Tilt

There are no such simple rules for predicting axial tilt and day length, so in choosing those you have more leeway. There are some constraints—for example, a planet that orbits quite close to its sun will have its rotation slowed by tidal forces so that eventually it will be locked into one of two kinds of synchronous rotation. (Tidal forces result from the fact that the gravitational pull on the parts of a planet or a satellite closer to its primary is stronger than on the parts farther away. They also cause ocean tides and make it impossible for a satellite to orbit too close to its primary, since the tidal forces would pull it apart.) Since locking a planet into synchronous rotation takes time, and won't happen for a distant planet, you can experiment with planets with all sorts of day lengths. Each, of course, will affect the lives of things that live there. The day-to-night temperature variation, for example, will be far greater on a planet where daylight and night each last a month than on one where they last an hour.

Axial tilt is the main cause of seasons, as shown in figure 3-5. Since the rotational axis always leans in the same direction as the planet goes around its sun, during part of the year one hemisphere leans toward the sun and the other away from it, while half a year later the hemispheres' situations are reversed. The hemisphere leaning toward the sun has "summer," with long days and high temperatures, while the other has "winter," with short days and low temperatures. The variation between summer and winter conditions is most extreme at the poles and least at the equator. That fact is the most important difference between arctic and tropic regions, with temperate zones lying between.

Other factors can influence seasons, of course. Ishtar, in Poul Anderson's *Fire Time*, orbits close to one star while a red giant orbits both in a highly eccentric orbit with a period of about a thousand years. Life there has had to adapt to prolonged periods of extreme heat at long intervals (whenever the red giant gets close), and anyone seriously interested in advanced world-building and the creation of exotic aliens would be well advised to study how it achieves that. For more prosaic situations, with a more or less Earthlike planet in orbit around a single star, axial tilt is by far

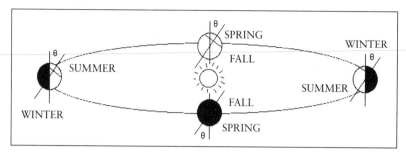

FIGURE 3-5 Axial tilt is the main cause of seasons. Here we see (not to scale!) a planet circling a sun with its axis of rotation tilted to the right by an angle θ from the perpendicular to the orbital plane. One latitude line, in the northern ("upper") hemisphere is shown. When the planet is at the rightmost position, that line spends most of its time in the dark region (winter), while in the leftmost position it spends most of its time in the sun (summer). In the intermediate positions, all parts of the planet spend equal parts of the day in light and darkness (the spring and fall equinoxes). In the southern hemisphere, the seasons are opposite those of the north, but for the same reasons.

the most important consideration. Even if the orbit is not quite circular, the variations caused by changing distance from the sun are small compared to those caused by the changing angle of sunlight.

Earth's axial tilt is 23.5°; others in the Solar System range from essentially 0 to more than 90°. (The "90 + " planet, Uranus, is effectively lying on its side and rolling "backward.") If you imagine tilts other than those shown in figure 3-5, you can see why changing the tilt would be so important. With no tilt, every part of the planet would get equal amounts of daylight and night, with the sun climbing to the same maximum angle above the horizon every day of the year. There would be no seasons, and there might be side effects such as aridity in the middle latitudes that are our temperate zones, since our temperate water supplies depend heavily on the spring melt of winter snow.

If you doubled Earth's tilt, to 47°, not only would seasonal variations be much more extreme, but odd things would happen to climatic zones. The counterparts of our Tropic of Cancer and Tropic of Capricorn (the highest latitudes at which the sun is ever directly overhead) would move out to 47° north and south, while the arctic and antarctic circles (the lowest latitudes at which the sun is ever above or below the horizon for a full day or more) would move down to 43°. Thus there would be no temperate zones at all, and the belt between 43° and 47° in each hemisphere would combine some of the harshest features of tropical and arctic regions!

Those examples serve as a good reminder of one of the most common mistakes to avoid in creating a world: the world that is "all jungle" or "all swamp" or "perpetually spring everywhere." Even as small a planet as Earth is, in human terms, a very large and immensely varied thing. Any real world will be, and any fictional world you want taken seriously had better be, too. Even a planet with no axial tilt, and therefore no seasons as we know them, will be far from homogeneous. Sunlight may arrive at the same angle every day at any point on the surface, but that angle will vary drastically with latitude. The equator will still be the hottest and the poles the coldest places, other things being equal.

Of course, other things won't necessarily be equal. Regional climates will also vary with things like elevation, atmospheric circulation patterns, the location and nature of bodies of water, geothermal activity, and the size and shape of mountain ranges. These in turn are influenced by things like surface gravity and escape velocity—which, though related, are *not* the same, or even proportional. (Surface gravity, again taking Earth's values as units, is $g = dD$, where d is the average density and D the diameter of the planet. Escape velocity, the minimum speed at which you have to launch something to keep gravity from pulling it back, is approximately $v_e = \sqrt{(M/D)}$ [M in this case referring to the planet.])

By now you should have a good feel for just how complicated a world is. I've given you some rudimentary tools for determining its most fundamental characteristics and shown you something of how they're interrelated, so you can't pick them in random combinations. If you want to develop your world in depth (as I hope you will, at least occasionally), you'll need more details and more tools than I can give you here. The References give a number of useful sources. The two Anderson articles have the special virtue of gathering some useful tools in one place (graphs in one article, equivalent formulas in the other) and working through a concrete example that was used in an actual science fiction story. Hal Clement's article "Whirligig World" similarly works through the development of Mesklin for *Mission of Gravity*.

Since these fields are changing so fast, some material in *any* book will have been superseded by more recent findings. Probably the single most useful source in my References is Stephen L. Gillett's *World-Building*, which is being written concurrently with this one. It is the most up to date, the most comprehensive, and the most specifically geared to the needs of science fiction writers. I also call your attention to the software packages listed, and urge you to watch for new ones as they become available. If you have access to a computer (as most writers now do), it may enable you to easily do exact calculations that just a few years ago would have been approached by mere educated guesswork. Some of them even let you play with possibilities—for example, trying slightly different values for a planet's location, size and mass, and quickly seeing a lot of the ramifications.

The aspects of world-building I've talked about in this chapter are independent of what, if anything, lives there—which is, of course, our primary concern in this book. What can live on a planet is very much shaped by the physical parameters we've been talking about—things like insolation, planetary temperature, surface gravity, and so on. From here on out we will assume that you've determined those things, to the extent of your ability and interest, and will then consider how your planet's characteristics shape its inhabitants.

And vice versa—for once a planet has life, that life can play an important role in shaping the world's further development. The large amount of free oxygen in Earth's atmosphere, for example, is almost certainly a consequence, not a cause, of life. And the effects that its one self-styled intelligent species (us) is having are currently a source of acute concern to scientists and politicians alike.

So the next thing we must do is look at life itself. What is it, and, given a world with particular characteristics, what forms can it take? That question has at least two parts, chemical and mechanical—and the chemical part comes first.

CHAPTER 4

Biochemical Basics

I n this book we shall take as a fundamental assumption that advanced life-forms must either evolve from more primitive ones and ultimately from an originally lifeless world, or they must be created by other advanced organisms that did so. Thus you cannot have humans, or their counterparts on some other planet, without the whole web of interdependent plants and animals that surround them—and the whole chain of ancestors that led from a raw planet to that ecosystem. You can imagine an apparent exception—a world on which one species has wiped out all other natural life-forms and invented entirely artificial means of sustaining itself (as some humans seem bent on doing)—but the exception is only apparent. If the other natural parts of an ecosystem hadn't been there originally, the surviving species wouldn't be there either.

LIFE ON EARTH

In thinking about how life originates and develops, we shall be forced to draw heavily on the one example we know of a planet on which that happened. As with stellar evolution, we have no eyewitnesses who watched the process, so we will have to rely heavily on inference and experiments with potentially pertinent chemistry. And (even worse than with stars!) we have no direct evidence about how typical what happened here is. Nevertheless, it's all we have.

At first glance, it might seem that this one little planet offers an enormous range of life-forms, many of them so obviously different that one might suspect them of representing a large sample of independent instances. Earthly life-forms include *Streptococcus* bacteria, basilisk lizards, lilies of the valley, zebras, aardvarks, sword-fish, rattlesnakes, giant sequoias, blue whales, hummingbirds, mo-rel mushrooms, the Great Barrier Reef, black widow spiders, alligators, and us—just to name a very, very few. There are lichens growing in the frigid wastes of Antarctica, and fish living in hot springs that would cook "normal" fish. In the past there were many others, such as tyrannosaurs, trilobites and giant dragonflies. Surely a diverse lot—yet at the fundamental level, they are all so similar that they are probably products of a single "biogenesis." All terrestrial life is, in a real and important sense, just *one* example with many variations on a basic theme.

That may seem an extreme statement, but there's a great deal of evidence to support it, much of which has just come to light in the last few decades. As wildly diverse as my examples seem, every one of them is composed of one or more cells. Those cells show a great deal of similarity in their structure and functioning. The same chemical reactions for extracting energy from food occur in organisms that would seem utterly unrelated. When important molecules exist in two versions (*stereoisomers*) which are mirror images, with no obvious advantage in choosing the "left-handed" or "right-handed" isomer, all organisms have chosen to use only one—the *same* one. And they all use the same kind of molecule, DNA (deoxy-ribonucleic acid), for storing and transmitting the information needed to make copies of themselves.

It's not easy to define life, especially with only one example to work with. Attempts to do so have commonly boiled down to saying, "I know it when I see it; now let's try to figure out what all the variants I recognize have in common." We can probably agree that living things, regardless of their specific form,

1. are highly *organized* structures.
2. take in energy from their surroundings and use it to maintain their structure and organization.
3. have the ability to reproduce, i.e., to make more or less exact working copies of themselves.

Each of these statements is subject to some qualification and clarification (for example, not every individual actually uses the ability to reproduce, and the offspring of sexually reproducing species are seldom identical to their parents), but given that, these are all characteristics that we expect of any life-form on Earth (and likely elsewhere). Others, such as the ability to move around or to learn from experience, are less general. We expect them of *some* organisms (such as a prospective tennis partner) but not of others (such as a stalk of broccoli to be served under *sauce hollandaise*).

Earthly organisms acquire the energy they need to maintain themselves in a variety of ways. Until recently, it was assumed that they all got their energy from the Sun, directly or indirectly. Green plants use sunlight directly, with water, minerals and carbon dioxide as raw materials, making carbohydrates, giving off oxygen and storing energy in their own tissues. Fungi or animals get their energy by eating those tissues and metabolizing the carbohydrates, and give off carbon dioxide that can be reused by plants. Still other animals (carnivores) can eat the animals that ate the plants; smaller organisms eventually recycle their bodies back into soil as plant nutrients. You see in this bare-bones summary the beginning of *ecology*: No organism exists in isolation, but all interact to keep *cycles* of chemical reactions going over and over, with chemicals being repeatedly reused and only energy added from outside.

The essential input is *energy*, not *solar* energy. We can no longer say, even on Earth, that the Sun lies at the root of all energy cycles. Recent deep ocean explorations have discovered whole ecosystems based on chemical synthesis on the ocean floor, far from Sol's reach. The food chain here starts with microorganisms that directly metabolize hydrogen sulfide and minerals in warm water seeping up through vents from the Earth's interior. (See the Ballard and Grassle article in the References.)

You can find chemical details in standard references, but central facts you should keep in mind are these: Biochemical reactions involve complex compounds of carbon, hydrogen, nitrogen, oxygen, phosphorus and sulfur, largely because of carbon's unique ability to form big, complex molecules (such as sugars, nucleic acids and proteins). In terrestrial life, these reactions normally take place in water solution—a liquid medium in which chemical "building blocks" can roam around and bump into others with which they can react.

The Importance of DNA

One kind of molecule is of unique and central importance because of its role in reproduction: DNA. By now practically everyone at least recognizes "the double helix," consisting of two very long

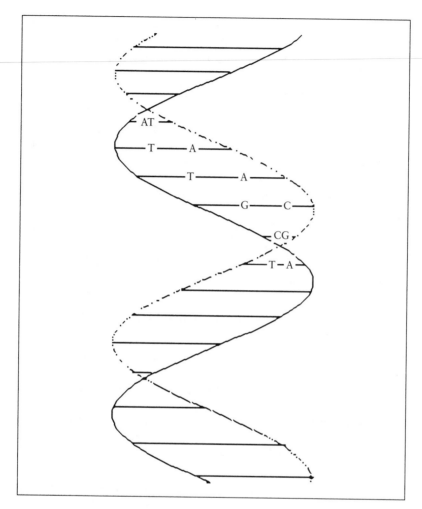

FIGURE 4-1 The structure of DNA (highly simplified schematic).

molecular strands spiraling around each other (see figure 4-1) in a way that looks remarkably like the caduceus long used as a symbol of medicine. Each strand is a string of building blocks called nucleoside phosphates. Each nucleoside phosphate in turn consists of still smaller units called sugars, bases and phosphates.

The crucial importance of DNA is threefold. First, it carries a complete set of instructions for building an entire organism. Second, it can make exact copies of itself. Third, if for some reason a copy fails to be exact—if a "mistake" is made in the process of DNA replication—the new DNA carries a changed set of instructions and will grow a changed kind of organism. The first two of these characteristics are the molecular basis of reproduction. The third is the basis of evolution.

I do not plan to go into the specifics of how the instructions encoded in DNA are carried out. The details of cellular reproduction in Earthly organisms are complicated and treated at length elsewhere. If you need them for a particular story, you can find them in the References. But you should have clearly in mind the basic picture of how DNA can carry information, how it makes copies, and how the copies can change.

The key to all that is in fact a kind of lock-and-key arrangement. Figure 4-1 may strike you as resembling a twisted ladder, with rungs consisting of pairs of bases, one sticking out of a nucleoside phosphate on each of the two strands. There are four bases that can be used: adenine (A), cytosine (C), guanine (G), and thymine (T). Only certain pairs of them can combine to form rungs of the DNA ladder: Adenine will combine only with thymine, and cytosine only with guanine. Nucleoside phosphates containing the four bases can be arranged in any order along one strand of a DNA molecule, but once you specify the sequence of bases along one strand, the sequence along the other is automatically determined. For example, if one strand contains the sequence A T T G C A, the corresponding section of the other strand *must* be T A A C G T. So the instruction book for growing a sea urchin or a senator is written in a four-letter code consisting simply of the order of bases along one strand of DNA.

Cells reproduce by dividing, and in that process the two strands of DNA separate, each rung breaking apart where its two bases join, a little like a zipper unzipping. Each strand has a row of bases sticking out, each of which would like to combine with another base of the one kind that fits it. An important function of the "maintaining reactions" mentioned earlier is to build up nucleoside phosphates from the simpler raw materials taken in as food, so each single DNA strand will now find itself in a medium well-stocked with the building blocks to replace the "missing" strand. When a nucleoside phosphate containing adenine bumps into a thymine projecting from the single strand, it can latch on. Eventually, complementary nucleoside phosphates will latch onto every base along each of the two strands of the original double helix. When that process is complete, each strand has grown into a new double helix exactly like the original. That process is the central event in all Earthly reproduction.

If it always worked perfectly, every organism would be exactly like every other organism—and since the first organisms must have been extremely simple, we would all be much too simple to write or read this book. Fortunately for us as a species, though unfortunately for some individuals, DNA replication doesn't always work perfectly. Factors such as radiation or chemicals in the environment can cause *mutation*—a change in the sequence along a DNA strand. A base might be deleted, replaced by another, or trade places with another. For example, if the second thymine in my sample sequence A T T G C A is somehow removed, you're left with A T G C A. That's a different genetic "word," and something about the organism built from the revised instructions will be different from the original—for example, eyes might be brown instead of blue. (Just *what* will be different is a more complicated question than you might guess, since each segment of DNA can influence more than one trait, and a trait can be influenced by more than one segment of DNA.)

Thus DNA, with the help of environmental disturbances, provides not only a mechanism for usually making identical copies, but also one for sometimes making something new. That is the first requirement for evolution. Once such a mutation has occurred, the new organism has a chance to reproduce itself, because the mutated DNA will (usually) replicate itself exactly like any other DNA. However, at the organism level, other influences may keep the mutated organism from making many more copies of itself.

Mutation is essentially a random process. Sometimes the resulting change in an organism will enhance its chances of surviving long enough to reproduce, but more often the effect will be inconsequential or harmful. It's a little like trying to fix a fine watch by dropping it off a tall building. If you drop enough watches off enough tall buildings, once in a great while one of them may land in just the right way to fix what ails it—but the vast majority of them won't.

So mutation is just one part of evolution. You need it to get new kinds of organisms, but then *natural selection* must operate. Mutations that interfere with an organism's ability to survive or reproduce will tend to die out. The few mutations that improve those abilities will tend to become more numerous. So mutations and the things that cause them are neither unmixed blessing nor unmixed curse. Too few of them in the past and we wouldn't be here; too many now and we'd be plagued with birth defects.

Evolution and Reproduction

Many other factors affect evolution, and I'll say more about them in the next chapter. For now, there's just one that merits special mention: sex. Sex is extremely important in biology because it provides an additional, and powerful, way for organisms to try out new forms, even in the absence of mutations.

The most primitive single-celled organisms on Earth—which for some three billion years were the *only* organisms—are the *prokaryotes* (or procaryotes), which include blue-green algae and bacteria. Prokaryotic cells are relatively simple and reproduce asexually. Each cell carries a single set of chromosomes ("genetic instruction books") consisting entirely of DNA, and reproduces simply by making an extra copy of that DNA and dividing.

Eukaryotes (or eucaryotes) have considerably more complicated cell structure, with internal membranes and substructures including a nucleus in which the genetic material is concentrated. Their chromosomes are also more complicated structures (though the genetic information is still coded in DNA)—and come in pairs. That's where sex comes in. Instead of a new organism being built from an exact copy of a single parent's DNA, it gets one chromosome governing a given set of traits from each of two parents. The offspring's actual makeup is determined by the combined effect of the two chromosomes. The details are too complicated to go into here, but are readily found in books and articles on genetics (such as Griffiths *et al*). The most important fact is that genetic information is distributed among several pairs of chromosomes (humans have twenty-three plus one "special" pair), and each parent contributes a randomly selected member of each pair. Thus sex allows essentially every new organism to try out a new design, by combining old characteristics in new ways.

The Origin of Life

How did all this begin? Again we must rely on educated guesses as to how it happened. Several theories have been put forth, and the votes aren't all in. From a science fiction writer's point of view, it's important to bear in mind that even if one of these theories could be proved to be The Way It Happened, that does not mean all the others must be relegated to the scrap heap. Life probably began only once here, and thus used only one of the proposed methods, but it may have originated in other ways in other places.

One hypothesis concerning the origin of life on Earth is that it didn't originate here at all. *Panspermia* is the idea that we evolved from dormant spores that drifted here from life evolved elsewhere. Some life-forms produce spores that can survive long periods of dormancy, even under the adverse conditions they might encounter in interplanetary or interstellar space. Under some conditions such spores could escape a planet's atmosphere, be blown out of their planetary system of origin by the "solar wind" from its sun, and eventually be captured by the gravity of a quite distant planet. Even if it didn't happen here, some version of panspermia could happen somewhere. The Threads in Anne McCaffrey's *Dragonflight* (organisms whose spores travel from one planet of a system to another when they are close together) are a good fictional example.

Panspermia does not really answer the general question of how life originates from non-life. Even if life on this or some other planet developed from spores evolved elsewhere, we're still left with the question of how it originated *there*. As it turns out, it's so easy to imagine ways that that could happen that most scientists find it an unnecessary complication to look for an extraterrestrial origin for terrestrial life. Any of several scenarios could have done the trick right here.

The original atmosphere of any planet is likely to approximate the composition of Jupiter's, with a prevalence of hydrogen, helium, methane, ammonia, carbon dioxide and water vapor. A massive planet far from its sun will retain that kind of atmosphere because its gas molecules will not move fast enough to escape its strong gravitational field. Small and/or close-in planets (like Earth) will tend to lose much of that atmosphere. Hydrogen and helium, in particular, are so light that they can easily escape a relatively weak gravity, especially if they're getting lots of thermal energy. Even if the original atmosphere is completely lost, though, it may be replaced by a new one consisting of "outgased" material—i.e., gases released from the planet's interior. Volcanos, for example, emit substantial quantities of gases, many of which can be too heavy to escape the planet's gravity.

Until recently, it was generally assumed that such a secondary (but still early) atmosphere would be much like the primary atmosphere, but without much elemental hydrogen and helium—in other words, methane, ammonia, carbon dioxide and water vapor. (You'll note that elemental *oxygen* is conspicuously absent from the list.) Both theory and simulation experiments suggest that, given oceans of water under such an atmosphere, the energy provided by such sources as solar ultraviolet radiation and electrical storms would cause chemical reactions producing complex organic molecules, leading in geologically reasonable times to the ones we call life.

Another model that has recently been gaining favor pictures an early Earth with an atmosphere heavy in carbon dioxide and nitrogen. This is not so favorable for "in-house" production of organic molecules, but there is also now evidence that those are sometimes formed *in space* and could have been brought here by comets and meteorites. Still others suggest that life could have originated not in the oceans, but in clays (which are soils consisting of very fine particles).

More study will be needed to determine which of these processes (or perhaps some other not yet identified!) was responsible for the origin of life on Earth. In the meantime, science fiction writers are free to consider any of them as possibly occurring *somewhere* and perhaps playing a role in a story.

Now, how about that oxygen atmosphere? Actually, of course, our atmosphere is only about 20 percent oxygen, most of the rest being nitrogen. (We would find an atmosphere containing much more oxygen toxic.) But the oxygen is the part that we use most directly, in the largest quantities, and simply can't do without. You'll recall that it was not a significant ingredient in any of the early atmospheres we've considered. Any elemental oxygen that was there would tend to combine into things like water and carbon dioxide. So how did it come to be the second most abundant ingredient of our present atmosphere?

Answer: It is a product of, and not a precondition for, life. The earliest life-forms on Earth had to make do without it, but some of them produced it as a by-product of photosynthesis. Since oxygen is highly reactive, it would tend to oxidize, or combine with, many other things, which would tend to keep much oxygen from accumulating in the atmosphere. (Hence the term "reducing" as a sort of opposite to oxidation—i.e., something else combining with oxygen.) That was a good thing for early life-forms, since they were among the things that could be oxidized. (As are we; as Carl Sagan wrote in *Intelligent Life in the Universe,* "In a very real sense, we Earthly organisms are living in a poison gas.")

However, one of the best reducing agents is hydrogen, which is also the lightest of all elements, and therefore the one that, in its elemental form, can most easily escape from the atmosphere. Ultraviolet radiation sometimes broke up molecules in the early atmosphere, and hydrogen thus liberated sometimes escaped. So, over long periods of time, the amount of hydrogen in the atmosphere declined, and the amount of elemental oxygen slowly increased. Eventually other organisms evolved that could *use* oxygen to extract more energy from food. So our world gradually moved toward the situation we now consider "normal," with an oxidizing atmosphere maintained by a balance between oxygen-breathing animals and oxygen-producing plants. This atmosphere would have been highly toxic to many of the earliest organisms, and the transition to it, although a slow process, might very well be viewed (at least from *their* standpoint) as the greatest ecological catastrophe in our planet's history.

ALIEN ALTERNATIVES

Which properties of life as described so far are universal characteristics of all life, and which are local peculiarities of our particular kind of life? The question is of special interest to science fiction writers, because our job is to explore as wide a range of possibilities as we can.

Some years ago I attended a colloquium at a well-known oceanographic institution, with the title "Is There Non-Aqueous Life on Other Worlds?" The title was a bit shortened for euphony; the speaker's actual subject was life with a chemistry not based on carbon with water as a reaction medium. To me and much of the audience, he seemed unduly determined to believe that the answer to his question was *no*. At one point, to support that view, he held up the *Handbook of Chemistry and Physics.* "There is simply no other element," he proclaimed, "that can form the great variety of complex compounds that carbon can. Just look at how many pages of this book are devoted to compounds of carbon, and how few to compounds of everything else."

"But isn't it just possible," asked an irreverent listener, "that the amount of space devoted to carbon might be influenced by the fact that that book was compiled by carbon-based, aqueous researchers?"

The question seemed to me a very good one. Naturally human beings, whose whole lives are based on carbon reactions carried out in water, would tend to consider them the most interesting area of chemistry. On the other hand, to be fair to that colloquium speaker, carbon does have an exceptional, if not completely unique, ability to form the kinds of complex molecules that life needs. Is that ability *really* unique, or are there other ways to do it?

Silicon is the one candidate that appears to show some promise. Its chemistry is in many respects similar to that of carbon, and it has the advantage of being highly abundant, especially on smallish planets like Earth or Mars. However, by itself it is not as well-suited to forming long chains as carbon is, and at temperatures like those on Earth, it tends to form hard crystalline structures. Some organisms use such silicon compounds because of their rigidity, in such structures as shells, but in general it's a disadvantage—life needs flexibility.

However, the "backbone" of an "organic" molecule doesn't necessarily have to consist of only one kind of atom. Silicon can form long chain molecules with properties better suited to the needs of life, called *silicones*, by alternating with oxygen, with methyl (CH_3) groups attached to the silicons along the chain as in figure 4-2. Poul Anderson and others have suggested that life based on silicones might occur in hot planetary environments. Isaac Asimov has taken the suggestion a step further: Fluorine might replace the hydrogens to form "fluorosilicones" that might serve as a basis for life on even hotter worlds. (Fluorine forms exceptionally strong bonds, so its compounds can be stable at higher temperatures than similar compounds of other elements.)

As a science fiction writer, you may find it useful to know that such possibilities exist. However, if you want to do much more than mention them in passing, you'll need to take a much closer look at their chemistry. Those are much beyond the scope of this book, and in fact these particular possibilities are so exotic that even a chemist would likely have to do some research before saying anything very definite about them. This is not intended to discourage you from using them, provided you're prepared to do the necessary

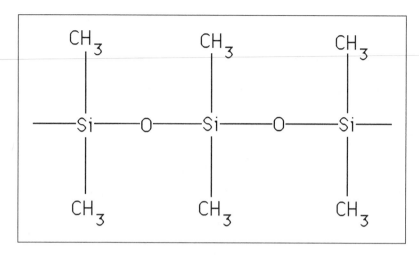

FIGURE 4-2 A portion of a silicone chain.

homework. Writers are often advised to "Write what you know." Less often heard, but no less important, is the corollary: "If you don't know it, learn it!" In writing science fiction you will often have to deal in some detail with something that you don't already know. So you need to be prepared to familiarize yourself with new areas, by means ranging from standard reference books to interviews with specialists.

However, you will have to decide how much research you want to get into in a particular case. If you happen to *be* a biochemist, you may want to tackle something as ambitious as working out the whole biochemistry and ecology, in the manner of Hal Clement, of a world where those things are based on fluorosilicones. If you have only a rudimentary knowledge of chemistry and want to get a reasonable amount of fiction written in a reasonable time, you'd probably better stick to more familiar territory.

Even there, things may vary considerably from what we're used to. I'll sketch some of the possibilities, any of which may be useful in stories, but always subject to the kind of caution I've just indicated. If you *can* imagine a really new kind of life, and make it convincing, that accomplishment will do much to make your story stand out from the crowd. But the more exotic you get, the more background work you must do, and the easier it is to make mistakes. As with so many other things, the potential rewards are roughly proportional to effort and risk!

What are some of the other possibilities for carbon-based life? For one, remember my earlier mention of stereoisomers. Experiments aimed at simulating the conditions that led to the synthesis of the first biological molecules on Earth produce equal quantities of "left-handed" and "right-handed" molecules of a particular type, yet terrestrial biology has chosen one version over the other. We don't know any reason why the handedness chosen should be intrinsically preferable; apparently evolution just happened to select one set. If that's true, another planet might evolve very similarly to Earth, but choose the opposite handedness for all the organic molecules that occur in two stereoisomers—or perhaps only some of them. In such a case, food evolved there that looked indistinguishable from something grown here would be quite indigestible for us (and vice versa).

How will genetic information be stored and transmitted on other worlds? Is DNA the only medium available, or might there be other molecules that can function similarly and have become the biological standard on other worlds? Even if DNA is used, the code may not be based on a *double*, but a *triple* helix. Such things occur in some Earthly cells, and Joan Slonczewski, in her story "Microbe," has imagined a whole ecosystem based on it.

Might plants on some planets use something other than chlorophyll in photosynthesis? It may be that some other molecule could play a similar role—and perhaps even play it better on a planet whose sun puts most of its energy into a different part of the spectrum than ours. For that matter, we have already seen, in the case of those deep-sea vents, that the energy input to drive an ecosystem can come from some other source altogether rather than from sunlight. Might geothermal energy play a larger biological role on some worlds than it does here? Arthur C. Clarke described one such system, on Jupiter's satellite Europa, in his novel *2010*.

How about the solvent in which biological reactions take place and the atmosphere in which the entire ecosystem is immersed? In our case, these are respectively water and a nitogen-oxygen mixture with smaller amounts of other gases. (Even many purely aquatic animals depend on elemental oxygen dissolved in the water.) Other types of planets, with different kinds of oceans and atmospheres, may use different reactions to survive and utilize local conditions. Poul Anderson has described several such possibilities in chapter five, "Life As We Do Not Know It," of his book *Is There*

Life on Other Worlds?

Some subjovian planets might have warm temperatures (thanks to the now-familiar greenhouse effect), liquid water and ample supplies of materials that can eventually produce life. Isaac Asimov suggested that early plants on such a world could use an analog of photosynthesis (catalyzed by something other than chlorophyll) to split water into hydrogen and oxygen, react the oxygen with methane to form carbohydrates and release the hydrogen. The hydrogen in turn could react with atmospheric carbon dioxide to form more methane. Such a process could eventually lead to an atmosphere consisting largely of hydrogen, ammonia and methane. The atmospheric balance could be maintained by hydrogen-breathing animals eating plants, breaking down their carbohydrates, and exhaling methane and water vapor. (For a more detailed account, see Asimov's article, "Planets Have an Air About Them.") In terms of the roles of oxidation and reduction, this is a sort of "opposite" of the balance we have on Earth; but it might work better where lots of free hydrogen is available but free oxygen isn't.

Anderson acknowledges that, for one reason or another, the exact scheme proposed by Asimov might turn out to be unworkable—but goes on to point out that many others can be imagined, some of which probably *are* viable somewhere. Cold planets with hydrogen atmospheres, for example, might have ammonia oceans, and ecosystems in which plants make unsaturated hydrocarbons instead of carbohydrates, which hydrogen-breathing animals eat, saturate and break down into simpler compounds, exhaling methane. Some variation of such an arrangement might be workable on a wide range of largish planets, from superterrestrials to jovians.

Thick atmospheres imply (again, because of the greenhouse effect) that the surfaces and deeper layers of such planets will be warmer than you might expect, even around weak suns or relatively far from stronger ones. However, they also make it hard for visible or ultraviolet radiation, needed for photosynthesis or similar reactions, to penetrate very deep into the atmosphere. This may imply that such reactions can take place only in the upper layers of such atmospheres. So be it: Much the same is true of Earth's oceans, yet rich ecosystems persist in the depths, fueled by materials that drift down after being photosynthesized near the surface. The analogy is even better than you might think, since pressures are so high deep in the atmosphere of a planet like Jupiter that conditions there are in many ways more like Earth's oceans than its atmosphere. For example, large animals could "swim" there, as in Arthur C. Clarke's "A Meeting With Medusa" or Rick Cook and Peter L. Manly's "Symphony for Skyfall."

Those Antarctic lichens and hot-spring fish show a startling range of temperature adaptations here on Earth, but do they really represent the extremes of what's possible? Probably not. An extremely cold planet with very high atmospheric pressure, for example, might have oceans of liquid methane. These could dissolve *lipids*, a class of compounds that includes oils and fats and can form things as complex as proteins. The life on Hal Clement's Mesklin, in *Mission of Gravity*, is based on such a system. On very hot worlds, as already suggested, silicones or fluorosilicones might provide a foundation for life. Or perhaps fluorocarbons (analogs of hydrocarbons, with hydrogen atoms replaced by fluorine), with liquid sulfur as a solvent.

Early science fiction stories sometimes featured aliens who *breathed* fluorine or chlorine instead of oxygen. As astronomers learned more about planet formation and the origins of life, this came to seem unlikely since neither of those elements is likely to be an important constituent of a primitive planetary atmosphere—but then, as Hal Clement pointed out, neither is free oxygen. Might there be planets on which life originated and then *created* a chlorine- or fluorine-based atmosphere, somewhat as life on Earth created an oxygen-based atmosphere? Maybe, subject to certain rather esoteric conditions. Dr. Stephen L. Gillett, in his article "Those Halogen Breathers," has expounded in some detail upon those conditions, and even dropped some hints as to how they might generate stories.

Dr. Gillett has also taken such a look at ways sulfur might play a central role in life, in the article "Fire, Brimstone—and Maybe Life?" Hal Clement's novel *Iceworld* features aliens from an extremely hot world who breathe gaseous sulfur; the "ice planet" they must deal with is Earth. In the light of later knowledge, Gillett is skeptical about the way Clement's aliens use sulfur (though he still admires the story). However, he goes on to explore a number of other possibilities that might hold up even under present-day scrutiny, including sulfur-based microbes on Io, sulfuric acid oceans that might exist elsewhere, and the difficulties intelligent aliens might face in building a technological civilization in such a place.

So . . . those three basic characteristics may be about all we can agree on for life in general: highly organized structures that take in energy from their surroundings and use it to maintain their structure and organization, and that have the ability to reproduce. Beyond that, there's a vast range of possibilities for a writer to explore. As for how life originates, any or all of the mechanisms suggested as candidates for Earth may operate somewhere. Life may form in one way on some planets, and in one or more quite different ways on others. Some of those ways may be completely different from *any* of the alternatives I've mentioned.

One new category in particular must be added—that of "created" or "engineered" life. Humans have already demonstrated an ability to produce life-forms different from any found in nature, such as mice that produce human hormones. This is just a beginning, and an intelligent species with more experience in this area may create things that we would have to call life that are *very* different from "natural" forms. My story ". . . And Comfort to the Enemy" portrayed a highly advanced technological society that we might not even recognize as such until it was too late, because its technology was entirely biological, all its "machines" being specially developed plants and animals. I can now easily imagine our own society going down that road, and alien societies going much farther. Naturally evolved life-forms are limited by what can be done with step-by-step modification of material that has already evolved. A civilization that can create life from scratch and to order might, for example, be able to create very strong or very smart creatures far larger or smaller than would be possible with the biological materials evolved on Earth.

Even that, of course, does not exhaust the possibilities. In this book I'm trying to tell you about a broad spectrum of the ideas that other science fiction writers and scientists have had—but if you can come up with a brand-new one of your own, that's even better.

HOW COMMON IS LIFE? THE FERMI PARADOX

How common is life, and in particular, the kinds of life that make good story characters? The only way to get a real, definite answer to that question is to take a close look at lots of stars and any planets they may have. However, we can make some educated guesses based on the universality of physical law, and those guesses suggest that life is pretty common.

There are a hundred billion or so stars in this galaxy alone, and we have pretty good reason to believe that they're all formed by the same basic mechanism. On theoretical grounds, that mechanism seems likely to produce planets in a goodly fraction of cases. Some theorists have even suggested that essentially *all* stars, with the possible exception of multiple stars and those far to the left in the Hertzsprung-Russell diagram, should have planets. These theories recently got some strong observational support when the Hubble telescope took an unprecedentedly detailed look at a nebula containing newly forming stars and saw what appeared to be protoplanetary disks around at least half of them.

So planets appear to be common. How many of those planets will develop life? If the processes leading to the development of life are simply a continuation of the processes that led to the development of a planet, it may well occur wherever the astronomical conditions are within certain ranges compatible with life. Since life can adapt to quite a wide range of conditions, this suggests that a large percentage of those planets—perhaps at least one in orbit around most single stars—is likely to have some sort of life. (Though not necessarily good "story" life—remember that for a majority of its life to date, Earth hosted only single-celled organisms, and those were confined to the oceans.)

Stephen H. Dole, in *Habitable Planets for Man*, attempted to estimate the abundance of planets on which human beings could live without life-support systems such as domes or spacesuits. That is a sharply limited subset of "all planets with native life." Dole assumed native life was necessary to create an oxygen-containing atmosphere that humans could breathe, but humans also have many other requirements that might not apply to all life. Dole made his estimate by making careful guesses (his reasoning is spelled out in chapter five of his book) at such factors as the fraction of stars that have suitable mass, the probability that a star has planets, the probabilities that at least one planet orbits at a suitable distance and has an acceptable axial tilt, etc. Even with all these restrictions, he estimated that there are something like 600 million human-habitable planets in our galaxy alone. Other galaxies should have comparable numbers. All of them may have additional planets where we couldn't live, but something else could.

Astronomers Frank Drake and Carl Sagan have made a different but related sort of estimate, about the number of *technological civilizations* with which we might be able to communicate, e.g., by radio. Their estimate, too, involves a product of factors, all of which have to be guessed. Some of them, such as the average lifetime of a technological civilization, are beyond the scope of this chapter, but we'll return to the "Drake equation" later. For now, just a bit of foreshadowing: Despite the wide variation possible in the guesses going into the final estimate, almost everyone comes up with a number so high that it would seem inevitable that we would have come into contact with at least one extraterrestrial species by now. This prediction, together with the lack of clear evidence that we have done so, is often referred to as the "Fermi paradox" (named for physicist Enrico Fermi, who asked bluntly, "Where are they?").

The Fermi paradox has reopened a great deal of speculation about such matters as the abundance of life. Could it be that we really are alone in the galaxy, if not the universe? If so, how do we reconcile that fact with the reasons already cited for thinking life should be abundant? If not, why has there been no apparent contact?

Trying to imagine explanations for the Fermi paradox is a fruitful field for speculation by scientists and science fiction writers alike. David Brin has speculated in both capacities (see his nonfiction articles and the short story "The Crystal Spheres"). It's a theme that will return to haunt us later in this book, but a fuller discussion must wait for a later chapter. (One of the factors in the Drake-Sagan equation, for example, is the probability of an inhabited planet developing intelligent life with manipulative abilities during the lifetime of their sun.)

However, even the beginning of an answer depends on making guesses about what forms life can take, and how likely the processes that lead to it are. That depends partly on chemistry, as we have discussed in this chapter. But it also depends on mechanical factors, and how they are shaped by the environment in which evolution takes place—for bodies and minds must be equipped to function in the environments they occupy.

CHAPTER 5

Engineering Organisms

Alien Bodies and Minds

I t is perfectly possible to write about plausible aliens who are essentially indistinguishable from human beings. After all, we're the one type of intelligent being that we *know* is possible. However, we also know that we evolved to fit particular conditions found on one planet, and that changing a number here or there in the astronomical description of a planet can change surface conditions dramatically. Since a planet is described by many parameters, each of which can vary through a wide range, the planets in any galaxy should offer a great variety of living conditions. We should not expect very many of them to produce lifeforms that look much like us.

Or should we?

CONVERGENT EVOLUTION

In the May and June 1939 issues of *Astounding*, a two-part article ("Design for Life") by L. Sprague de Camp looked at life from an *engineering* point of view, considering not only how life has developed on Earth but also what living things have to do and what engineering principles determine how those things can be done. He concluded that any intelligent being that evolved on any more or less Earthlike planet will probably be at least vaguely humanoid. Some of his assumptions need a bit of revision in light of more recent knowledge, but much of his reasoning holds up surprisingly well more than fifty years later. Could it be that we really *should* expect most intelligent aliens, at least from Earthlike planets, to look like us? Or is this another case where the conclusion is influenced by the fact that the speculator happens to be of the form he finds most plausible?

My personal guess is: a bit of both. The fact that we have spent all our lives on a planet where "our kind of people" have evolved and become dominant probably does make it harder for us to see alternative possibilities that might exist elsewhere. On the other hand, de Camp is quite right that there are some compelling reasons for believing that similar environments will produce similar life.

The first such line of reasoning is the empirical observation that precisely that has happened over and over in widely separated but similar environments on Earth. Biologists call it *convergent evolution*: two independent evolutionary paths leading to end points that look alike. De Camp cites the example of largish swimming animals. There are many, many species of such critters now, and there used to be even more. They belong to quite distinct lines of evolution—fish, reptiles, birds, mammals—yet they all have similarly streamlined body shapes.

The similarities are even more striking if you divide "swimmers" into subclasses depending on how they swim—e.g., "scullers" such as porpoises, ichthyosaurs, swordfish and sharks, all swim by waving a fin at the back end of the body while steering and stabilizing with other fins. De Camp identifies three such methods of swimming, and points out that virtually *all* largish aquatic animals use one of them, and have the general type of body shape that goes with that method.

Similar examples abound, sometimes involving whole collections of traits that may or may not be obviously related. South America has a family of birds called jacamars; Africa has a different family called bee-eaters. Even though the two families evolved independently, they have so many obvious similarities in both appearance and behavior (both types of birds catch insects on the wing and batter them to death against branches) that they're likely to strike even an untrained and not particularly interested observer as being related.

Why should this be? Why should only a few methods be used by all the many animals that have to propel a bulky body through water? Why should widely separated families of birds both look and act alike in so many ways?

In the case of the jacamars, I don't know. It's not obvious to me why there should be quite so many parallels. Why, for example, should the kind of color scheme favored by bee-eaters and jacamars so often go with their kinds of lifestyle? Probably there *is* a reason that simply hasn't occurred to me; jacamars, bee-eaters and probably some people who have written Ph.D. theses about them know more about what they're doing than I do.

The case of the swimmers is more straightforward, and leads us to the other line of reasoning that supports the expectation that similar environments produce similar life. The first was the simple observation that convergent evolution does occur. The second is the reason why it has to occur: Life that evolves is subject to the same engineering principles as any machine that's designed.

Evolution is an inefficient engineer; it depends far more on trial and error than any human engineer would be allowed to. But the ultimate requirement for both is the same: The product must *work*. It does not have to work perfectly, but simply well enough to compete successfully against whatever else is out there. No doubt you're painfully aware that this is true in industrial engineering: How many products that you buy represent truly optimal design and construction? It's especially true of evolution. An organism that can already use an available food source more successfully than anything else that's trying has no need to do it any better. (In fact, it might ultimately be an evolutionary disadvantage for it to do so. If it exploits its resources too efficiently, it may wipe out the supply and thus itself. Our own species could become a prime example of this, if it's not careful.)

Also, since evolution works so slowly, there's always a "phase lag" in its reactions to environmental changes. Most of the organisms in the early part of an ice age will be struggling to survive with equipment developed for warmer conditions. If the ice age lasts long enough, flora and fauna may eventually evolve that are well suited to the cold—but they will then be poorly adapted to the warmth when the ice age ends.

Either evolution or engineering will tend to produce devices (of which organisms are a special case) that are at least reasonably good at what they have to do. The ones that *aren't* will be squeezed out by others that are better; both evolution and engineers are constantly trying new designs. Whether or not a design works is determined by the same physical principles that govern everything else in the physical universe. For example, animals that live by swimming must be able to move rapidly through the water without wasting too much energy. A porpoise shaped like a porpoise can do this; a rectangular block cannot. Thus you find no rectangular swimmers, but many that are streamlined.

As an example of how pervasively an engineering principle shapes life, let's look at one particularly important principle and some of its biological consequences.

THE SQUARE-CUBE LAW

If you scale the linear dimensions of any object up (or down) by a particular factor, any *area* associated with it is scaled up or down by that factor *squared*, while its *volume* is scaled up or down by that factor *cubed*. For example, if you consider a glass sphere one centimeter in diameter, a sphere of the same glass *two* centimeters in diameter will have *four* times the surface area and *eight* times the volume.

In itself, this might seem a mere curiosity; but it has profound practical implications for life. Anything about the sphere that is proportional to area will also be changed by the linear scale factor squared, and anything proportional to volume will be changed by the scale factor *cubed*. For example, the amount of paint needed to cover the two-centimeter sphere is four times that for the one-centimeter, but the two-centimeter sphere weighs eight times as much as the one-centimeter.

Many quantities important to life come in related pairs, one proportional to the square and the other to the cube of the linear size. Since the two quantities of the pair don't change by the same factor when the size is changed, you *cannot* simply change the size of an organism arbitrarily, keeping everything else the same.

For example, consider body mass and strength. Humans often marvel that some insects can jump many times their own body length—but we could, too, if we were scaled down to insect size. A man might be 180 cm tall and a cricket 1.8 cm long. A 1.8 cm man—that is, a man scaled down by a linear factor of one hundred but otherwise constructed exactly like a normal man—would have one ten-thousandth the strength (proportional to cross-sectional area of arm and leg muscles and bones), but only one-millionth the weight (proportional to total volume). Thus he would have a hundred times as much force available to lift each gram of his body, and naturally could jump much farther.

If, that is, he could live at all. Unfortunately for our would-be Lilliputian, strength and weight are not the only things affected by scale change and the square-cube law. Reducing volume and hence mass by a factor of one million means there's that much less bio-mass that has to be kept supplied with food and oxygen; but it also means that the rate of heat loss by radiation from the skin is only reduced by a factor of ten thousand. Thus each gram of that little body is losing heat one hundred times as fast as each gram of a full-sized man. Since functioning as a human being requires main-taining a constant temperature of 37°C, the little guy, other things being equal, is going to have to eat and breathe one hundred times as much per gram as you or I. We might eat a fiftieth of our body weight in a day; scaled down by one hundred, we would have to eat twice our body weight—and have our breathing and pulse rates correspondingly speeded up to get enough oxygen in to oxidize all that food. This is why mice, shrews and songbirds have such high metabolic rates ("to eat like a bird" isn't at all what the colloquial usage implies!) and why you don't find warm-blooded critters much smaller than those.

There are other problems, too. Humans are composed of very large numbers of very small cells. If you try to scale one down by changing *every* linear measurement by the same factor of one hundred, this means that each cell is scaled down by that factor. Since no cells on Earth are anywhere near that small—all the cells on Earth only vary over about one order of magnitude in mass—we must suspect that cells of the required complexity can't be made that small with the materials used by Earthly life. Thus our tiny man would have far fewer cells of all types—including nerve cells. Since intelligence depends on having *lots* of nerve cells and lots of connections among them, the little man could not have anything like human intelligence.

While we're on the subject of cells, what does the square-cube law imply about the possibility of very large single-celled creatures, such as the "giant amoebas" sometimes found running amok in early science fiction? Their prospects are not good. A cell is essen-tially a bag of fluid. Make it very big, and the membrane can no longer support the contents. At best, such a creature will sprawl flat, effectively immobilized; at worst, the cell wall will rupture, spilling the contents out into a puddle. Thus we can expect macroscopic life-forms to be multicellular, wherever they occur. (Unless the environment itself provides lots of support—see William P. Jacobs's article for an exception in Earth's oceans.)

Meanwhile, back at that insect . . . how about the horror movie cliché of insects or spiders the size of horses or tanks wreaking havoc on the landscape? An insect-sized man could do dazzling athletic feats, but it works the other way, too. A man-sized insect couldn't even stand up. Scale its linear dimensions up by one hundred, and its legs can support ten thousand times the weight—but the new insect has a *million* times the weight. It also has additional problems. Most insects have extremely simple respiratory systems, consisting of a few tubes letting oxygen flow to the tissues where it's needed and carbon dioxide flow away. Such a system can't supply oxygen, and remove carbon dioxide, fast enough for an organism much bigger than the insects we have—that is, a few inches long.

There are, of course, special ways you might get around some of these problems. You can't simply scale up an insect a hundredfold without changing anything else—but that doesn't mean you can't have something that *looks* like an insect that size. It simply means that if you're going to do that, you have to make other changes to compensate.

The strength problem might be overcome by making the "insect" of sterner stuff—material with a much higher strength-to-mass ratio than what real insects are made of. To make this believable in a story, you'll have to imagine a way that your world has been able to evolve superior materials that four billion years of evolution haven't produced on Earth, or else assume that your insects are artificial creations of a technological civilization that's very good at materials science.

The respiratory problem you might solve by assuming that while the exterior looks the same, the innards are very different. Much greater efficiency could be achieved by using lungs or gills to aerate a very large surface, and a heart to circulate the gases to and from cells via pumped blood. Some prehistoric swamps sported dragonflies much bigger than any of their contemporary kin, but they could only get away with it because the air was denser then.

This little discussion of the square-cube law has served as a good illustration of how a simple physical principle can have far-reaching implications for every aspect of life. In this case, what it boils down to is that different mechanisms can serve a particular purpose, but each only works well in a certain size range. As a science fiction writer, you will be interested in all kinds of life, since any world you create will have many ecological niches to be filled. However, you will probably have a special interest in *intelligent* forms; so before surveying the kinds of problems that all life must solve, and the various means that can be used to solve them, we should look at some of the special requirements for intelligent life.

INTELLIGENCE AND THE ALTERNATIVES

The most basic special requirement for an intelligent species is a nervous system of sufficient size and complexity, which in turn puts some restrictions on possible size of an intelligent organism. The nature of intelligence will impose some other requirements, or at least guidelines, so this is a good time to ponder the questions: What *is* intelligence, and why should anything develop it?

Intelligence is, as L. Sprague de Camp put it, "an annoyingly vague term"—and a science fiction writer probably wouldn't want it any other way. One of the interesting kinds of things we can do in this field is speculate on different *kinds* of intelligence and different ways it might come about. (For an unusual fictional approach to the latter, see "Bluff," by Harry Turtledove.) So we wouldn't want to be limited by too narrow a definition.

We needn't look far to see that there are different kinds of intelligence, right here on Earth and even within our own species. We've all known people who were great at math but couldn't spell, or who wrote wonderful poetry but couldn't balance a checkbook. When I was teaching physics at a small college, I even saw amazing variations in how different students thought about the same physics problems.

Still, we will need at least an approximate definition of intelligence, and for that it would be helpful to have some examples of things that we would call something else. Let's define intelligence as including one or both of the following: the ability to learn by experience, and the ability to reason abstractly. The first of these can alternatively be thought of as forming conditioned reflexes in response to new stimuli; the second, as thinking about things that are not present and reaching conclusions that can be appropriately applied when they are present.

One might be tempted to include a host of other things as aspects of intelligence, such as self-awareness and emotion. For now, at least, let's treat those not as essential ingredients, but as special qualities that may be attached to particular intelligences. Trying to imagine intelligences that lack one or both can be an interesting science-fictional exercise. Emmett McDowell imagined a race without emotion (and found an evolutionary advantage in it) in "Veiled Island." Recent science fiction, spurred by real research on artificial intelligence, has imagined many computer programs that become self-aware, but can you imagine an intelligence that is *not*—i.e., that thinks intelligently about everything in its environment, but has no concept of itself as an independent player?

Intelligence is essentially a way for an organism to make decisions about what to do to solve the day-to-day problems of survival. For most organisms, those problems mostly fall into two categories: how to get food, and how to avoid becoming somebody else's food. For something that lives entirely in one place, like a dandelion or an oyster, those problems are simple. The dandelion simply absorbs light from the Sun and nutrients from the soil; the oyster opens its shell and lets currents bring food to it when not threatened, and closes its shell when it senses something might be about to eat it. Neither strategy is completely effective; some individuals of both types do get eaten, but their *species* survive by making many individuals. Intelligence would be of little or no value to a dandelion or an oyster, since neither is equipped to do anything different from its basic routine.

Something that can do something about threats or opportunities has an advantage; hence many organisms, mostly animals, have developed the ability to move around. A rabbit can run from a fox; a fox can pounce on a rabbit if it can sneak close enough.

A creature that can move needs a way to decide when, how far, in what direction and how fast to move. For most mobile animals, decisions are based on *instinct*, which is a simpler kind of programming than intelligence. Instinct may be thought of as "hard-wired" programming, built right into the organism, operational from birth and not subject to change. A baby snake, for example, fends for itself from the instant it is born or hatched. It drinks, catches and eats smaller animals, and flees when pursued just as an adult of its species does. For things that live simple, unchanging lives, instinct works fine and doesn't require an extremely complicated nervous system.

The next step up is "Type 1 intelligence," or the ability to form conditioned reflexes. This could, for example, enable a cow to learn to avoid an electric fence after being shocked a few times, even though cows never encountered electric fences until recently and so have no built-in instincts about them. Humans tend to think of this as a "primitive" form of intelligence, more characteristic of "lower" animals than themselves, but they use it, too. Learning to drive a car or play the piano is largely a matter of conditioning reflexes. A beginner has to think about every move and does them awkwardly, while an old pro does them automatically and much more smoothly.

Nonetheless, "Type 2 intelligence," or abstract reasoning, is what we think of as most characteristically and distinctly human. (Until recently, many of us rather arrogantly, if naively, claimed this as completely unique to humans, but it's become hard to deny that at least a few other species, such as chimpanzees and dolphins, do it too.) This kind of intelligence confers adaptability, allowing beings that possess it to figure out solutions to problems neither they nor their ancestors have ever faced before. Thus an intelligent being has a better chance of surviving a climate change or extending its range into regions for which it is not physically well-suited. Our own ancestors have demonstrated both of these abilities.

There is little evolutionary incentive for organisms to develop abilities, especially abilities that require complex physical equipment, unless those abilities significantly enhance their survival capabilities. Intelligence seems most likely to do this for an animal that moves around in an environment that poses many and varied challenges. De Camp considered this much more likely to happen on land than in the oceans; he considered the oceans to be too monotonous an environment to provide enough stimulus. (If the cetaceans [whales and dolphins] are as bright as they seem, this might be attributed to strides they made when their ancestors lived on land, as they apparently did for quite a while. Of course, that doesn't explain the octopus, which also shows considerable cleverness. . . .) In the case of our own remote ancestors, experience living in trees probably helped.

Since evolution proceeds by building on old traits, either modifying them or adding new ones, possessors of abstract intelligence may also carry remnants of earlier types of programming, like instinct. (See Carl Sagan's *The Dragons of Eden.*) One of their major recurring problems may be learning when to allow instinct to have its way, and when to let intelligence overrule it. (You would not want to stop and think about whether to pull your hand away from a hot stove; but neither would you want to trust instinct when landing an airplane, since most people's instincts tell them exactly the wrong thing to do in some situations.)

Intelligence allows a new capability that Alfred Korzybski called "time-binding": the ability to transmit learned information from generation to generation. This is crucial to the development of civilization, as it enables each generation to build on the accomplishments of its predecessors. Without it, each generation would have to learn everything for itself, repeating many of the mistakes of its ancestors, and none would have time to get very far. In humans, time-binding is achieved by having most of what we know taught by our ancestors during a long period of relative helplessness and dependency while growing up. This, of course, has far-reaching implications for the ways that human societies develop. But is it the only possible way?

Maybe not. A few years ago experiments were reported that seemed to show chemical transmission of learned behavior—e.g., flatworms that had learned to run a simple maze could be ground up and fed to "uneducated" flatworms, which would then show the same "learned" ability without going through the learning process. Attempts to repeat these experiments in other laboratories failed, and they came to be generally regarded as a false alarm. We still have no clear evidence of "chemical learning" in Earthly organisms, but it is not inconceivable that it has developed somewhere else. Marc Stiegler made fascinating use of this possibility in his novelette "Petals of Rose."

PROBLEMS AND SOLUTIONS: A CATALOG OF OPTIONS

We're now ready to survey the kinds of problems life must deal with, and some of the possible solutions that have been dreamed up by Earthly evolution and/or science fiction writers. I'll list quite a few of these as if they were separate, but over and over you'll see how they interact—i.e., the way chosen to solve one problem affects the ways available to solve others.

Unicellular or Multicellular?

Probably every world will have many single-celled organisms, in terms of both individuals and species. (Unless some civilization has made a very determined effort to get rid of them *and* to find another way to fulfill their functions—e.g., on Earth, blue-green algae play a large role in maintaining atmosphere oxygen.) However, as we've seen, single cells are quite limited in how big they can be and what they can do. So worlds that have *only* single-celled life (which may be common) will probably not be very interesting to human explorers (except perhaps as prospects for terraforming) or readers. On worlds of most interest, all but the simplest life-forms, and in particular any we'd call intelligent, will probably be multicellular.

Size

I've already said quite a bit about this in my discussion of the square-cube law, but there are still a few aspects that warrant special mention—e.g., what are the maximum and minimum sizes possible for A. organisms generally, and B. intelligent organisms?

Some bacteria of the genus *Mycoplasma* are smaller than 0.2 *micro*meter (or, if you prefer, a millionth of an inch, comparable to the wavelengths of visible light). Viruses are smaller, but are not unanimously considered truly alive, since they depend on other entities to carry out some of their life functions. At the other extreme we can find a variety of examples, depending on your additional requirements. On present-day Earth, the largest organisms are probably the giant trees of the genus *Sequoia*, which can reach heights exceeding 100 meters (or 300 feet). (Possible exception: Some fungi, long regarded as independent organisms, have recently been found to be mere parts of huge organisms that exist mostly underground.) Among contemporary animals, the largest is the blue whale (up to 30 meters or 100 feet in length), while the largest on land is the African elephant (up to 3.5 meters or 11 feet in height, but chubby, massing up to 6500 kg or 7 tons). Flying animals are much smaller, being limited to the 10 kg or so of condors and albatrosses.

Flying creatures are limited to much smaller sizes than land animals, and those in turn are much smaller than the biggest swimmers. That observation is highly significant for a science fiction writer, and is related to another: In some prehistoric periods, creatures of land and air grew much bigger than they now do. Some of the dinosaurs grew to 30 or more meters in length, with masses many times that of any contemporary elephant; and pterosaurs ("flying dinosaurs") have been found with bigger wingspans than many small airplanes. All of these facts illustrate that practical size limits depend on planetary conditions. The larger sizes of extinct land and air animals were apparently possible because their atmosphere was denser and richer in oxygen than ours, enabling a more efficient metabolism. Those that live exclusively in water can grow larger than on land because the buoyancy means they don't have to support their own full weight, as you can easily demonstrate for yourself in a swimming pool. However, it also means that they must stay in water. A beached whale is in serious trouble because it can't do basic things like breathing under the full force of gravity.

The full force of gravity, of course, can be more or less on other planets. On a planet with weak gravity, organisms would have something like the advantage whales get from water. Since the weight of every part (that is, the pull of gravity toward the ground) is less, the supporting structures don't need to be as strong as they would on a high-gravity world. Thus any type of thing—plants, animals, buildings—can be bigger and more graceful or "spindly" there. (See Martyn J. Fogg's article "On Beanpoles and Drum-Men.") If you want things built like insects or spiders, but man-sized or larger, a low-gravity world is where you have the best chance of making them work. The Overlords in Arthur C. Clarke's *Childhood's End*, tall and thin and with exoskeletons, originated on such a world. Hal Clement's Mesklinites, on the other hand, having to deal with extremely powerful gravity, are small and built low to the ground, rather like a foot-long centipede. You wouldn't want to be tall on a high-gravity world, either: On a part of Mesklin where the gravity is fifty times that on Earth, falling six inches would be like falling twenty-five feet here!

One can imagine still larger organisms, such as the planetwide silicon-based organism in Joseph Green's *Conscience Interplanetary* or the 150-million-kilometer intelligent nebula in Fred Hoyle's *The Black Cloud*. Those are getting beyond the scope of this chapter, but we'll take another look at such things in chapter eleven.

Restricting ourselves for now to life based on what we would consider more "ordinary" biochemistry, we return briefly to the question of what special constraints *intelligence* puts on possible sizes. I've already discussed reasons for suspecting that humanlike intelligence can't occur in a body built along the same general lines if that body is much smaller than ours. L. Sprague de Camp's guess of forty or fifty pounds as a lower limit for an adult being of human-like intelligence is probably as reasonable as any, at least in an Earthlike environment. My personal inclination would be to make it a bit smaller for the simple reason that scientifically careful guesses of limits have so often proved too conservative—there may well be an alternate way of doing something that we haven't thought of. This was part of my reasoning when I made the "chucks" in *Tweedlioop* comparable in both size and appearance to large Earthly rodents. (A more important reason, though, was that I wanted to play with the psychology of humans reacting to aliens that *looked* as if they belonged here but didn't, and those were the most convenient animals available in the setting I chose to use. I knew it very well, and in fact the opening scene of *Tweedlioop* was directly suggested by an encounter with a very real and slightly odd red squirrel.)

Very different environments may change the limits considerably. The neutron star dwellers in Robert L. Forward's *Dragon's Egg* (see chapter eleven) are much smaller than we are—but everything is necessarily much more compact there. Also, the embryonic field of nanotechnology suggests that *artificial* intelligences can be made far smaller than anything emerging from our kind of "natural" evolution—and it's entirely possible that some "aliens" we meet may be "artificial."

As for an upper size limit, it's hard to imagine a nervous system being intrinsically too big and complex to do whatever it needs to do. De Camp and Anderson put forth reasons for suspecting that intelligent land animals capable of building a civilization are not likely to be much bigger than a grizzly bear—say a ton or so. On the other hand, G. David Nordley has created in great detail a fascinating and believable race of extremely large amphibious intelligences, the Do'utians, for his "Trimus" stories. Fully aquatic beings can get quite large, and Earth's whales seem to show more signs of high intelligence the more we look at them.

Respiration

We've already established that if oxygen, hydrogen, chlorine or some other gas is available for use in highly efficient oxidizing or reducing reactions, an organism that uses it will get far more from its food than one that doesn't. Therefore, while primitive organisms using less efficient chemistry will survive in some niches, as they have on Earth, we can reasonably expect all but the most primitive to use the most efficient chemistry available where they live.

To get the oxygen (or hydrogen, or whatever) to their cells, larger organisms need more elaborate respiratory systems than small ones. Single-celled creatures simply exchange gases through their cell walls. Small multicellular land dwellers can use simple networks of tubes that open to the outside, like the tracheae of insects. Some small fish and amphibians respire directly through their skins, though amphibians doing that on land must keep their skins moist.

None of those methods can supply enough incoming gas, or remove enough outgoing, to satisfy the needs of a very large and/ or active creature. Such creatures must therefore find a way to make the square-cube law work *for* them. They can do this by increasing the surface-to-volume ratio of the structures through which vital gases pass, and/or the rate at which gases are moved to and from those surfaces.

Aquatic animals on Earth do this with *gills*, branched or feathery structures with many small blood vessels near the surface. They may simply protrude from the body, as in some larval salamanders; or they may be enclosed in protective cavities, as in most fish. They may be exposed to an effective flow of water by the motion of swimming, or the animal may have means of forcibly pumping water over the gills. Either way, dissolved gases are exchanged between surrounding water and blood through the thin walls of the gill branches, circulated through the animal's body in the blood, and passed through the walls of blood vessels to and from other cells along the way. The same mechanical principles would work just as well for animals that live in some other liquid solvent.

Lungs, used by creatures of land and air to get the same result, can be thought of as "inside-out gills." Gills pass a liquid over the outside of a repeatedly branched tissue structure; lungs draw gas into repeatedly branched hollow tubes, exchange gases with blood through the *inner* walls of those tubes, and expel an altered mixture of gases. Branching increases the surface area for gas exchange; breathing harder increases the rate at which gases are moved in and out.

Both lungs and gills can vary considerably in the complexity and details of their structure, and even in their number. Most snakes, for example, only have one functional lung. Both lungs and gills are mechanical devices for getting a large amount of gas into and out of the body as a whole, and depend on a circulatory system to get those gases to and from individual cells. That implies a system of blood vessels (veins, arteries and capillaries), one or more pumps (most of us in these parts have one heart, but a built-in spare or two could have advantages and might have evolved somewhere), and a circulatory fluid (blood). Blood itself is quite a complicated organ, containing several highly specialized structures. In us and our close relatives, oxygen is carried to cells by the molecule called *hemoglobin*, which gives our blood its red color. Other animals may use something else, and their blood need not be red. Some Earthly crustaceans and mollusks, for example, substitute the blue copper compound hemocyanin; but as a science fiction writer, you needn't limit yourself to compounds used by Earthly organisms. Those evolved elsewhere may find useful substitutes not even known to our chemists.

The kinds of respiratory and circulatory systems a creature needs will depend on the interaction of several variables. On an earlier Earth with a more concentrated atmosphere, simple tracheae sufficed for insects of a size that could not exist here and now. The centipede-like Mesklinites in Hal Clement's *Mission of Gravity* need no lungs and breathe hydrogen directly through skin pores because they are relatively small *and* they live in a dense atmosphere. Humans store little oxygen in their bodies and so must breathe frequently or die; seals and whales, which dive deeply, must have adaptations to let them go much longer between breaths. Giraffes, to get blood to heads that are five meters or more above the ground, must have a blood pressure that would kill a human— and that means they must also have very sturdy blood vessels (see J.W. Warren's article).

Eating

Another important function of a circulatory system is to distribute food to cells. What kind of food? That brings up a delicate but basic point: Every organism (except those at the bottom of the food chain, such as photosynthesizing plants) eats other organisms and eventually (barring artificial interference such as being mummified or sealed in a vault) gets eaten by still others. An ecosystem is a more or less stable collection of organisms that use different forms of energy to maintain a dynamic balance of the system as a whole. On the surface of Earth, solar energy is used directly by plants, herbivores use energy chemically stored in those plants, carnivores get theirs by eating herbivores, and ultimately they all get recycled back into plant nutrients.

Each organism occupies a unique niche in that web of relationships and in its environment. It needs certain kinds of equipment (i.e., anatomy and physiology) to fulfill the needs of any particular niche. Plants, mostly, don't "eat"; they just need chlorophyll and light-gathering surfaces to use it (though a few plants, such as Venus fly-traps, do eat small animals and have developed equipment for catching them). Animals eat either plants or other animals, and need means of catching and processing food.

Mouths take a wide variety of forms, depending on what they have to work on and what other requirements they have to be coordinated with. Many fishes' mouths are little more than holes large enough to gulp down a reasonable range of things smaller than their owners. Snakes seldom eat, and so must be able to handle prey larger than their own diameter if that's what's available. Lacking hands or feet to hold and manipulate their food, they use large numbers of small, backward-curved teeth to hold onto whatever they catch, and elastic skin and dislocatable jaws to accommodate oversized meals. Herbivores, like cattle and antelope, need teeth suited to cutting off plants and then crushing and chewing them. Carnivores, like cats, are better served by equipment for quick killing and tearing bite-size chunks off a carcass held down with paws.

An assortment of tooth shapes and sizes, together with manipulators that allow the gathering of many types of food, makes for an omnivore like you or me—with the advantages of versatility and adaptability. At the other extreme, some types of eating equipment become highly specialized. The native Hawaiian birds called honeycreepers evolved into several species, each with a different bill shape very well fitted to a particular narrow range of foods and useless for anything else. That's fine, as long as the required foods remain plentiful; but such specialization is risky in the long term, since environmental conditions do change.

Special features of eating equipment can be found beyond the mouth. Chickens, for example, must be fed not only food, but gravel to act as "internal teeth" in an organ called the crop. Cattle have multiple "stomachs" and regurgitate, rechew and reswallow food to get the most out of it.

How much food an organism needs varies and depends on several factors. Hummingbirds are small, active, warm-blooded and airborne, all of which increase their energy needs, making them eat almost constantly and consume amounts comparable to their own body weight every day. Snakes spend most of their time resting, are "cold-blooded," and therefore need very little food. (One who has been living in my house for the past decade eats a couple of meals a week in her "hungry" season, and little or nothing—by her own choice—during the cold months.)

Getting Around—Or Not

My earlier discussion of intelligence suggests that it is unlikely to develop in plants since they stay pretty much fixed—and in general, I'd bet on that to be true. However, science fiction writers take statements like that as challenges. If you can imagine circumstances in which plants develop intelligence, you can also imagine that they would have a very different perspective on things. For a memorable fictional example, see the Hlutr, the pensive "trees" in Don Sakers's "The Leaves of October." Plants aren't altogether static; if you doubt it, watch some time-lapse movies of plants growing, attaching themselves to supports, following the sun and blooming. The essential difference is that they do things very slowly. So if they were going to evolve intelligence, they would probably do it on a planet of a long-lived star (well toward the right on the Hertzsprung-Russell diagram) and their entire lives would be lived on a far less hurried time scale than ours.

How about active, mobile plants—beings that get their energy by photosynthesizing, yet move around like animals? In general, it doesn't work. In an Earthlike environment, a being of manlike size and shape could not photosynthesize nearly enough to meet its needs (see Hal Clement's "The Creation of Imaginary Beings" and V.A. Eulach's "Those Impossible Autotrophic Men").

Again, as a science fiction writer you may well take such a generalization as a challenge, and if you're willing to work at it, you may succeed. You could, for example, put your beings' planet closer to a hotter sun, thereby letting them get enough energy from photosynthesis to support a mobile lifestyle—but bear in mind that such a change will dramatically affect the nature of *everything* that lives there. Or you could create an elaborate system like the one in Paul Ash's "Big Sword." A being some six inches tall can move about, but spends much of his time basking to soak up sunlight through broad membranes filled with a very efficient photosynthesizing agent.

Developing something like that can become a major part of the story. For most purposes, your motile and/or intelligent aliens will probably be animals. How will they get around? Earth provides examples of numerous options, most of which have probably evolved in many other places to which they're well-suited.

One that Earth doesn't seem to have, at least at the multicellular level, is *rolling on wheels*. At least two explanations suggest themselves for this lack. First, since evolution works by successive modifications of preexisting structures, it's a little hard to see how an evolutionary branch might have gone from a multi-limb design to wheel-and-bearing in small steps; the basic forms are too fundamentally different. Second, rolling isn't a very efficient way to get around on most kinds of natural terrain. It works well on relatively smooth surfaces with relatively gentle grade and few major obstructions— in other words, on constructed highways. It works a lot less well where there are rocks, logs, ditches, bramble patches, trees, cliffs, etc. In such places strong, flexible limbs to climb over or around or push through are more effective.

If wheels ever did evolve here, they may simply have been out-competed before they could get very far. Still, you may be able to imagine circumstances in which wheels *could* evolve and compete successfully, as in Piers Anthony's *Cluster* or Keith Laumer's *Retief's War*. Even on Earth there are places where artificial wheels do pretty well without roads. Four-wheel drive vehicles travel freely over the deserts of the southwestern U.S. and the Serengeti Plain (although one I was riding in Tanzania got itself quite firmly, if temporarily, immobilized by an aardvark hole). In her story "Microbe," Joan Slonczewski imagined a world on which a whole ecosystem co-evolved with wheels basic to everything and plants grew in such a way as to provide "pavement" for wheel-like animals.

We've already talked about several versions of swimming that might be adapted to any liquid medium. To these we might add *jet or rocket propulsion* such as that used by octopi and squids to make a quick getaway. However, in those animals it's only practical for occasional short bursts, and it's a little hard to see how it could be adapted to routine, continuous, long-term transportation.

On and in land there are several possibilities, each of which comes in several variants. "Crawling" can mean at least three distinct modes of getting around in animals as similar as different species of snakes. All of them seem rather cumbersome and limiting to be very likely in intelligent forms. Some animals tunnel underground, using digging tools such as spadelike snouts or paws. Some spend all their time underground, which may make for too little variety to be conducive to the development of intelligence—though some species might develop a long way toward intelligence and then, for some reason, adopt subterranean ways. Many Earthly creatures burrow only to construct nests (which may be quite complex), while venturing out onto the surface to get food and water by such means as walking and running.

Walking and running are variants of the same basic idea, using limbs to throw the body off-balance and fall in a controlled way, landing in a new place. The principle has the advantage of great adaptability. A foot, unlike a wheel, can simply be lifted over an obstacle. The shape of a foot may be adapted to suit specific needs: The sprawling hind paw of a snowshoe hare helps it stay on top of soft snow, while the cloven and padded hooves of a mountain goat give it sure traction on steep rock.

How many walking limbs might a creature have? On Earth, the number varies widely, from two on folks like us and ostriches, to dozens on millipedes. However, all the largest forms use a basic four-limb design, with limbs coming in pairs, some of which may be modified for special purposes. Evolution tends to select the simplest design that works. Not only do you need to tie up less of your nervous system to supervise two or four limbs than twenty or forty, but a small number of long ones *work* better than a whole slew of short ones. So we can probably expect, on Earthlike worlds, that the larger animals will tend to have small numbers of limbs, like four or perhaps six. On less Earthlike worlds, something else may work better. I've already mentioned the centipede-like Mesklinites, designed to survive and prosper under very high gravity. I can also imagine cases in which factors like strong gravity or chronically heavy weather would favor a more stable design but not require anything quite that drastic. Such situations might favor tripod-like stability, obtained either by two walking legs and a sturdy tail (as in the Merseians in Poul Anderson's *Ensign Flandry*) or more complete trilateral symmetry and three legs (as in the Tripeds in Damon Knight's "Rule Golden").

Modification of basic limb design can greatly extend the possibilities. If one or more pairs of feet are modified into hands, climbing and *brachiation* (swinging by the arms from one handhold to another, like a gibbon) become possible.

Some creatures may go a step further and take up gliding. Flying squirrels have wide, extensible flaps of skin connecting their front and rear limbs, acting enough like wings to let them leap from one tree to another.

A step beyond gliding is flying: actively powered flight managed by flapping limbs modified into functional wings. Our most familiar examples are insects, birds and bats; in earlier ages we also had pterosaurs. On this planet, at this time, the biggest flyers run about twenty pounds for reasons again related to the square-cube law. With the biological materials used here, it becomes impractical to make a bigger creature that can have enough wing area and supply enough energy to its wings to keep itself aloft. Since that size is likely too small to support humanlike intelligence, Earthlike worlds seem unlikely to produce intelligence on wings.

However, a world with weaker gravity, denser atmosphere or both, might be able to do it. I've already mentioned that Earth seems to have had a denser atmosphere and much larger flying animals at times in the past. I've also mentioned the Overlords in Arthur C. Clarke's *Childhood's End*, who hail from a world of low gravity and thick atmosphere; they are a flying intelligence, and it shows in every aspect of the design of their cities. Could an intelligent flyer evolve on a more Earthlike world? Poul Anderson, in his 1963 book *Is There Life on Other Worlds?*, doubted it; but a few years later he took it as a challenge and came up with an admirable solution via improved biological engineering. The Ythrians, in his 1972 "Wings of Victory" and 1973 *The People of the Wind*, have a "supercharger," a mechanism for increasing their air intake and thus their efficiency.

Shape

Body shapes don't happen arbitrarily; evolution selects those that are well suited to the way an organism lives. Thus, as we have already seen, successful swimmers tend to have streamlined bodies. Plants tend to maximize surface area, by growing leaves, to photosynthesize efficiently—though in some cases they must make compromises to meet other needs at the same time, such as the various mechanisms desert plants use to conserve water.

We've already seen that the square-cube law limits how big or small you can make an organism of any particular design and materials in any particular environment. The flip side of that is that size and environment impose constraints on shape. You could not, for example, remake an elephant in the form of a gazelle. A gazelle makes good use of its slender legs to move its smallish body around quickly; an elephant needs thick, strong legs just to support all that weight. However, if you could otherwise adapt an animal of elephantine mass to live in Martian gravity, it *could* be considerably more slender.

A few other features seem likely to be shared by most active creatures. A head seems likely to be of such value as to evolve almost anywhere—i.e., a package located high and/or far forward on the body, containing major sense organs and probably the most important nerve center (brain). Having sense organs concentrated high enables the owner to notice potential food or danger as far away as possible. Having them forward makes sense because, as Poul Anderson so deftly put it, "Even when fleeing, an animal has more need to know where it is bound than where it has been." Having the sense organs close to the brain enables data to be processed and acted upon as quickly as possible, since nerve impulses travel considerably slower than light or sound.

Of course, some sense organs can't be located near the brain because their purpose is to detect things happening to other parts of the body. On the other hand, you can imagine multiple "brains" distributed through the body. This would have the advantages of allowing faster action on certain kinds of signals and making the overall nervous system less vulnerable to any local injury. However, it would have the disadvantage of making much nervous communication slow and unwieldy. I suspect that the disadvantages would usually outweigh the advantages, so most intellectual activity would be concentrated in a single heavily armored brain. On the other hand, there may be cases where more than one would have enough advantage to evolve, and this would certainly create interesting fictional possibilities.

A fascinating fictional variant on this theme is the Puppeteers in

Larry Niven's "Neutron Star" and *Ringworld*. A Puppeteer has only one brain, but two heads housing sensory clusters and mouths. The brain, located in a bony hump between the two necks, enables the two mouths to carry on simultaneous, independent conversations. (This is not, by the way, as far-fetched as it may sound. The human brain has two "hemispheres" which in many respects function independently. Normally they communicate through a structure called the *corpus callosum*, but experiments on patients in whom that link has been destroyed show some fascinating results, which surely suggest possibilities for fictional aliens. [See the Gazzaniga and Holmes articles.])

The Puppeteers' mouths also function as *manipulators*, a class of devices often considered prerequisite for the building of any kind of civilization. In recent years this assumption has been called into question, in the light of research suggesting that at least some cetaceans (whales and dolphins) have complex social structures and perhaps highly developed languages. ("If they're so smart," someone once asked me, "why haven't they *done* anything?" To which I replied, "How do you know they haven't? Do everybody's accomplishments have to look like *our* accomplishments?") However, that possible exception aside, it does seem likely that in at least many environments, those beings that can develop their lives farthest beyond what nature has given them will be those with some means for manipulating their environment—reshaping it to their own needs and making tools to make that process even easier. Imagining skyscrapers does not make them part of your culture unless you have ways to build them.

Manipulators are not limited to extremely "advanced" animals, of course. Lobsters and crabs have claws shaped to serve particular manipulative ends. Cephalopods (octopi and squids) have prehensile tentacles equipped with suction cups. The elephant's *nose* is modified into a pretty good manipulator, though it's better suited to pulling than pushing.

Animals like raccoons have paws modified into handlike shapes that allow rather fine grasping and manipulation. Making one or more fingers *opposable*—a thumb—produces a quantum jump in the degree of manual control attainable. Next to the brain, the thumb is the most important single feature that has enabled humans to build what we call civilization. Something like it will very likely be found in many species with technological civilizations. At least three fingers (including thumb) seem necessary for a true hand (i.e., one significantly more capable than a lobster's claw). More than six or seven seem unlikely to give enough advantage to warrant the extra neural circuitry needed to operate them.

Other species in other environments may find different ways of achieving similar effects. G. David Nordley's huge Do'utians, in his "Trimus" stories, have repeatedly branched tongues that function as manipulators at levels ranging from coarse to fine. Why not modified feet? Because, being so massive, they need all their limbs simply to stand and walk.

Different numbers of limbs also lead to different possibilities. A centaur-like being, walking on four legs with two arms free for manipulation, could not come out of the same Earthly evolution that produced us. By the time reptiles and birds and mammals branched off, we were all down to four limbs maximum. There are straightforward evolutionary ways to modify or lose a pair of those, but not to add a new one. But on a world where the analogs of those classes had *six* limbs, one pair might well develop hands while the other four kept feet. Or one pair might become hands and another wings, leading to flyers both intelligent and dexterous. You might think Anderson's Ythrians would have to be such; Anderson himself did when he wrote *Is There Life on Other Worlds?* But by the time he wrote the story, he'd figured out a way to evolve them from four-limbed ancestors (their "feet" are actually their hands, while their wings double as feet when they must walk). It's a good example of how unobvious possibilities may become a lot more likely when you take a close enough look at a problem!

Structural Support

We've already looked at some of the design features needed for an animal of given size to exist in a given gravitational field. An important part of the problem is providing enough stiffness for the critter to keep its shape, move around and exert forces on other objects. For buoyant beings in liquid (or dense gaseous) surroundings, this isn't much of a problem; but for land animals, it's crucial. An octopus at home does just fine with a boneless body and tentacles, but a land crab or a lumberjack needs stiffening.

Most Earthly animals use either the land crab's solution (an *exoskeleton*) or the lumberjack's (an *endoskeleton*). At least one other approach is possible, but has found only limited application in our biology. An intrinsically soft (hollow or porous) body or body part can be stiffened by filling it with a gas or liquid under pressure. This is convenient for something that only needs stiffening occasionally, like a copulatory organ or the inflatable sac that a blowfish uses to make itself big and hard to swallow. It is not so good for something that must always be stiff—a leak could be lethal. For permanent support, some form of skeleton is preferable. The material isn't particularly important; a serviceable skeleton need only be made of suitably strong and hard stuff, and several different materials are used by different kinds of creatures on Earth.

The more important question is: Should the skeleton be internal or external? Almost all of the most advanced animals on Earth carry their bones inside, probably for reasons related to the need for . . .

Growth

Every creature I know of starts out as a smaller structure produced in the body of one or more adults of its kind. To become an adult itself, it must grow. An endoskeleton seems to provide the easiest way to do this, so it has become the usual approach in things that grow very large. Skeletons generally get their strength from hard substances that are *produced by*, but not *part of*, living cells. If your bones are inside, the softer tissues on the outside can grow continuously. The bones must do some growing, too, of course, but this is relatively easy to arrange since they are surrounded by blood vessels to keep their growth cells supplied with what they need.

An exoskeleton is less convenient. The ones on Earthly animals do not allow continuous growth; the shell itself, once made, stays the same size and so forces its contents to do likewise. Different groups of arthropods use two solutions to this problem:

1. Crustaceans, like crabs and lobsters, periodically shed their shells. The shell splits open and the animal, now without its usual armor, crawls out. For a brief period, while "soft-shelled," it can grow. Then a new, slightly larger shell forms and hardens and growth stops until next time. The main drawback is that an animal in its soft-shelled phase must hole up and hide till its defenses are back in place.

This seems awkward for a creature that aspires to intelligence and civilization, and will probably be out-competed if endoskeletal beings like us chordates have already become established in the same neighborhood. On the other hand, there may be places where that doesn't happen, and civilization may in fact evolve from something like lobsters. Defenseless periods are inconvenient, of course, but the long childhood of primates like ourselves is such a period, too. Not only do we survive it, but it's essential to our being what we are. When most of your behavior is learned rather than instinctive, you need time to learn and protection to survive while doing so.

2. Many kinds of insects use complete metamorphosis. A larval form (e.g., grub or caterpillar) hatches from an egg, spends its part of the life cycle eating, then sequesters itself in an immobile case (pupa, with or without cocoon). There it rearranges its entire body to emerge some time later as an adult (e.g., butterfly) that mates and produces eggs to repeat the cycle.

This type of arrangement would not seem to lend itself well to an intelligent species, if only because the radical reconstruction of the body between larva and adult would seem to preclude time-binding. The adult seems unlikely to retain memories from its larval phase, so larvae can't be educated for adulthood—*unless* a line of evolution has developed something like the chemical learning I mentioned at the end of the section on intelligence. This is the case in the fictional example I mentioned before, Marc Stiegler's "Petals of Rose," which postulates some of the most intriguing aliens ever imagined. Their adult lives are astonishingly brief periods of frenzied activity, completely dependent on the transmission of ancestral memories in the larval "bloodfeast [the last act of metamorphosis], in which the larva consumes the bulk of the brainblood of its bloodparents."

An utterly different example of aliens with a complete metamorphosis can be found in Susan Shwartz's *Heritage of Flight*. Here is the caterpillar-butterfly dichotomy writ very large; the "eater" larvae are objects of terror even to their own parents—and the source of an exceedingly painful dilemma for humans who must try to live among them.

A sidelight I must mention in connection with metamorphoses is the old science-fictional standby of the shape-changer, found in memorable stories at least as far back as John W. Campbell's "Who Goes There?" and A.E. van Vogt's "Vault of the Beast." The alien capable of assuming any shape at will is certainly a powerful image that lends itself to strong stories, but it's not an easy thing to make scientifically believable. Not that it's impossible—caterpillars turning into butterflies are living proof that shape-changers exist. But the shape-changers we know about must follow one preset plan, take a long time, and use nearly all of the organism's stored energy resources. Changing *quickly* would require *lots* of energy and generate lots of waste heat; being able to change into many different designs would require far greater flexibility of programming. The time may be ripe for a new shape-changer story that hits today's readers as hard as those two hit their first readers, yet makes itself fully believable in terms of today's science. A hint if you'd like to try: Learn all you can about nanotechnology!

While reading my descriptions of solutions to the growth problem used by Earthly arthropods, you may have wondered about a third possibility. Bones grow; why not simply build enough growth cells into an exoskeleton to let that grow, too? The problem there is that the growth cells would have to be supplied with blood, which requires a network of blood vessels both inside and outside the shell. That in turn implies a structure to carry the blood vessels on the outside—something like the velvet on a deer's antlers. It might happen somewhere; but the endoskeleton seems to get the same advantages so much more simply that if you do choose to use the velvety-exoskeleton model, you should be prepared to explain why that won the evolutionary race.

Reproduction

The problems of growth are closely tied to those of reproduction. For reasons discussed in chapter four, we can generally expect asexual reproduction in some primitive organisms, but some form of sex in more advanced ones. Two sexes are enough to confer large evolutionary advantages, but some evolutionary lines may have more (like the three in Isaac Asimov's *The Gods Themselves*). On the other hand, some Earthly animals evolved from sexual ancestors have found ways to reproduce parthenogenetically—there are entire species of lizards whose members are all identical females. (See, for example, O. Cuellar's article.)

The specific manner of delivering young into the world can vary greatly and have large effects on lifestyle. Many animals lay eggs that, when fertilized, contain genetic instruction packages (DNA) and raw materials (food) to build a new organism capable of existing outside, with or without help. Eggs can be produced in numbers from one to millions, fertilized internally or externally, and cared for diligently or left to chance. In some fish, a female discharges vast numbers of eggs into the water, a male ejects a cloud of sperm into the same general vicinity, and they go their separate ways; many eggs are eaten by predators, many hatchlings from the surviving eggs go the same way, and only a tiny percentage survive to adulthood. Birds fertilize internally, lay small numbers of eggs, guard them diligently until they hatch into young who can't yet care for themselves, and feed and teach them until they can. Some snakes are "ovoviviparous," growing young in eggs but hatching them internally.

A couple of species of mammals lay eggs, but the vast majority use one of two methods of producing and caring for live young. In both cases a fetus is connected to the mother's bloodstream, with provision for supplying nutrients and oxygen and removing wastes. In *marsupials* this system is relatively inefficient, and the young must be born quite early. Tiny and undeveloped, they spend the first portion of their "outside" lives in a pouch outside the mother's body, leaving it more and more frequently as they become more able to fend for themselves. *Placental* mammals have an improved system for feeding fetuses and removing their wastes, and use it until a more advanced state of development. After birth, both kinds of mammals live on milk secreted by their mothers for the first part of their lives.

Science fiction writers have often dabbled in inventing new kinds of reproductive cycles, particularly ones whose workings are not obvious to their first human observers. In Susan Shwartz's *Heritage of Flight*, the adult flyers and larval eaters are initially thought to be two different species, one very attractive and the other utterly repulsive to humans.

Warm-Blooded or Cold-Blooded?

The animals we know are often loosely categorized as "warm-blooded," meaning they have an internal mechanism for keeping their body temperature within a narrow range despite environmental fluctuations; and "cold-blooded," meaning they don't, and therefore become warmer (and more active) or colder (and less active) whenever their surroundings do. "Cold-blooded" is, in at least some cases, an unflattering oversimplification. Many reptiles control their body temperatures quite closely (within a degree or so) as long as they have the opportunity to move back and forth between warmer and cooler places. However, they're very dependent on having that choice, and in practice tend to spend much of their time simply lying in places where the temperature feels right. A warm-blooded animal, with a built-in means of optimizing its temperature, can remain active under a much wider range of conditions. The disadvantage is that it must be active more of the time, and eat much more, than its cold-blooded counterparts. Intelligence probably has more chance to evolve in warm-blooded creatures—and a strong incentive to do so since they can't go as long without food.

Warm-blooded animals, in many climates, also need a body covering to help them retain body heat. (How badly they need it depends on size—in general, large animals need it less, since their low surface-to-volume ratios help them conserve heat.) Body insulation can be hair or feathers, or it could be something like foam insulation. In humans, and perhaps in other intelligent species, the insulator is not built in, but added voluntarily in the form of clothing. In the climates where the first humans evolved, there was not much need for body insulation, which may explain why they lost most of it. Later, when they expanded into other climes, the ability to make artificial insulation greatly increased their adaptability.

Body coverings are not just for insulation, of course. They also provide protection and may have to serve other purposes as well, which is likely to influence their exact nature. Feathers lend themselves especially well to flight, and so have become standard equipment for birds; bats, however, prove that they're not necessary for flight. Marc Stiegler's Rosans, who must generate lots of waste heat during their frenetic adulthoods, are covered with "hundreds of delicate cooling fins, the Rosan equivalent of scales or feathers," but looking to humans much like flower petals.

Senses

Equipment for deciding on a course of action in response to what's happening around you is useless unless you have ways to know what's happening around you. Thus any successful organism needs senses for getting information about its environment. Even a plant needs to "know" where the sun is and which way is up.

In places where light is readily available and travels freely, *sight* is probably the most useful of senses. It can carry a great deal of information, carries it faster than any other medium, and carries it with very high precision. For example, you can look at a distant football field in the midst of a play and tell exactly where every player is. Doing so, of course, requires highly developed eyes. Eyes probably originated as simple photosensitive spots that did little more than tell the owner where there was more or less light. The compound eyes of insects are little more than clusters of such spots, allowing crude recognition of shape and motion, but little detail—so they're not very likely in highly intelligent animals. The most intelligent animals on Earth, on a couple of major evolutionary routes (chordates and mollusks), have independently evolved the "lens-camera" type of eye, in which a lens forms a detailed image of an object and projects it onto a retina, where densely packed photoreceptors can send the brain signals constituting an accurate map of the object.

Two eyes have a large advantage over one: They enable depth perception and help judge distances. (However, that's not the only way they can be used. African chameleons use their two eyes to scan, more or less independently, two separate fields of view.) The advantage of more eyes than two is less obvious or general, though you can certainly imagine specific cases in which they would have one. An eye or two in the back of the head could be useful if you were frequently pursued by more than one attacker (or teaching fourth grade). In "Tinker's Spectacles," Gregory Bennett has imagined a situation in which an extra eye (and a different kind of neural wiring) might provide an extra *kind* of vision useful under special circumstances. The Pled life cycle depends on their fighting fast-moving predators called gyrbirds. To do that they've evolved a set of three eyes, two of which provide range information but can't adjust very fast, while the third eye acts with them to judge how fast range is changing.

It's relatively easy to imagine modifications that might fit eyes for special jobs. A telescopic eye, or a "zoom" eye, could be concocted, though it's not clear under what conditions it would be really necessary. Earthly birds of prey achieve astounding acuity with more "conventional" eyes optimized for high resolution at long distances. "Four-eyed fish" found in the tropics really have two eyes, but each has two irises and two retinas, one for vision above the water and the other for underwater. Nocturnal animals often have a reflective layer behind the retina to give them a second chance to use light

that would be wasted by a diurnal animal's eye. In my story
"... And Comfort to the Enemy," I took this a step further: The
tsapeli, one of the few nocturnal civilizations I can recall, have
"searchlights" built into their eyes. Some animals do generate light;
the tsapeli must do that at unusually high power levels *and* focus
the light into a beam where it's needed.

How about eyes using other parts of the electromagnetic spectrum? What we call visible light is likely to prove, at least approximately, the most useful on other planets as well, since it's a part of
the spectrum in which atmospheres tend to be relatively transparent. However, there's no need to assume that other beings will see
exactly the part of the spectrum that we do. They might tend to
favor the colors produced in greatest abundance by their own star
(and transmitted best by their own atmosphere). They might see
an even narrower part of the spectrum than we do, or a somewhat
wider one—extending into the ultraviolet and/or infrared. (Some
animals on Earth already do such things; some insects see ultraviolet but not red, and the snakes called pit vipers have organs for
detecting infrared from warm-blooded prey.)

They are not likely to use wavelengths very much shorter or
longer than "visible light." X-rays and gamma rays are not abundant
enough in most environments to provide a reliable source of illumi-
nation—which is fortunate since they tend to be destructive to
living cells. Radio waves share the availability problem, and also
would require a relatively enormous eye to form an image of useful
resolution.

In some environments, sight is not particularly useful because
it is in short supply and or doesn't travel reliably. Under many
such conditions, *hearing* is better—and since even beings who rely
primarily on sight sometimes have to deal with such conditions,
they tend to have pretty good hearing, too. In a jungle, lines of sight
tend to be so short that any enemy you can see, you see too late.
Sound, however, has much longer waves than light and travels
around obstacles, so you may be able to hear something long before
you can see it. If you add refinements such as paired ears and
external ear funnels of complicated shapes (like ours), you can
even get a pretty fair idea of where the sound source is. On nocturnal animals like certain desert foxes, the external ears may be very
large for the same reason astronomical telescopes are very large:
to gather as much energy as possible and enable the owner to hear

very faint sounds.

Land animals generally use a relatively limited range of sound frequencies, though the exact range chosen varies. For healthy humans it's about twency to twenty thousand hertz; or, since going up an octave means doubling the frequency, about ten octaves. That's still a lot more than our visual range, which is slightly less than one octave. By being able to perceive and distinguish such a wide range of frequencies, we make up to some extent for our inability to hear the kinds of detail—i.e., images—that we see with light. We've also learned to distinguish a lot of auxiliary properties of sound, such as the shape of the wave (which we hear as "tone quality") and variations in pitch and amplitude. This has made it an excellent way to transmit information, so many animals have also developed sound-*producing* organs for signalling to each other—and in some cases, those signals develop into language.

In animals for whom vision is of little use, sound senses may be even more developed, sometimes in ways resembling the ways we use light. Dolphins can hear and produce sounds over a much wider frequency range than we can—up to perhaps two hundred kilohertz. In addition to using sound for communication, in ways whose sophistication we are just beginning to grasp, they use it as "sonar" for navigation and food location. A dolphin can send out a burst of high-frequency sound and, by analyzing the echos, learn not only where objects are, but quite a bit about what kinds of objects they are and what they're doing. Visibility in water is often quite limited, so sound is the best available way to form "pictures." Sound waves are all longer than light and therefore can't form images of such high resolution; but *high-frequency* sound can do a pretty good job. In an environment where light can't do the job at all, high-frequency sound is a winner.

Chemical senses such as *smell* and *taste* also have their uses. For us, the latter is of value mainly for confirming that the food we already have in our mouths is in fact what we think it is. It also encourages eating by providing positive reinforcement in the form of pleasure. For some other animals, it does considerably more than that. Dolphins seem to use a sense perhaps best-called taste for learning a great deal about the water in which they swim. Salmon use it to find their way back to where they were hatched to lay their own eggs.

Smell provides a way of detecting a variety of things, from food to predators, that are *not* yet in hand or mouth, but are close enough to warrant serious consideration. It's particularly useful in places like the aforementioned jungle. Some predators, such as dogs and cats, have developed it to something far more sensitive and refined than our relatively crude version. However, it seems unlikely to serve well as a principal long-range sense, carrying highly detailed information with the precision of sight or sound. Scent works by detecting and identifying trace molecules that have travelled through atmosphere or liquid medium from the smellee to the smeller's nose (or whatever passes for one). The problem with that is twofold: Such molecules travel much slower than light or sound waves, and they are likely to be deflected by collisions with other molecules en route. Thus they can't provide reliable information on fast-changing conditions, and they don't give a very precise idea of where they originated. (Except, of course, under highly specialized conditions, such as those in Hal Clement's "Uncommon Sense," where an airless environment allowed molecules to travel [usually] in nearly straight lines. Thus his aliens could use organs resembling pinhole cameras to "image" food or prey, using molecules instead of light or sound.)

Most organisms will also need some short-range senses to keep them informed of conditions in and very near their own bodies, such as a sharp object, a hot iron or an ice cube pressing against their skin. The semicircular canals in our ears provide a balance sense that enables us to maintain the improbable upright posture that most of us take for granted. The lateral lines of fish keep them up to date on fine variations of water pressure and currents. Some fish can detect (and produce) electrical fields. There is some evidence that birds monitor the Earth's magnetic field as an aid to their long-distance migrations (which may get them in trouble the next time that field reverses, as it does periodically). In inventing aliens for new environments, you may find that still other specialized senses are both desirable and plausible.

Frills

We've now surveyed many of the basic characteristics you'll want to consider in concocting your aliens, but you'll still have room to play with many less basic ones. Remember that evolution does not always come up with the very best possible solution to a problem, and that the correlation between genes and traits is not one-to-one.

If evolution selects for one trait, such as a long neck, it may happen that the same set of genes incidentally produces another trait, such as green eyelids. As long as the "by-product" trait doesn't carry enough evolutionary disadvantage to cancel out the advantage of the "principal" trait, it may spread freely through a population. Some traits are "evolutionarily indifferent"; in humans, for example, whether you have brown or blue eyes is seldom a life-or-death matter. Others may be slightly detrimental, but not enough to have any significant evolutionary effect. Our wisdom teeth (apparently left over from a time when our ancestors had longer jaws) now cause many of us pain and bills and bring few of us any conspicuous benefit; but neither do they often kill us or keep us from reproducing.

Such traits I lump here as "frills"—"extras" that an organism can have but doesn't have to. They can be literal frills, in the form of "decorative" bits of skin or hair, or things like color patterns, the precise number of toes or an ability to change color. Such options can provide you as a writer with some of your best opportunities to have fun with your aliens, giving them character and individuality. And in some cases they may take on more significance than they originally had. Color changes, for example, may be inconsequential under some conditions, but under others prove quite useful for camouflage or communication.

Self-Modification

Finally, we must note that once a species gains the ability to reengineer its own genetics, all these constraints about natural evolution get seriously weakened. Humans, as we now are, are quite incapable of living continuously underwater without technological help. But we can imagine creating genetically modified humans with gills instead of lungs, who could live *only* underwater. Similarly, we may meet, either here or on their own turf, aliens who have reshaped themselves into forms quite unlike the ones their "natural" ancestors inherited. This could lead to interesting misunderstandings, say, if a human party is trying to guess where a party of aliens came from by analyzing their appearance and lifestyle.

SOME CLOSING TIPS

If we limit ourselves to naturally evolved forms, though, the gist of the preceding arguments does tend to agree with de Camp that a more or less humanoid shape—at least as human as a monkey, a *Deinonychus* (a type of small dinosaur), or a kangaroo—is favored under Earthlike conditions. But note also that even for those, appreciable differences will usually occur, and one shouldn't make a habit of writing about aliens that are *just* like people. Those would require conditions just like Earth, and considering the range of possibilities, those will be very rare indeed.

And never forget that the range is considerably broader than "Earthlike conditions." Even planets that are fairly similar to Earth will usually be somewhat different, and some planets will be a *lot* different. For those, life may be wildly different from what we're used to, and you must design it to fit its environment.

The overriding principle, regardless of how like or unlike Earth your planet is, is this: If you want to create believable, interesting aliens, you cannot simply scale some Earthly creature up or down, or cobble together features from two or more (such as putting an elk's head on a grizzly bear's body). Every being must fit the environment that produced it. And form and environment together will shape its way of life and the kind of culture (if any) that it builds.

CHAPTER 6

Creating Alien Societies

Show me a being that thinks as well as a man," John W. Campbell told writers, "but not *like* a man." To do that, you must have a realistic idea of what it means to think like a man (or, in today's preferred language, a human). Chances are that your idea of the answer is far too narrow. Since most people spend the vast majority of their lives in a single culture, they tend to assume, consciously or subconsciously, that that culture's ways are equivalent to "human nature."

In fact, human ways cover a much broader range of possibilities than the few selected by any one society; and any individual's personal thinking and habits are even more influenced than he or she probably realizes by the culture in which he lives. About the closest I've come to identifying a genuine "universal" of human nature is this: Most people in *any* culture consider *their* culture's ways "just normal," and any others that differ from them "strange" and probably inferior (savage, barbaric, pagan, etc.).

We often hear, and most people in the culture I grew up in seem quite willing to accept, that "Humankind is by nature warlike." Yet in *Patterns of Culture*, anthropologist Ruth Benedict observed, "Only our familiarity with war makes it intelligible that a state of warfare should alternate with a state of peace in one tribe's dealings with another. The idea is quite common over the world, of course. But on the one hand it is impossible for certain peoples [such as the *Yanomamö*] to conceive the possibility of a state of peace, which in their notion would be equivalent to admitting enemy tribes to the category of human beings, which by definition they are not even though the excluded tribe may be of their own race and culture. On the other hand, it may be just as impossible for a people [such as the *Inuit*] to conceive of the possibility of a state of war."

That is but one example of how differently peoples can see the world and their role in it. A science fiction writer who hopes to create societies that are truly alien, yet believable, would be well advised to start by studying cultural anthropology, through books such as Benedict's and more recent studies in the same area. One of the commonest faults with science-fictional aliens is that they are little more than "humans in funny suits." Or, more precisely, "humans-of-the-author's-own-place-and-period in funny suits": Many real human cultures are far more alien than many fictional aliens. To avoid that pitfall, you must learn something about the range of human cultural possibilities—partly because they will suggest story ideas, and partly to stretch your imagination beyond its usual parochial limits.

Even that is not enough. Diverse as human cultures are, they are all *human*. They are ways that a single species of animal has found to live in the relatively narrow range of environments on a single planet. On a different planet, with a different kind of sun or a different axial tilt or a richer or poorer supply of heavy elements, even a single species would come up with quite different solutions. Other species, with different evolutionary backgrounds, would come up with still others, some of which might evolve into different kinds of intelligence and culture. Since the cultural patterns of intelligent species must have evolved gradually from the behavior patterns of their less intelligent ancestors, you should also learn something about *ethology*, the science of animal behavior. Marine cephalopods, herd-dwelling herbivores, arboreal omnivores and pack-hunting carnivores will, if they develop civilizations at all, develop extremely different *kinds* of civilization. Learning about the kinds of social interactions such animals and others already show may give you ideas of what kinds of societies they might eventually produce.

Ethology is, of course, a huge subject. The National Geographic Society's book in the References is a good layman's introduction, and will provide more in-depth references to topics that particularly interest you.

Since we are the only species we've had a chance to observe that has developed societies of human complexity (though we've recently learned that several other species have done far more in this area than previously suspected), much of our thinking will have to be guided by existing or historic human cultures. Our basic plan will be to survey some of the elements that have developed in human cultures, and then to think about how they might develop differently—or be replaced by others—in beings with different evolutionary roots. As in the last chapter, you'll notice repeatedly how the things I've listed as separate topics are in fact inextricably intertwined.

ELEMENTS OF CULTURE:
OUR PAST AND ITS IMPLICATIONS

Our species evolved from omnivorous primates in Equatorial Africa. One of the earliest known hominid species, *Australopithecus afarensis*, seems to date back at least four million years or so and to have held its own quite successfully for a million years or so (see Stephen Jay Gould's "Lucy on the Earth in Stasis"). According to many contemporary evolutionists (including Gould), successful species often remain pretty much unchanged for such long periods, until abrupt environmental changes, such as a shift from forest to savanna conditions or the beginning of an ice age, force them to develop new adaptations. Eventually one such burst of evolutionary activity split off several new species of *Australopithecus* and also the new genus *Homo*, to which you (I presume) and I belong.

Most of the primates already showed several features we think of as characteristically human, probably largely as a result of their arboreal origins. These include large and complex brains, long gestations to let those brains develop, long dependent childhoods to fill those brains with useful education, unspecialized and therefore adaptable bodies with "hands" on at least two limbs, and a tendency to live in groups. To these, the hominids added some tricks of their own, most notably a fully upright and bipedal posture and increasing complication of social structures. Let's look at some of these traits and their contributions to the development of human culture, as well as some others that came into play later on. (For further reading on these matters, see L. Sprague de Camp's "The Ape-Man Within Us.")

Living In Groups

This is probably a basic prerequisite for culture. Since culture is by definition a body of knowledge and behavior patterns shared by a group, it's hard to imagine it arising in a species of solitary habits. (Science fiction writers are, of course, welcome to take that claim as a challenge!)

Relatively complex family and social structures were already well established in many kinds of primates, but probably got an extra boost when ancestral forests began thinning out to savanna. With traditional food sources scarcer than before, continued prosperity required learning to use others that were *not* found in trees. Mouths and digestive systems equipped to handle a wide range of foods were clearly useful for that, as was the ability to stand upright and get around easily on the ground. But perhaps most useful of all was the formation of social structures that could cooperate in defense against predators and enemies, the capturing of large food animals, and sharing such large units of food.

Since meat was not the only food source, early cultures were based on hunting and gathering, with some people doing the hunting and others the gathering. Here is a beginning of division of labor and specialization of tasks. It is probably *not* a beginning of distinct roles for the two sexes; that sort of thing is already found in many other species of animals. It is not surprising that the sex roles assumed by early humans were continuations and extensions of those in their ancestors. Since gathering was generally safer than hunting, and females were more indispensable than males for at least the early stages of child-rearing, it was almost inevitable that males would do most of the hunting and females most of the gathering.

Reproduction and Childhood

The behaviors associated with reproduction and that long period of dependency played central roles in how social structures developed and worked, and this has remained true throughout history. Another advantage of living in groups is that it can provide extra safety and support for dependent children, including baby-sitters and backup mothers for orphans. But the central importance of such matters also requires that social units include mechanisms for minimizing conflicts, determining who mates with whom, and ensuring that the young actually are raised and trained. Thus arose a whole elaborate system of rules and rituals. In humans, at least, such systems are largely *not* instinctive, so they have developed quite differently in different cultures.

However, certain broad characteristics are widespread. Most cultures have some form of marriage (though not necessarily monogamous, and varying greatly in the rights and obligations it involves). Most have rites of passage to formalize the transition from childhood to adulthood (which can range from ritualized physical torture and mutilation to high school graduations and debutante balls).

In creating new cultures for science fiction, you can imagine many ways things might develop differently. If there are more than two sexes, their roles and relationships might define themselves differently. Even with only two sexes, their roles might be quite different. Among lions, the usual family organization is a "pride" with one male, several females and their cubs—and from time to time a new male will forcibly oust the old one, and immediately slaughter all his cubs. What kind of culture might evolve from such an arrangement? Some interesting speculations along those lines can be found in Eric Vinicoff and Marcia Martin's "The Weigher" and C.J. Cherryh's *Chanur* books. In "The Weigher," for example, civilized feline females go into wilderness to have cubs; if the cubs survive long enough, they may be captured, trained in the ways of civilization, and eventually challenge their elders for job, territory and life.

Language

This is the mortar that lets generations build on the achievements of those that went before. It allows the transmission of large bodies of complex information, not only from adults to children, but from adults to other adults of their own or later—even much later—generations. Among humans it likely grew out of gestures and sound signals used for such activities as coordinating hunts and warning other group members of danger. Its role in building and sustaining culture is so centrally important, and its nature so directly pertinent to the storytelling process, that the next chapter will be devoted entirely to it.

Conflict and Cooperation

The history of humans and many other animals involves an ongoing counterpoint of competition and cooperation. Societies exist in large measure because of the benefits the members of groups can get by cooperating: sharing work and food, responsibility for child-rearing, and the good feelings they get from companionship. Yet the mere fact of many individuals living together sets the stage for conflict: competition for food, for mates, for power over other members of the group. The counterpoint can be seen in microcosm in any baboon troop, small town, high school or corporate boardroom. Societies have had to evolve mechanisms for controlling the conflicts. Typically these mechanisms have involved hierarchies or "pecking orders," in which one individual somehow acquires general recognition as The Boss and everyone else must submit to that one's will.

Conflicts occur not only within a group, but between groups. If one nomadic tribe encountered another on a favorite hunting ground, or at an oasis with limited supplies of food and water, each might feel threatened by the other. Each group might try to drive the other off so it could keep all the goodies for itself—which, if the goodies were indeed scarce, might make evolutionary sense. It has been suggested (see L. Sprague de Camp's "The Ape-Man Within Us") that many of our currently continuing problems of intergroup hostilities represent a genetically programmed hostility to "outsiders" that once was a survival trait but now is a liability. There is probably some truth in this, though there also seems to be some difficulty in reconciling it with Ruth Benedict's observations on the Inuit and war.

In any case, our history has been largely shaped by the tension between the pulls toward cooperation and conflict, both within and between groups. Many of the benefits of civilization have resulted from successes in cooperation within groups, and sometimes between them—though the latter, not surprisingly, are much harder to achieve.

In their rawest forms, conflicts take the form of bludgeoning and bloodshed: mayhem and murder at the individual level, warfare at the tribal or larger level. There are clear advantages in finding less bloody ways to resolve them, so many animals have found ways to do so. Males of many animal species fight for mating rights, but in quite a few of them (such as bighorn sheep) the combats have become so ritualized that they are unlikely to end in death. The more civilized humans get, the more they tend to ritualize their battles. It's debatable how far beyond ritualization we can go. Some believe the tendency toward combativeness is built-in and outlets will always have to be found for it. Others suspect it's largely a cultural artifact and can (with great difficulty) be trained away. Whatever its actual origin and nature, it seems that, at least now and in many human cultures, such a tendency does exist, and such activities as organized sports exist partly as a relatively harmless outlet for that kind of energy.

The other view of sports is that it is simply an outgrowth of play. Playfulness—an urge for young animals to experiment with their environment and each other and to imitate the behavior of the adults around them—is a vital part of training to *be* adults in most animals of appreciable intelligence. Its value is such that this is likely to be true of species on other planets, too; and survival of parts of it into adulthood may well lead to things like our culture's fascination with sports. On the other hand, it may also be that many aliens would be astonished and perplexed by the fact that so many of us are so enthralled by the antics of a handful of grown-up strangers playing with a little sphere. Why, they might well wonder, should more of our newspapers be devoted to *that*, of all things, than to any other single subject?

Or they might have their own sports, but of quite different character reflecting their different origins. The tension between conflict and cooperation probably exists in most intelligent species, but their relative importance and the way they're handled may vary considerably. Many of us are at least casually familiar with power struggles and dominance hierarchies in such species as baboons. Less well known is the existence of species with lots of cooperation and very little conflict (see Natalie Angier's article on cotton-top tamarins). In his story, "Touchdown, Touchdown, Rah, Rah, Rah!," W.R. Thompson shows how a species whose history emphasized cooperation more than conflict might develop a sport quite different from any of ours.

Bagdrag is a ritualized survival of a preagricultural time when herds, inherently cooperative entities, sometimes had to compete with other herds for food. Three teams drag a heavy bag around on a hexagonal field, each side of which is a goal line. Each team has a home goal, and the line connecting two of those is a shared goal for those two teams. Any team can get one point by dragging the bag across its home goal, but if two teams cooperate to drag it across their *shared* goal, *each* gets *two* points—and players prefer a tie to a game with a clear winner and a clear loser.

Agriculture, Villages and Cities

The earliest hominids were nomadic; they went where the action was, in terms of available food and water. Somewhere along the line, some of them made a crucial decision: to settle down and become villagers and farmers, forcing food to grow where they were instead of constantly having to go where it was. As told in J. Bronowski's *The Ascent of Man* (chapter two), the real revolution took not only that decision, but also a fortuitous biological accident. It is one thing to decide you're tired of traveling and will settle down and live on what you find around you; it is another to find that you can actually do that in a style to which you'd like to become accustomed. Most wild plants just aren't that bountiful.

In the case of Old World humans, the lucky accident was wheat. Its wild form was just another grass, producing seeds that were edible, but requiring considerable effort to gather enough to be very nutritious. But two hybridizations and a mutation led to a new form producing plump, nutritious seeds, yet incapable of distributing them by natural means as its ancestors had done. The combination gave humans a strong incentive to settle down and devote themselves to cultivating the new wheat, seeing that some of the seeds got back into the ground and using some as a reliable "staff of life" for themselves. Such early agriculture actually seems to have been more labor-intensive than the life of hunter-gatherers— but more reliable.

And it meant the beginning of cities. Not large cities, at first, but places where sizable numbers of people gathered to dwell permanently in one place, living off the crops grown there. In surrounding nomads, subject to the uncertainties of natural food sources, permanent settlements with controlled, dependable food sources of their own were bound to evoke covetousness. So farming villages had to fortify and defend what they had. . . .

And so on.

How unlikely were the biological accidents that led to this revolution in human life? Perhaps not terribly; they, or something enough like them, seem to have occurred independently at several times and places on Earth. Might there be worlds on which they *didn't* happen? If so, civilization might be rarer than we'd guess; and human explorers might find many worlds with intelligent beings stuck at what we would consider "early" stages of development.

In places where the agricultural revolution does happen, cities are likely to grow bigger and bigger, as they've done on Earth. But as a writer creating such places, you must never forget how they originated and how they work. A common mistake in science fiction is to depict huge, highly advanced civilizations without supplying, either explicitly or implicitly, the physical infrastructure that could make them work. In our own civilization, many cities are so big and so isolated from the farms that many of their residents have no real conception of where food comes from. You must not fall into that trap; you must never forget that, even if they're out of sight, the farms (or something that serves the same purpose) must be there. If the places where food is produced are distant, there must be a transportation system for getting produce—and other raw materials—to the users. And the more users there are, the more essential it becomes that there be means (which may have to be large and elaborate) for disposing of their wastes.

Domestic Animals

Closely related to the agricultural revolution, and of comparable importance in the development of human civilization, was the domestication of animals. A wide variety of animals, from dogs and cats to tarantulas, have been kept as pets; but domestication means more than that. In the strict sense it means not just taming and keeping animals, but selectively breeding them (and thereby modifying them from their wild ancestral forms) to serve human purposes. And, as Jared Diamond points out in his article "Zebras and the Anna Karenina Principle," that has implications that are far more profound and wide-reaching than you might expect.

It's perhaps obvious that big domestic animals are highly valuable to societies that have them. They serve as reliable sources of high-energy, high-protein food. Their body coverings provide insulating material for clothing and shelter. Their excrement can also serve as a building material, and as fuel. As fertilizer, it improves the cultivation of crops. The animals themselves made possible a technological leap in agriculture by serving as draught animals to pull plows and other implements in the field, and wagons to carry produce to distant markets. These advantages allowed human populations to grow larger and denser and societies more complex, with some people freed from agriculture and able to devote their time to other specialties such as crafts and writing. Thus domestic animals directly contributed to many aspects of civilization. But their influence goes even further than that.

Much of human history is a record of who conquered and subjugated whom. How different might human history have been if Africans and Amerindians invaded and colonized Europe before Europeans got to Africa and the Americas? The fact that history's major empire-builders came from Europe and Asia is directly attributable to the fact that they had domestic animals like horses that gave them a powerful advantage over peoples who didn't have them. Eurasians have sometimes flattered themselves that this historical accident somehow demonstrates their innate superiority, but Jared Diamond makes a convincing case that it *was* a historical accident. Eurasians had a decisive edge simply because they had several domesticable animals available and other peoples didn't. Not all animals lend themselves to domestication. Some grow too slowly to be economically worth raising; some can't be fed economically; some don't breed well in captivity or have dispositions or social structures that make it impractical to keep or raise them. Only a handful of species on Earth *don't* have at least one of these disadvantages, and it just happens that almost all of those are native only to Eurasia.

There was a time when the Americas also had several animals that could have been domesticated, but they were hunted to extinction when humans came to the New World; most were gone by 11,000 years ago. Why this happened in America but not Eurasia provides yet another example of the importance of historical accident and timing. In Eurasia, the process of domestication began before humans had the ability to hunt most animals to extinction; so humans, animals and their domestic relationships all developed together. By the time humans came to America, they were too good at hunting for their own good, and the animals they encountered had had no opportunity to develop a healthy fear of them.

That bit of prehistory neatly disposes of the popular myth that primitive peoples in general or Amerindians in particular lived in harmony with nature and had little impact on their environment. It also suggests one of several speculations about how things might have developed differently, any of which might provide good material for science fiction. What if humans had come to the New World much earlier, so that their relationships with local animals could develop as they did in Eurasia? What if the land bridge they came over was destroyed shortly after their arrival, so that human cultures *with* domestic animals could develop independently here and there for several years? Harry Turtledove's *A Different Flesh* shows an alternate history based on a variant of this idea. (*Homo erectus*, a slightly more primitive hominid, crossed to the Americas, but *Homo sapiens* didn't. So the first English colonists found the land occupied not by "Indians" but by *Homo erectus* who had not been quite clever enough to exterminate things like mammoths and sabertooths.)

We now have only one species of hominid on Earth, but in the early millions of years there were several. Sometimes two or more existed at the same time; recent evidence suggests that sometimes two or more tool-using species were neighbors. Might one have treated the other as domestic animals—and if so, what effect would that have on both? Even after we were down to one species, humans often enslaved other humans, sometimes justifying the practice by claiming that the enslaved group were "not really human." We know better now—but what might happen in a situation where the same world held two species, one of which really was conspicuously less intelligent than the other, yet conspicuously more so than most other species?

The Aztecs had the wheel, but it apparently never occurred to them to use it for anything except toys. What if they'd had horses, or something like horses, much earlier in their history? Might they then have made the leap to wagons and beyond? That question leads us to . . .

Other Technologies

Having hands developed for tree life opened the possibility of using tools. Acquiring the habit of walking upright left one pair of hands free to do so much of the time. (And made the other pair unnecessary; human feet have now adapted to be more useful for walking than grasping, leaving us the only primates without prehensile toes.) Couple those physical abilities with long childhoods and a playful tendency to experiment, and it was probably inevitable that early primates would discover that sticks and rocks could be used to facilitate food-gathering. Later they found that rocks could be used to modify other rocks into still more effective shapes. This is not, by the way, to suggest that such skills are "primitive." Chipping flint takes a good deal of skill, and few of us today could do it because we've concentrated our learning on other skills.

Such activities snowballed, slowly at first, but at a rate that increased inexorably (and is still doing so). Every time a member of a clever species learns to do something new, and teaches the method to others, it becomes increasingly likely that somebody will see still other new applications of an old technique, or new ways to *combine* old techniques into a new one. Thus paleolithic humans learned to use rocks as tools (e.g., weapons and digging implements) and neolithic humans used them to make better tools for a wide range of purposes (e.g., hunting, fishing, carrying liquids and making clothing and shelter).

Clothing and shelter were of minimal importance in the times and places where the first hominids evolved, but became increasingly necessary as they expanded into regions of harsher climate— or regions of harsher climate came to them. Perhaps the latter came first, when the glaciers spread toward the equator. Worsening climate forced people to develop protection against the cold—but once they knew how to do it, they could move into regions their ancestors would have considered uninhabitable.

A particularly powerful ally in coping with inclement weather was fire. Primitive hominids must have encountered it in nature, as a result of lightning; learning to keep a fire going and to start one at will opened up many new possibilities. It could keep a shelter more comfortable under even more conditions. It could help keep pesky animals away. By cooking food, it could enhance flavor and variety. It made it possible to refine and work metals, producing greatly improved tools and ornaments of copper, gold and silver, later alloys of copper, and eventually iron. I hardly need to emphasize how important these things have been to our civilizations' development. Natives of a world on which heavier elements are quite scarce might never get beyond a stone age, for lack of materials (see Jack Vance's *Big Planet*). But might they compensate by learning to do more than we have with lighter elements? Conceivable, but doubtful. In this century we've been doing things with light elements that our ancestors could not have imagined, but it's not clear that we could have done them without first having long experience with the easier things that can be done with metals. On the other hand, if your light-element planet orbits a late-class star, the inhabitants may have a lot of time to learn. . . .

The use of clothing and shelter probably originated as a necessity for coping with bad weather. Both have grown greatly in sophistication, both as technologies and as arts. The increasing tendency of large numbers of people to live in compact areas also forced the development of improved sanitation methods such as indoor plumbing and sewers, though these were quite late in coming to most areas. Until quite recently, largely because of poor sanitation and ignorance of how diseases are transmitted, life expectancies were much lower than they are now in developed areas. Attempts to cure disease probably led quite early to experimentation with plants, some of which proved to have medicinal value. Such experiments gradually evolved into an increasingly sophisticated bag of medical tricks.

Religions and Sciences

Attempts to cure disease, and to understand and deal with such traumatic and uncontrollable events as birth and death and storm and famine, probably also contributed to the development of religion. In primitive societies, a person who had acquired some knowledge of medical practices that worked—whether through experience or being taught "the secrets" by earlier practitioners—would be in a position to wield considerable power. To reinforce and retain that power, such people might be tempted to fortify it with an imposing array of rituals to impress the uninitiated and make sure they took the whole business seriously. Enough humans seem fond of ritual that the strategy would often work and allow the development of a firmly entrenched priesthood.

The origins of the oldest religions are lost in prehistory. The ones of which we have more or less detailed records came much later and were influenced to varying extents by those that went before. So it's difficult to say whether the earliest religions were more creations of particularly influential individuals, or outgrowths of shared folklore. It seems fairly safe to say, though, that most religions include rituals related to a belief in one or more powers higher than human, stories to explain the origins of world and life, and teachings aimed at inculcating and perpetuating a moral code.

Religion in some form has existed in most, if not all, human cultures. Its exact shape has varied greatly, as has the degree of its influence on the surrounding culture. A writer who wants to create an original religion for an alien culture would be well advised to do some reading on human religions. However, he or she would also be well advised to ask questions that go beyond merely comparing human religions and trying to add another to the catalog.

For instance, would aliens necessarily have religions at all? There seems to be something in the built-in programming of humans that impels them to seek answers to the kinds of questions that religions ask, and to create or willingly accept the kinds of answers that religions give. It may be too much to assume that all intelligent species have the same kind of impulses. Some, for example, might have intense interest and curiosity about the details of everyday life, yet either have no interest in the Big Questions or consider the Big Answers too far beyond comprehension to waste time on.

Often, in science fiction, a religion and the culture of which it is a part will be designed to serve specific needs of the story. In "Unhuman Sacrifice," Katherine MacLean needed to show a culture with a ritual (hanging youths upside down for a week or so right before adulthood) that was obviously stupid and barbaric to human eyes, yet absolutely indispensable to the race that practiced it (it was an essential part of their life cycle). In *Newton and the Quasi-Apple*, I had to put an alien race's analog of a key scientist from our own history (rather like a bit of Galileo and Newton rolled into one) into conflict with a theocracy like the one Galileo faced—but not *too* much like it.

As the last example illustrates, science and religion have many of the same concerns—and don't always see eye to eye about them, even though some prominent scientists have been churchmen. Religion, though, has developed far more often in human history than science. Why is that?

First, you must understand that science and technology are not the same. Technology began when the first hominids used rocks or sticks to change the shape of other rocks or sticks. Learning to use fire and make spears and arrows and canoes were large technological advances. That sort of thing can be done without science—that is, without an analytical understanding of the underlying principles. A great deal can be accomplished simply by tinkering and building on the tinkering of your forebears, experimentally finding things that work and using them, regardless of whether you understand why they work.

But there are limits. Poul Anderson, in his speculations on the nature and origin of science in chapter eight of *Is There Life on*

Other Worlds?, doubts that it's possible for such purely pragmatic craftsmanship to produce a sophisticated ship or an airplane. I'm not sure I agree that it's impossible, but it would at the very least be a much slower process, likely taking more time than most species have.

Science adds an extra element that helps: theory. Scientists observe, both personally and through the accumulated observations of others. They attempt to formulate systems of rules that precisely describe the observations made so far and can be used to predict things that haven't been observed yet. They then do experiments to test those predictions. If the experimental results agree with the predictions, they provide support for the theory—additional reason to believe that it is, if not an exact description of the real world, at least a good and useful model. By "useful" I mean, among other things, that it can be used to design things that are expensive to build—things like bridges and airliners—and be reasonably sure they will work.

So there is a *connection* between science and technology. Science makes possible kinds of technology that would be difficult to imagine, much less execute, without it. But Anderson suspects, and I suspect he's right, that its development is far from inevitable. (My *Newton and the Quasi-Apple* shows how a fundamental breakthrough crucial to a species' development of science could be derailed by untimely exposure to a bit of advanced technology that doesn't seem to fit the theory. What if Newton had seen an "apple" [in this case an artificial construct of advanced physics called "quasimaterial"] that *didn't* follow the law of gravity?) Scientific method seems to have originated only once among humans, and the fact that it did seems to have depended on several social conditions coming together in a somewhat improbable combination. It happened in the Renaissance, and required the fusion of several ideas or attitudes that had all existed before, but never all at once, including the Hellenistic interest in mathematics and logic, the medieval Judeo-Christian emphasis on trying to establish rigorously which theory was *right*, and the emphasis on trade and handicraft during the Dark Ages.

One interesting question raised by Anderson concerns the relationship between the "hard" or physical sciences (such as physics, chemistry and astronomy) and the "soft" or "human" sciences (such as psychology, sociology and economics). We can easily imagine a world on which the physical sciences have not progressed very far, but that may not imply anything about the state of the "soft" sciences. They could, in fact, be better developed there than here. Conceivably, the rapid progress of the physical sciences on Earth has *interfered* with the growth of the human sciences, partly by attracting talented researchers away from them and partly by creating a perceived compulsion to use the methodology of the physical sciences in an area where something else might be more appropriate and effective.

Arts

Still another major area of intellectual activity that has occupied our kind since its very early days is that group of pursuits called "the arts." Wall paintings in ancient cave dwellings depict the dwellers' lives and world with considerable sophistication, and artifacts that are clearly musical instruments leave little doubt that they had discovered the charms of patterned sound. Other species will likely have developed similar pursuits—but how similar? It has been suggested that one of the few things that might be worth carrying in interstellar commerce would be arts and crafts. Would different species be able to understand each other's artistic productions enough to make it worthwhile?

My guess is: yes and no. You don't need to look beyond our own species to see that there can be considerable gulfs between one culture's ideas of beauty, or what a set of symbols represents, and another. The glib proverb notwithstanding, music is *not* a universal language. To a typical American, the popular music of Japan or Bulgaria is likely to sound quite strange, and not at all likely to evoke in him or her the same things it evokes in a Japanese or Bulgarian who grew up with it. (Of course, it works the other way, too!) Yet it *is* likely to evoke *something*, if only a vague impression of exoticness. Even though music does not communicate perfectly across cultural borders, it often communicates far more than the spoken languages of the same cultures. And there are sound physical reasons for that.

Part of it is that our nervous systems are all wired similarly—which will not be true of us and most alien species. But another part goes even deeper: The relationships of sound that human music incorporates tend to be ones that have special significance in a purely *physical* sense. It's no coincidence, for example, that the sequence of notes that a European or American harmony student knows as a well-voiced major chord is precisely the set of natural frequencies produced by many common natural vibrating systems, such as air columns or strings. Certain relationships of frequencies occur naturally so often that beings who can distinguish frequencies at all will almost inevitably home in on them and use some of them in their music. The wishful thinking of atonalists notwithstanding, there is something special about the relationships on which scales and harmony are based.

Similar arguments could be made for visual arts. Representational drawing is a fairly simple form of mapping reality, and likely to occur in forms at least approximately recognizable to many intelligences that feel the urge to record their surroundings.

Still, which elements of their surroundings they choose to concentrate on, and how they choose to map them or weave them into song, can vary considerably. Humans are all built to recognize the specialness of an octave or a fifth, but European music is practically unique in the importance it places on harmony. Other cultures are likely to use scales, such as the pentatonic one that occurs independently in many parts of the world, that are based in a different way on the same physically special relationships; but they are also likely to place more emphasis on other aspects of music, such as melody or rhythm.

And any culture's arts are likely to evolve quite far from their physically simple origins. In music, for example, people in this part of the world have expanded their palettes to include chromatic scales and the complex harmonies of Stravinsky or modern jazz, while others elsewhere use intervals even smaller than those in our chromatic scales. In painting and sculpture, some later practitioners have moved away from straightforward representation to cubism and surrealism. Artists of other species, even if their starting points were similar to ours, are likely to experiment in still other directions.

And, of course, some species may have such different senses or nervous programming that they will have whole areas of art with no close counterparts among us. A species that does not distinguish colors or pitches would be unable to perceive many of the most important features of our art; but may make up for it by creating artistic patterns with things that *we* can't perceive, like the polarization of light, subtle nuances of scent or electromagnetic field patterns. Dolphins use sound, but they use it over such a wide range of frequencies that we can't hear much of it. Your aliens' art may be only incidental to your story, but if you want it to be more than that, and interesting in its own right, keep always in mind that it would have developed to please and move *them*, not us.

Trade, Money and Credit

If neighboring cultures discover that each of them has natural resources or skills that the other lacks, both can benefit by exchanging what they have too much of for what they have too little of. Such a situation may arise for the obvious geographical reasons: You live where there is plenty of water, I live where there is plenty of salt. Or it may result from a difference of lifestyles. Jacob Bronowski describes the example of the Bakhtiari, nomadic herders who roam parts of Iran with flocks of sheep and goats— and little else. Having to carry all their possessions, they do not carry nonessentials or things that they need only rarely. They cannot afford the time or carry the equipment to make things like metal pots, so they barter for them with settled peoples who do make them.

Barter is the most basic form of trade: a simple exchange of different kinds of goods or services. Money has proved such a useful invention that most cultures have adopted some form of it. A compact medium of exchange can both simplify transactions and increase flexibility. If we agree that your ton of coal is worth my camel, we *could* meet somewhere and trade, but that requires physically getting both to the meeting point and then back to their new homes. If we agree that each is worth a thousand dollars and I don't really need the coal right away and can't store that much at a time, I can sell you my camel now, pocket the thousand dollars, and buy as much coal as I need, when I need it. Such a system will inevitably generate some kind of banking system, so I can even loan a third party some of the thousand dollars and let it earn interest while I wait for coal-burning season.

At present we're moving toward a system that takes the money system a step further: The money doesn't even have to be a physical object, but can be numbers processed by computers reflecting who owes and can afford what. That, too, seems likely in species that develop computers and use them as widely as we do—but it's not inevitable.

Whatever the method or medium of exchange, some form of trade seems likely to develop wherever two or more cultures exist within reach of each other and have enough in common to be able to use some of the same commodities. When it does, it's likely to be one of the most powerful forces shaping the course of history. Exploring expeditions, for example, are more likely to be financed by rich people who hope to get richer importing exotic goods than by those who are merely curious about what's over the next hill. Many science-fictional scenarios are driven largely by trade and provide ample occasion for interspecies contact—as in Poul Anderson's *Trader Team* (part of his larger Polesotechnic League series).

Trade is not likely to happen unless 1. both parties have some interests in common, and 2. it is cheaper to get what they want from the trading partner than from some other source closer to home. The second requirement casts immediate suspicion on any plot involving, say, bringing iron and silicon to Earth from a similar planet of Alpha Centauri. There's so much iron and silicon right here that it wouldn't be worth it. (See Warren Salomon's article on "The Economics of Interstellar Commerce" and John Barnes's "How to Build a Future," which is largely about constructing plausible economies.) The first requirement seems obvious, but is subject to change with technological advancement. If it turns out that dolphins have humanlike intelligence, it might have seemed until recently that they and we would have few common interests or conflicts. Now, of course, both are running short of fish, and dolphins in some areas are threatened by human-produced pollution. So they and we would certainly have things to talk about.

Government

While that last example might be an opportunity for trade between two species living in alien environments—e.g., dolphins bringing hard-to-mine submarine minerals to humans in exchange for farm-raised fish—it appears even more clearly an occasion for conflict resolution. I have already touched briefly on the growing importance of this as people (or aliens) live in larger and larger groups and come into more contact with other groups. A major impetus for the development and evolution of governments has been the need to maintain order within a society and to protect it from outside dangers (which usually means other governments, so the concept is clearly a mixed blessing).

Humans have experimented with many forms of government, but most of them are pretty obviously modifications and extensions of the kinds of hierarchies found in baboon troops. Even those that take great pride in being democracies tend to have at the top of the hierarchy an "alpha male" with suspiciously many of the trappings of royalty. Nevertheless, all the steps that have given previously excluded classes (such as the unpropertied, former slaves and women) a voice in their own government surely represent some of the most important kinds of progress ever made. So it seems, at least, to most of us—but might another species see it differently? In *Tweedlioop* I show a culture that to humans seems obviously older and wiser than our own—so they're shocked when it turns out to be a strict dictatorship. A very different kind of dictatorship than any in human history, but a dictatorship nonetheless; and I like to think their Ambassador makes a good enough case for it to disturb readers into some hard thought about both their system and ours.

A general tendency through much of our history has been toward larger governmental units: families, clans, tribes, city-states, nations, empires and various forms of international alliances and confederations. At the moment there seems to be a trend in the opposite direction, with an epidemic of Balkanization sweeping the world. Whether that is a significant new trend or just a passing aberration remains to be seen. I rather hope the latter; even though I mistrust governments as much as anyone, it's becoming clear that many problems now transcend national boundaries and will have to be solved on a global level if they are to be solved at all. For that reason I suspect that most planets that have equaled or passed Earth's present population density and technological level will have some form of world government.

What form I will not venture to specify. I suspect there are many answers, and part of the business of being a science fiction writer is to imagine some of them and work out how they might function. Whatever the level of development of your aliens, you'll need to be careful to let their governments and social institutions grow out of *their* history, not ours. W.R. Thompson's kya, for example, have a society that grew naturally from their background as herbivorous herd animals, which generates quite different answers to such basic questions as "How shall we pick leaders?" and "Do we even *need* leaders?"

The Other Government: Custom, Etiquette, Social Pressures and Morality

Formal government is by no means the only force governing individual action. Here, and likely elsewhere, it was a relative late-comer, growing out of established customs that in turn grew out of earlier animal behavior patterns. Intelligent animals can modify their habits as changing conditions warrant, but they do so reluctantly. Thus, for example, many humans still see "Be fruitful and multiply" as something they should do as well as they can, even at a time when the problem is no longer too few people, but too many.

Even in the presence of formal governments, the "unwritten laws" of custom, etiquette and social pressure remain important influences on individuals' lives—and an important source of the little details that add verisimilitude for a writer trying to bring an alien culture to life. Our lives are full of tiny gestures and nuances that carry a surprising wealth of meaning—things like a raised eyebrow or holding a door open for someone. The lives of aliens will similarly be full of such things, though of course they will be different from ours. The novels of C.J. Cherryh are known for their richness in such details, and particularly commendable for recognizing that they will be different not only from ours, but from each other.

Even within a single species, social attitudes, strictness of control over individuals and the significance attached to gestures can vary greatly from place to place and from time to time. In our culture it is rude to belch at the dinner table; in some others, it is rude *not* to. When I grew a beard as a young professor at an American college in the early seventies, some of my colleagues said, "It makes you look like one of the kids!"; but my grandmother (who grew up in a time when only old men wore beards) complained, "It makes you look so old!"

To a Japanese visitor to America, a piece of pie presented with its point toward a diner might be taken as an expression of hostility, while it would never occur to an American to attach any significance to the pie's orientation. Contemporary American culture has abandoned many of the symbolic requirements of etiquette and emphasized tolerance of individual choice in many (though by no means all) areas. Japanese culture, perhaps as a result of its high population density, has retained a great many social rituals and attaches great significance to any deviation from them. A great deal of life in such a culture consists of role-playing according to an elaborate script, which everyone is supposed to know. Putting food on the table the wrong way really *can* express hostility, if everyone present has been taught that it does; but reading that into it in a culture where everyone *hasn't* been so taught would be unjustifiable.

Formal religions tend to be particularly full of such strictures and rituals, and also play a large role in determining what kinds of behavior are treated as moral or immoral. Cultures that don't have formal religion or observe it strictly will have to find other ways to define, justify and enforce their moral codes—but many people on Earth already do that. Any culture will need moral codes to define what is acceptable in such areas as killing or injuring other individuals, taking or using their property, and so on. Many social dictates of acceptable behavior involve such areas as reproduction (a society must control fighting over potential mates, ensure that children are raised acceptably, and so forth), eating and elimination.

Most human cultures are quite firm about the clothing that people must wear or not wear, and read great symbolic meaning into individual choices—even in climates where clothing is not a functional necessity. Even though each society has its own ideas about what is "proper," no two necessarily agree on such things. My brother was once refused admission to a restaurant in the South Pacific because he wasn't wearing a skirt; not too long ago, it was considered scandalous for women not to do so in this country.

To make alien cultures live and breathe, you will want to give ample attention to details of custom, gesture, morality and clothing; and you will want all of these things to grow out of your particular aliens' nature and background. Additional good examples can be found in the kya stories of W.R. Thompson, the Trimus stories of G. David Nordley, and the "Noah's Ark" stories (*ReGenesis*) of Julia Ecklar.

Advanced Technologies

In the last few centuries, our species has undergone a technological explosion whose consequences have radically altered virtually every aspect of life. This or something comparable is likely to happen to any intelligent, tool-using species that has science as well as technology. It may also happen, though more slowly, to longer-lived species whose technology must develop unaided by well-developed theory.

Since you're living in the midst of this explosion, many of its features are already familiar to you, though your view of them may still need a bit of stretching. Many people tend to assume, at least subconsciously, that the conditions they live under represent the final phase of development. They don't, of course; the pace of change has been accelerating steadily, and shows no sign of ceasing to do so. Since aliens you write about may be at any stage of development—before, at or after ours—I plan in the next few paragraphs to survey briefly some of the major areas that have already brought radical changes to our lives. In the next section, I'll hint at what still more radical changes might be yet to come.

Advances in agriculture, sanitation and medicine have all contributed to a greatly increased, and still rapidly growing, population. Lifespans have increased so much, thanks to disease prevention through sanitation and treatment through medicine, that people have been accumulating at an unprecedented rate. So far we've been able to get away with it, at least marginally, because improvements in agricultural technology and plant and animal breeding have also allowed us to feed more people. It remains to be seen how far that combination of circumstances can continue, but at the moment agriculture is getting a new boost from genetic engineering, which allows more drastic modification of existing plants and animals than conventional breeding.

Closely related to improvements in food production are improvements in storage and distribution. People have long used methods like salting and drying to preserve summer's food for winter consumption, or for use on long trips. Refrigeration has revolutionized the whole business, making it possible to eat food of near-fresh quality at any time of year. Portable refrigeration and rapid transportation have made it just as easy to have products grown or made in one area distributed and used in any other.

Transportation has developed dramatically, with the advent of self-propelled motor vehicles such as cars, trucks and trains, enhanced by infrastructures like high-quality roads and railroads. In this century we have even moved beyond the surface of our home world, with flight making transcontinental or transoceanic travel a routine matter of a few hours instead of the arduous adventure of months or years that it once was. All of these developments, being reasonably straightforward applications of universal physical principles, are likely to occur in some form in any technologically inclined culture that also has a scientific bent. (Though not necessarily in the same way. Imagine, for example, a world on which the conditions that led to the formation of coal and oil occurred less often or less widely than on Earth.)

Note also that there's more than one approach to many problems, some of which we've tried and abandoned in favor of an alternative. There was a brief period, for instance, when humans used lighter-than-air airships (blimps and dirigibles) that floated unhurriedly through the atmosphere. Here these have been almost entirely superseded by faster, heavier airplanes, but you can easily imagine an alien culture in which airships survived and flourished as the favored mode of flight.

We have now demonstrated, but barely begun to use, the possibility of spaceflight, going even beyond the atmosphere. It's relatively easy to see the potential value in exploiting sources of raw materials, and moving messy industry, outside our home planet's immediate neighborhood. Some of us can also see value in establishing additional "home planets," be they actual planets or artificial habitats in space. There is strong evidence that Earth has been repeatedly subjected to planet-wide catastrophes that wiped out large numbers of species. If we really care about the long-term survival of our species, we'd do well to make sure this little planet isn't the only place it's represented.

Colonies in our Solar System will of necessity be largely artificial, ranging from pressurized domes containing small artificial habitats to whole planets, such as Venus or Mars, that have been "terraformed," or artificially transformed to make them more Earthlike. This will probably be true of other races in other solar systems as well. Except under very rare and special circumstances, two planets in a single system are unlikely to be so similar that natives of one could live unaided on another.

There is, however, another possibility for using a planet different from the one where you evolved. Terraforming means adapting a planet to new inhabitants; the new and rapidly developing field of genetic engineering (which also has profound implications for medicine) will enable species to remake themselves to thrive in a new and alien environment. Humans and/or other species may eventually decide that this approach is preferable, especially in cases where a planet they want to colonize already has an ecosystem. Terraforming would involve destroying that ecology to make room for ours; adapting ourselves to fit it might be a gentler and ethically more acceptable alternative. (If this consideration seems trivial or far-fetched, think of the Golden Rule and imagine an alien party wanting to "terraform" Earth!)

I can't leave this brief discussion of advanced technologies without mentioning electricity and electronics. They've been implicit in all the foregoing, since cheap, easily distributed electric power and electronic instrumentation have played central roles in all the areas I've mentioned. They have made possible a greatly increased standard of living in many parts of the world, and have made the world, as the cliché says, a much smaller place. With light-speed communication taken for granted, the ways that business and government and arts operate have changed radically. If I'd been writing this book a couple of hundred years ago, and wanted to get my editor's opinion of a proposed change in its organization, I would have had to write him a letter and wait weeks or months for his reply. Now I simply call or e-mail him, regardless of where either of us is, and the matter is taken care of in seconds or minutes.

The branch of electronics dealing with computers has so revolutionized so many aspects of life so fast that it's almost an embarrassment to the science fiction profession. Few, if any, published stories imagined that computers would ever be as small, powerful and ubiquitous as they've become in the last couple of decades. Virtually any new appliance, camera or car now contains at least one computer, giving it abilities that would have seemed like magic just a few years ago. Computers have wrought major changes in the way banking, government, medicine and the arts are done. By making it quick and easy to do calculations that couldn't be done at all without them, they've played a major role in making that explosion of new science, technology and social change happen even faster.

Will the explosion continue, here or among aliens? We'll consider that in the next section. Meanwhile, I should point out that this section has skimmed lightly over many interrelated and interacting aspects of human history. As a science fiction writer you'll probably find it helpful to know as much as you can about our own species' past, and in particular how various fields of endeavor have influenced each other. Such knowledge is likely to give you ideas for stories, both in terms of what circumstances are likely to produce what kinds of responses, and in terms of how things might have developed differently if conditions were different. Two books I've found particularly useful for such studies, in addition to the ones I've already mentioned, are H.G. Wells's *Outline of History* (even though it necessarily stops well short of the present and includes some outdated opinions) and Bernard Grun and Werner Stein's *The Timetables of History*. This last has an unusual and particularly instructive feature. It shows events in different areas of human endeavor in parallel columns, so you can see at a glance what was happening in many areas at any time.

IN TIMES TO COME: OLDER AND WISER?

Once a civilization reaches a stage comparable to our present one, there is the potential for a great deal of further development, at an ever-increasing rate. All the fields I've mentioned in the last section are changing rapidly, and every new development opens up previously unsuspected possibilities. Furthermore, activities in different fields are synergistic, finding applications in seemingly unrelated fields. Computers, for example, were originally developed to assist mathematicians and engineers with number-crunching, but they have also greatly accelerated the development of every other field of science, radically changed the ways that arts and publishing are done, and made possible such medical advances as the CAT scan. So important is this synergistic effect that almost any forecast of when a particular advance is likely to happen will be much too conservative—*if* such progress is allowed to continue and accelerate. K. Eric Drexler in *Engines of Creation* and Vernor Vinge in *Marooned in Realtime* have, independently and in different language, extrapolated the rapidly climbing curves of progress to foresee a "Singularity," a time when the curves of change grow so steep that humanity undergoes a sudden, radical transformation to something new and so utterly different that we can barely imagine what it might be. Some intelligent species may already have undergone such a transformation.

Or it may be quite rare. It's relatively easy to imagine reasons why the current rates of change, and acceleration of change, may *not* continue. A growing anti-scientific element in our own culture has already significantly reduced the emphasis on basic research, and could, if it goes far enough, lead to another "Dark Age" in which little new knowledge is learned and much old knowledge is lost. Or we (or any other species in a comparable situation) could destroy ourselves, accidentally or foolishly—because, at least so far, human progress has been closely tied to controlling larger and larger amounts of energy. In this century we have learned to use (and abuse) nuclear fission, and are currently struggling to put reins and harness on fusion. There is no reason to assume that, if we can survive those, we might not move on to still bigger things.

As described in Shklovskii and Sagan's *Intelligent Life in the Universe*, astrophysicist N.S. Kardashev suggested dividing possible technologically advanced civilizations into three classes according to their energy use:

I. A civilization with energy use and technology levels comparable to contemporary Earth.

II. A civilization capable of using the entire energy output of its primary star. (Science-fictional example: Larry Niven's *Ringworld*.)

III. A civilization able to use energy at the rate produced by an entire galaxy.

The Kyyra in my novels *The Sins of the Fathers* and *Lifeboat Earth* fall somewhere between Kardashev classes II and III—intentionally closer to II (they move planets and induce supernovas as a means of producing raw materials) and accidentally closer to III (an industrial accident on a scale far beyond our present capabilities sets off a chain reaction of supernovas, exploding the entire core of a galaxy). If we continue to use larger and larger quantities of energy, we or our descendants may eventually undertake projects of comparable magnitude—and have to deal with corresponding risks.

Tiny Technologies?

On the other hand, the trend toward more and more energy use may not continue, or at least may not continue to steepen so precipitously. We might instead (or in addition) learn to accomplish more with less energy. Some of our efforts have already turned in this direction. Automobiles are more fuel-efficient than they were a few years ago, and expected to become still more so. The computer on which I'm writing sits comfortably on an old typewriter table and wields far more computing power than the one I used in graduate school, which filled a very large room and required far more electricity. Those and other movements we have already seen toward making things smaller and more efficient will probably be mere drops in the bucket compared to some we can anticipate.

Perhaps the most profound of these is *nanotechnology*, the embryonic technology of building virtually anything atom by atom, using programmed *molecule*-sized machines called assemblers. Possibility in principle is demonstrated by our own existence. Biological systems are naturally occurring nanotechnological systems in which DNA carries full instructions that direct active molecules to build and operate complete macroscopic organisms. As K. Eric Drexler points out in his book *Engines of Creation* and in his shorter article with Chris Peterson, the fact that nature does it means that we can learn to do it at least as well—and perhaps better and with a wider range of applications. Drexler's arguments are scientifically conservative; nanotechnology looks likely to transform our lives, and those of any beings who decide to explore that road, so profoundly that I can only hint at the possibilities here and urge you to read his books.

Another emerging technology that may reduce the energy needs of its users is *virtual reality*: computer-generated sensory experiences that mimic reality so convincingly that they can *replace* reality for some purposes. Rocket pilots, for example, might receive much of their training by "flying" virtual rockets, requiring only a little electricity instead of tons of rocket fuel. They might even conduct actual explorations by means of virtual vehicles, using the closely related technology of *telepresence*. Virtual reality, as the term is usually used, means a "reality" that is *generated* by a computer and may be completely fictitious. Telepresence feels the same to a user, except that the virtual reality he experiences is a simulation of an *actual* reality, transmitted by another computer which is operating one or more robots there. Thus a "pilot" might explore a new planet through the artificial senses of a small, agile robot probe with no need for life-support systems. We may do this ourselves, or we may meet aliens only through *their* robot probes. Or you can imagine a radically different scenario: Instead of using telepresence to explore the real universe, a species might retreat into virtual reality and abandon most contact with the "real" world.

Non-Technological Hurdles

Whichever way we or any other species might choose to jump (and there's no reason an entire species has to jump the same way!), it's pretty clear that once a species reaches our current level or something comparable, it will have to clear some important *non*-technological hurdles to get much further. We have progressed to the point where we can do a great many things we couldn't before—including destroying ourselves by such means as nuclear war, runaway industrial pollution or overpopulation. Our species is currently trying to learn to cope with these things; its prospects for future survival and prosperity will depend on its ability to do so.

Will we succeed? I hope so. . . . In the universe at large, how likely is any species to succeed? We have no data on which to base a definitive answer, but for a science fiction writer's purposes it may be enough to say that *some* species probably will. There may be as many ways to succeed as there are to fail, and most of both may be as hard for us to visualize or understand as it would be for a gibbon to understand the appeal of Tolstoy. However, it is the science fiction writer's business to try to imagine some of the possibilities, and to make them seem real and comprehensible.

In early science fiction, aliens were commonly little more than clever monsters bent on destruction, for reasons that were at best vaguely defined. It's hard to get that sort of thing past editors now; we now expect any species' actions to make sense in terms of its own nature and background. But even our own species' future attitudes are likely to change so much, so fast, that we might have difficulty understanding them. If you try to imagine our own great- or great-great-grandparents reading a description of America in the early 1990s, you may get some inkling of how hard they might have found it to believe, much less understand, our current tax rates, dress codes, moral standards and so forth.

So it will be quite a stretch to imagine beings who are older or "more advanced" than ourselves, even if they started out quite similar to us. When I wrote ". . . And Comfort to the Enemy," about an advanced civilization with an all-biological technology, both my editor and I thought I was depicting something so alien that we wouldn't even recognize it as an advanced civilization. Within ten years I could see hints that we ourselves were starting down a road that could easily lead to such a future.

So where might we, or aliens more or less like us, be after an additional hundred or thousand or ten thousand years of history? Natural evolution seems unlikely to make much difference in our physical form. If punctuated-equilibrium theorists like Stephen Jay Gould are right, major evolutionary changes occur only in response to major environmental changes, and civilization by its nature tends to minimize evolutionary pressures. A couple of qualifications: If we stay on one planet, which is increasingly shrunken by easy transportation, racial separations are likely to blur and gradually disappear. On the other hand, if we colonize other planets and the colonies have little contact with each other, the isolated populations will tend to diverge, eventually becoming separate species. And, of course, any species that gets heavily into genetic engineering may remake itself in one or more ways that nature couldn't have.

That and other ways that cultures learn to cope with the problems mentioned above may seem quite strange and perhaps distasteful to contemporary humans. My Kyyra, for example, have forgotten the concept of war, but they have also forgotten pets. To deal with large, growing populations and ecological problems, they long ago learned to replace natural ecosystems with simplified, completely engineered and controlled artificial systems, with no natural life-forms left except themselves. Such an idea likely seems repugnant to you, but I find it all too easy to imagine our own species following a path leading there. The Kyyra have eliminated interpersonal and interfaction stresses by going far beyond what we think of as world government—their "Coordinator" is an enormously complex computer that continually monitors minds and makes adjustments as needed to ensure that everyone gets along.

The possibility of such things suggests that, while the heavy-handed alien invaders of yore now seem quaint and unlikely, neither can we assume, as some have, that any species that has achieved starflight will be so morally advanced that they would be no threat to others. They must have found some way to avoid destroying themselves; but their way of doing that could easily involve one of their factions destroying or dominating all others, and that tendency could just as easily extend to other species they met in their travels.

Really Big Civilizations

How likely are such travels, and how far might they extend? I have already said a little about travel within a species' native solar system. So far this has been done mostly with chemical rockets, which is extremely expensive—but then, chemical rockets are quite an inefficient way of going about it. A large part of the problem is that they must carry their own fuel with them, and many designs routinely discard major parts of the vehicle itself (both of which pose special difficulties for round trips!). So a lot of thinking has gone into ways to avoid these problems, including reusable spacecraft, nuclear rather than chemical rockets (which run into large problems with public acceptance), and rockets designed to collect return fuel at a destination (see the first two Zubrin references). Others have suggested ways to get in and out of Earth's gravity well more efficiently, as in Arnold and Kingsbury's article "The Spaceport," about an orbiting spaceport that stores energy and momentum released by a docking spacecraft for use by one departing later. Still others propose completely non-rocket propulsion systems such as electromagnetic catapults and sails using light and the particulate "wind" from the sun or light from ground-based lasers. (See, for example, Zubrin's "The Magnetic Sail.")

Until fairly recently, most people *other* than science fiction writers tended to assume that manned interstellar flight beyond the solar system was impractical. The distances are huge (the closest star is more than four light-years from the Sun), and the amounts of energy required to reach even that in a human lifetime are enormous. However, a variety of ways around those problems have been explored by science fiction writers—and more recently but quite seriously by actual physicists (some of whom, such as Robert L. Forward and Geoffrey A. Landis, are also science fiction writers).

One early way around the energy and distance problems is the generation ship: a relatively slow ship that might take hundreds or thousands of years to go from one star to another, with generations of crew living or dying on board. An obvious problem with that, even if you can develop an onboard life-support system that can be trusted for so long, is that crew born aboard ship are likely to have little conception of, or interest in, either the "home" planet the ship started from or the destination that it's bound for. The ship is their universe and likely to develop a peculiar culture of its own (as in Robert A. Heinlein's story "Universe").

Another approach, if you can get enough energy, takes advantage of the relativistic effect called *time dilation*. I won't go into the details here, but if you want to see them (and you should, if you plan to make this an important part of your story) I recommend Taylor and Wheeler's *Spacetime Physics*. The essential result for storytelling purposes is that if you travel at a sizable fraction of the speed of light, the trip appears to you, the traveler, to take less time than it does to an observer back at the spaceport you left.

The relationship is

$$t_{ship} = t_{port}\sqrt{(1 - v^2/c^2)} \, ,$$

where t_{ship} is the trip time measured aboard the ship, t_{port} is the trip time as it appears to a non-traveling observer at either end, v is the ship's speed relative to starting point and destination, and c is the speed of light. At low speeds, the time dilation factor (the square root) is so close to 1.0 that it's hard to notice the difference between the two times. But as v gets close to c, the trip time experienced by the crew gets smaller and smaller, as shown in table 6-1. It also gets harder and harder to accelerate the ship any further, and Einstein's theory of relativity (with support from experimental data) at least suggests that the speed of light is a strictly enforced limit beyond which we can't go.

How to attain such speeds? It isn't easy, but physicists have

v/c	t_{port}	t_{ship}
0.1	43	42.784
0.2	21.5	21.066
0.3	14.333	13.673
0.4	10.75	9.853
0.5	8.6	7.448
0.6	7.167	5.733
0.7	6.143	4.387
0.8	5.375	3.225
0.9	4.778	2.083
0.92	4.674	1.832
0.94	4.574	1.561
0.96	4.479	1.254
0.98	4.388	0.873
0.99	4.343	0.613
0.999	4.304	0.192

TABLE 6-1 Trip Time from Sol to Alpha Centauri
The left column shows travel speed as a fraction of c, the speed of light. The middle column shows the length of the trip at that speed in years, as measured by an observer on Earth or a planet of Alpha Centauri. The last column shows the length of the trip as measured by the travelers aboard ship. Shipboard time is always less than "port" time—only slightly so, until v/c gets fairly large, but very dramatically when v is quite close to c.

worked out several methods in considerable detail, including anti-matter rockets, beamed energy systems, solar sails and fusion ram-jets that gather sparse interstellar material for fuel. An excellent guide to these and other aspects of interstellar flight (which inci-dentally tells you a good deal about more ordinary propulsion *within* a solar system, and contains lots of in-depth references) is Eugene Mallove and Gregory Matloff's *The Starflight Handbook*.

These considerations of spaceflight will obviously be of interest a couple of chapters hence, in connection with human-alien interac-tions. Our present interest in them stems from their relevance to the question "Can a society (human or alien) get bigger than a single planet?" An old standby in science fiction is the galactic em-pire, republic or federation. How likely is that?

Even for a much smaller interstellar civilization—say, one includ-ing a few solar systems in a region of space spanning a dozen or so light-years—the problems are large and the rewards not neces-sarily commensurate. Assuming that we're limited to the kinds of physics we've considered so far, travel or communication between member worlds will take years and cost fortunes. What would make it worthwhile? You don't go light-years afield to import commodities that you can make far more cheaply at home. You don't mount expensive expeditions to defend yourself against beings so remote that they can't afford to mount expensive expeditions against you. Interstellar colonization seems more likely to lead to a proliferation of largely independent civilizations, though there may be a limited trade in information and alien artifacts. George Ochoa and Jeffrey Osier devote a chapter of *The Writer's Guide to Creating a Science Fiction Universe* to the problems and possibilities of galactic-scale civilizations.

Of course, everything I've said about why interstellar civiliza-tions are likely to be smallish and loosely knit could change dramati-cally if one or more species discovered new kinds of physics allow-ing faster-than-light travel and/or communication. In the last couple of decades, physicists have been noticing possible loopholes in rela-tivity that just *might* mean the speed limit isn't as absolute as we thought. (See Dr. Robert L. Forward's *Analog* article "Faster Than Light.") And it's by no means inconceivable that someone will even-tually discover whole new areas of physics that suggest ways to go quickly, easily and cheaply across interstellar distances. I won't say much about those now, since for the time being we're limiting ourselves to what can be foreseen with *present* scientific knowledge. However, such a technology could open up the possibility of a very far-flung yet closely knit and fluidly interacting civilization, so I will say a bit more about such "new science" in chapter eleven.

For now, the important fact for a writer about aliens is that any possibilities that we can imagine for ourselves are just as plausible for other intelligences somewhat like us. Anything we can do, or clearly see the possibility of doing later, somebody else can do, too.

AND IF THEY AREN'T LIKE US?

Throughout this chapter, I've sprinkled fictional examples of how some aspect of an alien society might develop differently from the same aspect in ours. Could a society be so alien that some of its features have no counterpart in ours (or vice versa)?

An advanced society might evolve, for example, from something analogous to our social insects: bees, wasps, termites and ants. These have elaborate social structures in which thousands of individuals are highly specialized to serve very specific functions in the operation of the hive as a whole. Individual actions are determined by a combination of hard-wired programming and messages exchanged between individuals by such means as coded chemicals or the "dancing language" of honeybees. The actions of any one individual (except the queen) are not very important; individuals are largely interchangeable and expendable, and none can live very long except as part of the hive. In a sense, the hive is more like an intelligent animal than a herd, and the constituent individual insects more like its cells. Considering the complexity already achieved by some of these insect societies, it's not too hard to imagine some developing to a point comparable to our cities or even larger units. In such a society, concepts such as "individual rights" and "democracy" might be almost incomprehensibly alien; indeed, the concept of an individual as a complete being might be so. The Taurans in Joe Haldeman's *The Forever War* appear to have a hive-like mentality.

To dolphins, or similar beings evolved elsewhere, cities themselves might be a hard concept to grasp, with their implications of many individuals living virtually their entire lives in crowded locales full of artificial boundaries. My "Pinocchio" is a product of a type of culture that bottlenose dolphins might have. My speculations were based on actual research results, and we still can't completely rule out the possibility that they might have such a society. (Even if they don't, something much like it may still exist elsewhere!) Their lifestyle is even more nomadic than that of human nomads; they roam over vast distances in a world that is essentially three-dimensional (ours is largely two-dimensional) and they don't build artifacts because they don't have hands. Fire is impractical where they live, so the notion of cooking food would probably seem quite odd to them. Lying and deceit, so deeply entrenched in virtually all human cultures, might be hard for a dolphin to imagine. Visceral reactions associated with emotional stress would be hard to hide, since dolphins' bodies are literally transparent to each other's sensing sounds!

Still other very alien cultures can be imagined, often by starting with some group of animals found on Earth and imagining how it might evolve—such as the starfish-like Radiates in Naomi Mitchison's *Memoirs of a Spacewoman*. Most cultures are likely to have *some* elements that correspond recognizably to aspects of human cultures, but may also have some that don't. In general, the more different your animals are from primates, and the more different their environment from the one in which primates evolved, the more different the cultures will be.

Habitual flight, for example, would have lots of consequences. The Overlords in Arthur C. Clarke's *Childhood's End* have cities without walkways and with doors placed at arbitrary elevations. The Ythrians in Poul Anderson's *The People of the Wind* don't have real cities, and that vision may be more likely. Their mobility makes permanent crowding unnecessary, and the great energy needs of flying have made them voracious carnivores, who must live thinly spread, maintaining and defending large territories.

Numerous other fictional examples are scattered through the literature. You might find it helpful to browse in *Barlowe's Guide to Extraterrestrials* for a quick introduction to several, and then track down the original stories to read in more depth about some that interest you.

You'll probably also find it helpful, as a source of ideas, to read widely about Earthly animals and imagine what kinds of societies might evolve from them. What sort of attitudes might we have toward death and the value of life, for example, if our parents laid thousands of eggs and knew that only 1 percent of them would produce children who would survive to adulthood? If we shed our skins, like snakes or lizards, might our parents decorate the house with shed skins from childhood the way some human parents put pencil marks on a wall to track their offspring's growth?

The best general advice I can give a writer who would write about alien societies is this: Learn all you can about ethology, anthropology and history—in their broadest senses—and then go beyond them. Let them suggest directions for you to go, and then follow those leads as far as you can.

CHAPTER 7

Alien Language

A - i   a - m-e   u   a-e   e - z-e-a- u.

That's as close as I could come, in symbols widely understood on Earth, to transcribing a key sentence from my first story that ever attracted any serious interest from an editor. The story ("A Devil and a Deep Blue Sea") had other problems and never sold, but it did draw a genuine letter of encouragement from an editor who had previously sent me only printed rejection slips. Not too long after that he bought my first story, and was soon buying them regularly.

What did this story have that its predecessors didn't? The most important element to catch the editor's eye, I think, was the careful attention it paid to the role of language in contact between two alien species. I wrote it in part because I couldn't remember ever reading another story that showed the actual process of a human learning an alien language. I consciously set out to do so—though of course the main thrust of the story revolved around what the aliens said once communication was established.

To show the process of learning the language, I had to know quite a bit about the language—in other words, I had to invent it in considerable detail. This isn't always necessary, of course. You may never need to show an alien language in that much detail. But you will almost certainly include at least a few words—names, if nothing else—and likely some general description of what the language sounds or looks like. As with any other aspect of writing, the more you know about your background, the more convincing the part you tell will be—because the reader will sense that what's on the page is part of a larger and self-consistent whole. One of my most satisfying moments as a writer was the time a copyeditor caught a grammatical mistake in an alien language for which I had not spelled out any rules.

As with organisms and cultures, the range of shapes languages can take is wider than you may suspect, even on Earth. So let's start this discussion of how aliens might communicate by surveying some of the ways humans communicate, starting with the most familiar and then going farther afield. What I'm about to do is not intended as a comprehensive and orderly introduction to linguistics, but rather a quick tour of some of the tricks human languages have come up with, to give you a feel for just how much variety is possible. For a more detailed and methodical study, you might start with something like Victoria Fromkin and Robert Rodman's *An Introduction to Language*, which will in turn refer you to many other sources. Also, I've found it both instructive and entertaining to browse in the articles on languages and linguistics in the *Encyclopedia Britannica*.

TOOLS OF THE TRADE:
A MINI-MUSEUM OF LINGUISTIC CURIOS

If English is the only language you've used or studied, you've encountered some grammatical terms and concepts, but not others. Languages differ enough that you need different vocabularies to describe their features. Swahili, for example, does not have participles, while English does not have simultaneous and consecutive tenses. There's some overlap in what those things do, but a lot of difference in how they do it—and even their functions are by no means equivalent.

I will assume here that you have at least a passing familiarity with such basic features of English as consonants and vowels, nouns and verbs, adjectives and adverbs, pronouns and prepositions, and past and present tenses. Starting from there, I'll remind you of some features you might have encountered in other languages commonly taught in American schools, and then move on to still others found only in languages you're less likely to have encountered.

If you've studied French or Spanish, for example, you've met verb *conjugations*. A conjugation is a pattern for changing the form of a verb to express person, number and tense. In English this is so simple you were hardly even aware of it. The simple present tense has two forms (*go* and *goes*) and the past only one (*went*); the future is formed by placing an auxiliary verb in front of the basic form (*will go*). In French or Spanish things are immediately more complicated because for each tense you need to learn (approximately) six forms: one each for *I*; *you* (singular/familiar); *he, she* or *it*; *we*; *you* (plural/polite); and *they*.

Moreover, there is not a single pattern that always works. Spanish verbs are classifiable into three different conjugations, and French four. If that's not enough, both languages contain lots of verbs that are "irregular"—that deviate in small or great ways from any of the standard conjugations, and so must be memorized. Since that's true to an appreciable extent in all the languages commonly taught in North American schools, you may assume that languages have to be full of irregular verbs. (They don't; more on that later.) On the bright side, while such languages require you to learn more forms, they also give you some extra flexibility. When the person and tense are implicit in the verb form itself, you don't always have to explicitly identify the subject. Spanish usually skips the subject pronoun unless it's needed for clarity or emphasis (e.g., *hablo* instead of *yo hablo* for *I speak*).

In learning French or Spanish conjugations, you also discovered that *tenses* aren't necessarily defined the same way in different languages. Where English has one simple past tense, Spanish has two. The *preterite* (corresponding roughly but not exactly to what French teachers often call "past historic") refers to an action that took place once at a definite time (*"I read the book yesterday"*) and the *imperfect* to an action that took place repeatedly or continuously over a period (*"I often read a book when I got home from work in those days"*).

In French or Spanish or German, you also have to distinguish *levels of address*. In speaking to any individual, you must decide whether to address him or her familiarly, as *tu* or *tú* or *du*, or formally (politely), as *vous*, *Usted* or *Sie*. The familiar forms are used in addressing animals, children and people younger or of lower status than yourself; the polite forms in addressing those older or of higher status. The difficulty (and pitfall) lies in the need to make a decision about which class is appropriate for anyone you're addressing. It can get tricky, and guessing wrong can get you into trouble. Contemporary English (now that *thou* has fallen from popularity) spares you that decision. The closest English now comes is the choice of first name or title plus last ("John" or "Mr. Smith").

Treacherous as the distinction between polite and familiar address may seem to someone encountering French or German for the first time, it can be and sometimes is worse. Polish has 45 versions of "you" (not 45 separate forms, admittedly, but 45 separate situations [combinations of number, level, gender, case, etc.] that must be distinguished to know which form to use). Japanese has an elaborate system of honorifics and degrees of floweriness that must be carefully chosen according to the relative status of speaker and person addressed.

One thing you were probably pleased to discover in Spanish or German is that spelling and pronunciation can be more straightforward and logical than they are in English. On the other hand, you may have been dismayed to find that you had to learn to make new, unfamiliar and perhaps "difficult" sounds such as the rolled *r* and the German vowels *ö* and *ü*. (Would it make you feel better to know that English is just full of sounds, such as *th* and the continually changing vowel in the American word *can't*, which occur in few other languages and are strange and difficult for almost everybody else?)

If you studied German or Latin, you had to learn about *cases* and *declensions*. These are to nouns, adjectives, articles and pronouns what conjugations are to verbs. English contains vestigial traces of them, but *only* vestigial traces, in the different forms of pronouns used as subjects and objects (*I* and *me, he* and *him, she* and *her*). In German and Latin *every* noun, adjective, article (if any) or pronoun has to be put in the correct form (case) for its role in the sentence. German has not two, but four cases; Latin has seven. And, of course, each language has several patterns of declension, and a generous sprinkling of exceptions to the rules.

All my examples so far have been from languages commonly taught in our schools and more or less closely related to English. If we go a bit further afield, things become even more interesting. If we go a *lot* further afield, they get a *lot* more interesting.

All of the languages I've mentioned belong to a large family called Indo-European; English and German belong to the Germanic subfamily and Latin, French and Spanish to the Romance subfamily. Yet even within that group we found one language, Latin, that doesn't use articles—words (*the, a, an*) that we use constantly. Many languages get along quite comfortably without using them at all. Examples can be found both inside the Indo-European group (Slavic languages such as Russian and Polish) and outside (such as Chinese, Japanese and Swahili). Speakers of such languages, when learning English, may find it hard to see what purpose articles serve and to know when to put them in. Scandinavian languages do use them, but the definite article is a suffix *added* to the noun instead of a separate word in front of it (Swedish *hus* = *house, huset* = *the house*).

Slavic languages also include a verb classification called *aspects*. Remember the distinction between the preterite and imperfect tenses in Romance languages? Now imagine the same kinds of shades of meaning being divided in all tenses. Slavic languages have (at least) two separate, fully conjugated verbs to translate a single English verb. One, the *perfective aspect*, is used in situations with a feeling of definiteness or completeness, like the Romance preterite. The other, the *imperfective aspect*, is used for continuing or habitual actions, rather like the Romance imperfect.

Any language is a set of tools for expressing ideas. Just as one toolbox may contain a crescent wrench and another may not, some languages contain tools that others must make do without. One particularly useful tool that English lacks, but Slavic and Scandinavian languages have, is a full set of *reflexive* possessive adjectives and pronouns. In English, if "Joe told Henry he loved his wife," Henry may be a bit edgy until he ascertains whether the wife in question is Joe's or Henry's. In Russian, there is no ambiguity. "His" is one word if it refers to Joe (the subject of the sentence) and a completely different one if it refers to someone else (such as Henry). (Of course, this isn't always an advantage: English jokes that depend on such ambiguity can't be translated into Russian!)

Another tool that English lacks is a third-person singular "gender-noncommittal" pronoun. In recent years, many people have been trying to get such a thing established (e.g. "s/he"), but it's hard to introduce language changes at such a fundamental level as pronouns and so far none has been universally accepted. "It" does not fill the bill. In English it implies a lack of sexuality, which most people find insulting when applied to themselves. What I'm talking about is a pronoun that implies that the person does have sexuality, but doesn't specify it. Many languages (e.g., Swahili, Japanese and Hungarian) have only that kind of pronoun, offering no easy way to specify "he" or "she." (In practice, this doesn't seem to guarantee a sexism-free society.)

Gender, by the way, thoroughly pervades most Indo-European languages. English, again, has shed all but traces. In Spanish or French or German, *everything* has gender, which does not necessarily have anything to do with sex: A French table is "feminine," a German maiden is "neuter." Adjectives must agree in gender and number with the noun they modify, and in Polish and Russian even past tense *verbs* vary with the gender of the subject.

Outside the Indo-European group, the differences can be much larger and more fundamental than anything I've mentioned so far. Here's a sampling of things you might encounter:

Really Different Sounds

Semitic languages such as Hebrew and Arabic make extensive use of guttural sounds. "Guttural," by the way, is probably the single word most misused by writers trying to describe alien languages; it refers quite specifically to sounds produced in the throat, such as the German or Scottish *ch* or the Arabic *q*. (Yes, I know it's sometimes loosely used to mean "strange, harsh or unpleasant," but those are too vague, especially for science fiction. Science fiction readers will interpret "guttural" in its more precise sense, and be annoyed with you if you don't seem to be using it that way.)

Several southern African languages use "clicks" that are so different from any of our sounds that English speakers have trouble even hearing them as speech. You can hear samples in the movie *The Gods Must Be Crazy*. When you hear a Bushman speaking, it's likely to sound like someone speaking a "normal" clickless language, with an unidentified separate source making clicking noises in the background.

The set of sounds that human speech organs can make is considerably larger than the subset used by any language. Babies in all cultures try them all out in the early stages of learning to talk; their culture reinforces the ones they'll be expected to use, and they soon forget how to make the others.

Different Methods of Inflection

"Inflection," in linguistics, means changing the form of a word to express shades of meaning or related meanings, such as *leading, led* and *leader* from *lead*. That example illustrates two methods used in Indo-European languages: changing an ending and changing an internal vowel. The latter method is relatively rare in Indo-European languages (in Germanic languages like English and German it occurs mainly in a few "strong verbs" such as *sink, sank, sunk*), but it's the central *modus operandi* in Semitic languages. There a basic word root consists of a group of consonants (commonly three), with related words derived by changing the vowels interspersed among them. If English worked like Arabic, *postal, pastel, pistol* and *pustule* would all look like forms of the same word, or at least very closely related; while *kisses, kisser, kissed* and *kissing* would look unrelated.

Tones

In many African and Oriental languages, the tone in which a word is pronounced is integral to its identity and drastically affects its meaning. English makes limited use of intonation to express things like attitude—e.g., the syllable "Oh" can be pronounced in different tonal patterns to express resignation, astonishment, delight or skepticism—but truly tonal languages like Chinese go much further. The same combination of vowels and consonants (say, "blurp") pronounced in four tones—e.g., high level, low level, rising and falling—can make it four completely unrelated words, with meanings as different as *spinach, carburetor, politician* and *entropy*.

Completely Different Types of Grammars

Most Indo-European languages are predominantly *inflectional*, meaning they do most of their grammar by changing word forms. There are other ways to do it; most languages make some use of more than one method, but one predominates. English is an atypical Indo-European language in that it has lost most of its inflectional forms and become largely *isolating*. In an isolating language—Chinese is a good example—words don't change form, but derive much of their meaning from the order in which they're assembled. The same word can not only represent different tenses, numbers or cases, but different parts of speech, depending on where they occur in a sentence. *Walk*, for example, can be either a verb or a noun, and if it's a noun, it can be any case. Word order is much more critical in a highly isolating language than in a highly inflected one. In the English sentence "The dog bit the man," you know who bit whom from which participant precedes and which follows the verb. If you change it to "The man bit the dog," the meaning is reversed and newsworthy. In German or Russian, you can express either meaning with either word order, because "the man" and "the dog" will have different forms depending on whether they're subject or object.

A third major grammar type is *agglutinative*, in which the rules of grammar deal largely with how to *build* words by stringing together elements, each of which has a definite form and meaning. At first glance, these may look similar to Indo-European inflectional patterns, if the things added to a basic form are suffixes and there aren't too many of them. In Turkish, for example, *ev* is *house*, *ler* is a plural suffix, and *evler* is *houses*. But you can add multiple suffixes: *den* is an ablative case suffix, meaning *from*, so *from the houses* is *ev* + *ler* + *den* = *evlerden*.

The added elements don't have to be suffixes. In Swahili, most of the grammar is done with prefixes. The plural of *kikombe* is *vikombe*; the singular of *watu* is *mtu*. If you encountered the word *kilichotutosha*, what you would look up in the dictionary is *tosha*, meaning *to be sufficient*. To understand the whole word you would have to recognize four prefixes and know that when they occur in this order *ki* is a subject prefix for a particular class of nouns, *li* is a past tense prefix, *cho* is a relative pronoun for the same class of nouns as *ki*, and *tu* is a first person plural object pronoun. So *kilichotutosha* means *(that) which was enough for us*.

This may all sound rather formidable, but that's mainly because it's so different from what you're used to, not because it's intrinsically difficult. In fact, agglutination can make for a refreshingly logical and regular language. A beginning Swahili text can introduce three or four verb tenses in the first lesson and immediately expect you to be able to use them on any verb in the language, given its root. In marked contrast to French or Spanish, this is not only reasonable, but easy; learning three tenses just means learning three two-letter prefixes.

This doesn't mean that agglutinative languages are necessarily *totally* simple, regular or easy. Sometimes, for example, they use *vowel harmony*, in which the vowels in suffixes or prefixes (or in-fixes, inserted in the *middle* of a word!) must change to agree with those in the root word. In Turkish, vowels are divided into "front vowels" (including *e* and *i*) and "back vowels" (including *a* and *o*). In my example above, the plural and ablative suffixes were *ler* and *den* because *ev* contains a front vowel. If the root word contains back vowels, like *oda* (*room*), the suffixes must also contain a back vowel, so *from the rooms* becomes *odalardan*. I mentioned that the "pronoun prefixes" in my Swahili example were for a particular noun class; noun classes are roughly equivalent to grammatical gender, but there are eight of them. The plural of *kitu* is *vitu*, the plural of *mtu* is *watu*, and so on; and each class has its own set of "concords" (prefixes and other building blocks for various pur-poses). Some languages such as Eskimo (sometimes called "poly-synthetic") carry the agglutinative principle to dazzling heights where a long and complicated English sentence becomes a single word.

Different Writing Systems

Many languages are written in an *alphabet*, in which a few sym-bols are used to represent the basic sounds of a language and there-fore can be used to write all of its words. How closely spelling corresponds to pronunciation varies widely. English has drawn words from many sources and its spellings and pronunciations have not evolved consistently or at the same rate. Thus there are many inconsistencies in English spelling and a good deal of memorization is required. Nevertheless, with enough practice you can usually make a pretty good guess at how to pronounce an unfamiliar word. In Swahili and Turkish, the match is so close that you can *always* pronounce a new word correctly on the first try, or spell one you hear for the first time.

Numerous alphabets are used, and other methods of writing are possible. Japanese and Cherokee use *syllabaries*, in which a symbol represents not a vowel or a consonant, but an entire syllable. The earliest writing was almost certainly *pictograms*—stylized pictures intended to represent literal objects such as a man, a woman or a tree. (These have been making a comeback lately in such areas as international traffic and "No Smoking" signs.) The use of picto-grams gradually expanded to include representing ideas *associated* with an object (such as *heat* with the Sun) or the sound of the word representing the object (such as a pictogram for *Sun* used to represent the English word *son*). Alphabets are a late stage of the latter kind of evolution. A surviving example of the former is the set of several thousand *ideographs* or *characters* used to write Chinese. Each must be memorized, so they're far less convenient and conducive to widespread literacy (and typewriter or computer keyboards) than an alphabet. On the other hand, they have the virtue that they can be read by educated people from all parts of China, even though their spoken dialects are mutually unintelligible.

And So Forth

I could go on listing such things for a very long time, mentioning such things as inclusive and exclusive forms of *we* (depending on whether the person addressed is included or not), audible question marks, words that can mean either *yes* or *no* depending on how the question was worded, and the twenty-six moods of the verb in the Australian language Aranda. But space doesn't permit, and by now you have the idea. If you want your aliens' languages to be truly alien, learn as much as you can about human languages–both general principles and the particulars of a few sample languages. I strongly recommend studying at least one non-Indo-European language. But even that is not enough as a basis for inventing alien languages because, diverse as they are, all the languages I've mentioned have one very important thing in common, which will not be shared by your aliens.

BEYOND HUMAN

All my sample languages were, of necessity, *human* languages, evolved for use by human speech and sense organs and nervous systems. I've already mentioned that all human babies try out all such sounds and their cultures select a subset of those to use. Something similar seems to be true of grammar. The kinds of grammar humans use seem subject to certain broad limits imposed by the hard-wiring of their nervous systems. (See Bickerton's article on "Creole Languages.")

Except under very special circumstances, your aliens will not be human. Neither their nervous systems nor their anatomical equipment for making and detecting sound are likely to be very similar to ours. They may not be able to produce our sounds—or we theirs. To get a better idea of what range of speech sounds might be used by intelligent beings elsewhere, you should listen not only to French and Arabic and Chinese, but to the whole range of sounds produced by all kinds of animals: the buzzing of bees, the long songs of whales, the eerie laughs and howls of loons and prairie chickens and oropendolas. . . .

A typical field guide to birds will try to describe a bird call with some rather fanciful transcription like "Good Sam Peabody" or "Whee-wheeoo-titi-whee." (I'm not making these up!) Such a transcription may be somewhat useful as a mnemonic to help you recognize the actual bird, by suggesting its general rhythm and intonation. But the vowels and consonants in the transcription aren't even vaguely approximated in the real thing.

The sounds birds and cetaceans make are simply too different from ours to be mutually pronounceable, or for theirs to be represented with any accuracy by our spelling systems. The situation with beings evolved independently on other worlds is more likely to be like that than like humans who simply grew up in different cultures.

The sentence with which I opened this chapter *has* to be written in musical notation because it's in a language in which absolute pitch and length of syllables are essential to meaning. Every syllable is one of seven vowels or semivowels (the speakers have froglike lips and flexible mouth walls, but no tongues), pronounced on one of thirteen pitches and with short, long or medium duration. Musical notation is the best way we have to write such things. They, of course, have their own—a syllabary in which each vowel or semivowel is represented by a basic geometric form (a vertical line, a horizontal line, a circle, etc.) with embellishments to indicate its pitch and accompanied by dots or dashes to indicate length. Their script is written in a counterclockwise spiral from page margin in toward the center, "framing" any accompanying matter such as illustrations. Few humans could speak this language. While most human languages make at least some use of relative pitch patterns, this one requires speaker and listener to have what musicians call "perfect pitch," which few of us do.

The Kyyra language in my *Lifeboat Earth* series (the most detailed references are in *The Sins of the Fathers*) is somewhat similar in that it uses absolute pitch and length. It differs in that the Kyyra do have tongues, and rather agile ones, so they can and do use the whole human range of vowels and consonants, and then some.

They can learn any human language more easily than any of us can learn theirs, simply because their built-in speech tools are more versatile than ours. They have at least one kind of inflection at their disposal that humans don't—they can conjugate verbs by transposing them. They can, at least in principle, convey more information faster, since they have more ways to vary each syllable they speak.

Of course, your aliens may not even use sound as their principal medium of information exchange. Other forms of communication are not only possible, but used right here on Earth. I've already mentioned that bees "dance" to direct their coworkers to food supplies. Many animals use chemicals called *pheromones* to convey such messages as, "I'm ready to mate." Those messages are pretty simple, though, and the methods may be limited in applicability by the nature of the media. Smells, for example, tend to be too sloppy in both spatial and temporal resolution to lend themselves to holding esoteric discussions like this one. However, I've already mentioned one possible exception, in Hal Clement's story "Uncommon Sense." For another fictional example of sophisticated chemical communication, see Joan Slonczewski's *Still Forms on Foxfield*.

In general, the likelihood of a particular medium developing as a major means of communication will depend on considerations already discussed in the section of chapter five on "Senses." Some beings could use modulated light (octopi use complex changes in body coloration to express emotional state), but that has a line-of-sight limitation. Sound seems likely to be the best compromise for many environments, at least environments at all similar to those found on Earth, since it lends itself to a fair degree of precision and speed under a wide range of conditions. So I'd guess that many of the universe's beings do speak, in one way or another, with sound.

But not necessarily with words or sentences even as similar to ours as the ones I've already described. In earlier chapters I've mentioned an alien of at least moderate intelligence that lives in the oceans of Earth: dolphins. Living in a water world that is far more three-dimensional than ours, they use a much wider frequency range of sound than we do, both for communication and as sonar, for navigating and locating food. While researching my novelette "Pinocchio" (which also appears as the third section of *Lifeboat Earth*), my studies led me to suspect that, since their means of communication and perception were so closely linked, intelligent dolphins might find the human concept of "word" odd and difficult to grasp. "Our language," Pinocchio explains to a human contact, "grew out of descriptions, and our descriptions are much more graphic than yours. You might say we talk in pictures. . . . [For example] instead of saying 'A fish just swam by above and to my right,' I'd say 'I made such-and-such kind of feeling noises, and this is what I heard.' Another dolphin, when I repeated my echoes, would literally see that fish—what kind it was, how big it was, where it was, how fast it was going, and what was around it."

We still don't know whether Earth's dolphins actually have such linguistic or cultural sophistication, but even if they don't, dolphin-analogs elsewhere could (an interesting variant can be found in G. David Nordley's "Final Review"). The point is that when you invent aliens, you should, insofar as possible and to the extent that you're interested, let their languages be a logical outgrowth of the rest of their natures.

PRACTICAL TIPS

When preparing to write about aliens, ask yourself how much you need to know about their language, and then how much you'd like to know. Some stories require very little; others demand a lot. In *Tweedlioop*, I knew little about the aliens' language except that it included a lot of birdlike whistles and a sound system so different from ours that they couldn't even begin to speak human languages, or vice versa. In "A Devil and a Deep Blue Sea," the detailed structure of the language was so integral to the story that I had to invent it in considerable detail. In *The Sins of the Fathers* I didn't have to, but I chose to, as part of the process of "bringing the Kyyra to life" for myself and the reader. In *Newton and the Quasi-Apple*, I didn't actually include much of the language in the story, but I figured out the basics anyway, to ensure that what I did include was consistent with a larger context. In this case it was fairly easy—the story had to be about a very humanoid species on a very Earthlike planet, so the languages were mutually speakable.

By personal preference, I usually work out at least the basic structure of an alien language, and encourage others to do so, too. But that doesn't mean you have to write a complete, detailed grammar, much less an unabridged dictionary. If the language is so different from human ones as to be mutually unpronounceable, and its structure doesn't play a key role in your story, you may need no more than a general description of how it sounds to humans and how the two species manage to communicate. If it lends itself to at least approximate transcription into our alphabet, though, you'll probably want to know at least a few ground rules.

In my experience, the minimum needed to include a modest number of words in the story is a list of what letters are used in spelling its words, and any restrictions on how they can combine. Among human languages, for example, the combination *cs* at the beginning of a word is a very strong suggestion that the word is Hungarian, while initial *cz* is characteristically Polish. Polish adjectives (at least when used with masculine singular nouns in the nominative case) often end in *ski*. (With other genders, numbers and cases they take different endings.)

That last example illustrates that you're also likely to want to know a few grammar rules. In Italian, singular masculine nouns and adjectives usually end in *o* and singular feminine nouns and adjectives in *a*. If you were writing a story that included quite a few Italian noun-plus-adjective phrases, even a non-Italian-speaking reader might have the vague feeling that something was not quite right if you used the phrase *giardino bella* (*beautiful garden*, but with a feminine adjective after a masculine noun) late in the story.

It was something like that that enabled the copyeditor to spot that grammatical error in my *Newton and the Quasi-Apple*. I don't remember exactly what it was, but I do remember that the language was agglutinative, using both prefixes and suffixes to convert a basis root into things like the name of a place, an inhabitant of that place, several inhabitants of the place, the language spoken there, etc. I never explained all that; but the fact that I *used* the rules consistently made the language feel more real (and let the copyeditor catch me when I slipped).

In deciding what letters to use in an alien language, it's a good idea to keep in mind anything you know about its speakers' anatomy and physiology. For example, the speaker quoted in my opening sentence, with no tongue, couldn't produce many consonants. To keep the reader on your side, you'll probably want to use things that are reasonably pronounceable—that is, from which a reader can easily imagine a working pronunciation—even if things often might not be that way in reality. Most readers can invent a way to imagine "Kangyr" being pronounced when they run across it, or even (perhaps grudgingly) "Bdwdlsplg." But using nonalphabetic symbols, as in "A%$th*s," conveys no information about what the word actually sounds like, and is likely to achieve nothing except annoying the reader. Since annoyed readers may turn elsewhere for their entertainment, such practices are generally best avoided.

In closing I might mention a couple of additional pitfalls to watch out for in inventing alien languages. Beware of speaking of languages like "Martian"; they're on a par with "Terran" or "Human," and if you expect your reader to believe an entire species or planetary population speaks a single language, you'd better be prepared to explain how it got that way. And if you're giving many examples of a language, don't be tempted by such shortcuts as simply changing all the vowels in sample words from some obscure human language. If you do that, your alien language will have the same underlying structure as its human model. That just isn't likely to happen, and somewhere out there is likely to be at least one reader who will catch you in the act.

Laying a solid linguistic foundation can add a lot to a story. It can be fun, and it's a fairly wide-open field, since writers so often shy away from attempting it. If you do try, your best bet is what I've already suggested. Learn the basic principles of linguistics. Study at least a couple of real languages, including at least one non-Indo-European, in some depth. Then take some of the elements you've learned—preferably enhanced by some new ones of your own invention—and work them into something fresh, new, interesting and believable.

CHAPTER 8

Interaction With Humans

I n this chapter we begin to shift our emphasis from *creating* aliens to *writing* about them. An idea is only the starting point for a story. The essence of story is conflict—the struggles of at least one character trying to solve a problem. Usually the problem and struggle will be at least partly an interaction between characters, so the first stage in conceiving a story worth telling is to imagine two or more characters and how they might interact.

Aliens will have their own stories—their own wars, loves, quests and other conflicts for which we have no names. But telling a story containing only aliens, in a way that human readers can understand, empathize with and enjoy, is a very challenging proposition. Few writers attempt it, and even fewer succeed. I'll say a bit more about that in the next chapter, but for now let's consider a more common, and generally easier, situation. A large percentage of stories involving aliens involve their interaction with humans—a matter that can be broken down into three main problems:

1. How do we contact them or vice versa?
2. Why hasn't it already happened (or has it?)
3. Once in contact, how might humans and aliens interact?

Let's look at each of these and bear in mind that much of what we say will also apply, with little modification, to contacts not between aliens and humans, but between two different kinds of aliens.

MAKING CONTACT: THE PHYSICAL PROBLEM

Contact can be unilateral or mutual, and direct or indirect. Perhaps the most unilateral and indirect is the archaeological, in which members of one species discover another and must learn what they can about it (and perhaps themselves) from an artifact. A good example with an obvious tie to the preceding chapter is H. Beam Piper's "Omnilingual," in which human explorers must find a way to read the language of a long-dead Martian civilization. A newer example is Maya Kaathryn Bohnhoff's "The Secret Life of Gods," showing the perils of jumping to conclusions about what an artifact means or how it was used (an archaeologist is determined to interpret everything about a site in terms of religion, but its real explanation is much more prosaic). Others abound, as different as Arthur C. Clarke's "The Sentinel" (the basis of the movie *2001*) and *Rendezvous with Rama*, and Michael F. Flynn's "Eifelheim" (in which the encounter occurred long ago but left traces that gradually emerge from historical records). An unusual variation is Kevin J. Anderson and Doug Beason's *Assemblers of Infinity*, in which the artifact is building itself—onstage—as the story unfolds.

Mostly, in this chapter, we'll be concerned with two-way contact, since that has the most possibilities for *interaction*. Direct, or face-to-face, contact requires getting us to where the aliens live, or them to where we live. (Or at least partway. In Murray Leinster's "First Contact," two ships, human and alien, meet in deep space. Both must figure out how to go home without attracting the other's hostile attention to their home world.) In chapter six I indicated some of the difficulties in this—intelligent aliens seem unlikely to occur in other parts of our Solar System, and travel to any other star would be very expensive in time and money—but I also indicated that a number of ways around those problems may prove possible, even without new physics.

The ways we know about and can imagine in detail are, at best, expensive and slow. This has led many people to believe that indirect contact—the interstellar equivalent of a phone call—is likely to come first (and perhaps only). Even that is difficult because of the times involved. If we sent a radio message from Earth to Alpha Centauri, we would have to wait 8.6 years for an immediate reply sent the same way. This makes for an awkward conversation, at best. The original sender could easily die, lose interest or forget what he said before the reply came back. If the message was somehow garbled and the recipient of the original message got only enough to want to say, "Say again, please?," the excruciatingly drawn-out non-communication could be frustrating for both sides.

And lack of results could lead to funding being cut off for attempts to detect interstellar signals. Programs do exist on Earth for SETI (Search for Extraterrestrial Intelligence), but they require expensive equipment to devote large amounts of time to searching for something that may or may not be there. Even if the galaxy is full of intelligent searchers for alien intelligence, all their efforts may come to naught if nobody is making an active effort at *Contact* with Extraterrestrial Intelligence (COTI), as in Ian Randal Strock's story "The Ears Have It."

What type of message could you send to beings at a great distance, whom you've never met and who will have to understand it on the first try, if at all, since there will be no opportunity for clarification? I.S. Shklovskii and Carl Sagan devoted several chapters of *Intelligent Life in the Universe* to this problem. The fastest and perhaps the technically easiest methods use electromagnetic radiation: radio waves or laser light. Shklovskii and Sagan discuss in considerable detail the advantages and disadvantages of both, what wavelengths might be best to use, and the kind of message that might have the best chance of being deciphered.

Their answer to this last question, which is the most plausible I've heard anyone suggest, depends on a fact that John W. Campbell summed up in three words: "Hydrogen isn't cultural." That is, while art and philosophy may vary so much that no species can assume any element to be shared with any other species, all species are based on the same laws of physics and chemistry. Any culture that studies physical science will have descriptions of the same chemical elements, the same laws of gravitation and electromagnetism, and so forth. If scientists of one culture write enough about such things, especially with the graphic accompaniments so often useful in science, scientists of another may be able to recognize familiar patterns and so begin to get a handle on the first culture's language.

This is the key to Piper's "Omnilingual"—the "Rosetta stone" for the Martian language is a periodic table. Shklovskii and Sagan described a pictorial message that could be sent in binary code by radio or laser pulses, schematically showing such things as our general shape, the elements on which our biochemistry is based, and the general layout of our Solar System. The space probes Pioneer 10 and 11, which will drift far out among the stars, carry an etched plaque showing similar information in more clearly pictorial form.

Even if nobody makes a deliberate effort to send a message to nearby stars—and some have suggested that it might be unduly risky to try to attract such attention to ourselves—contact *could* still occur. Humans have been broadcasting radio-frequency signals for close to a century. The vast majority of them have not been intended for aliens, but for fellow humans on Earth—but the signals are not confined to Earth, and could be noticed and analyzed by beings quite far away. Thus we can imagine aliens making a flamboyant entrance to our world, already versed in its ways and talking like a hodgepodge of old radio and TV characters as a result of studying our broadcasts on the way—as in Stephen L. Burns's "Showdown at Hell Creek." Or casually logging onto one of our computer nets, as in Roger MacBride Allen's "Phreak Encounter" or F. Alexander Brejcha's "Looking Through the Personals."

Another possible method of contact is by robot probe—that is, an uncrewed spacecraft that can carry a message and/or send signals back to Earth. Our Pioneer and Voyager probes are relatively primitive examples, designed to conduct remote explorations of other planets of our Sun and then to wander off into interstellar space carrying one-way messages for anyone who might happen to find them. (See the book *Murmurs of Earth*, by Sagan *et al.*) Many variations can be imagined (Shklovskii and Sagan describe several), such as probes designed to check a succession of stars for signs of civilization and send back a report of any positive findings. Or, since it's easier to construct spacecraft that don't have to support life than ones that do, several civilizations in different solar systems might communicate only by the exchange of information and physical artifacts carried by robot ships that arrive every generation or two. A more sinister possibility is the plague of war machines programmed to destroy organic life in Fred Saberhagen's *Berserker* stories.

For the most part, I've restricted my discussion to things that are pretty clearly possible and can be imagined in considerable detail using only science that is already well known. However, from the science fiction writer's point of view, these do impose stringent constraints on the kinds of interaction that can occur—and even from an open-minded physicist's viewpoint, they may not be the only possibilities. If you as a writer want to have a multistellar empire, or group of empires, engaging in lively commerce or warfare, you need a way for them to travel, or at least communicate, across interstellar distances.

Thus many writers have used various forms of faster-than-light (FTL) communication and space to allow brisker interaction of widely separated beings. Ursula K. Le Guin invented the instantaneous communicator called the *ansible*, in *The Dispossessed* and other stories; both word and concept have passed into the general science-fictional vocabulary and toolkit, along with such other standard equipment as robots, spaceships and FTL itself. Several writers have used various means to let their characters travel faster than light, ranging from vaguely defined "spacewarps," to extrapolations of real possibilities such as "wormholes" (see the Cramer and Donaldson articles), to new kinds of physics such as that postulated in my *Sins of the Fathers* and *Lifeboat Earth*.

My general advice is this: If your story doesn't need faster-than-light travel, don't use it. If it does need it, go ahead and use it—but carefully. You have two basic "safe" approaches: Take for granted a general type of FTL principle that other writers have rationalized and used enough that readers can accept it easily; or invent a new one of your own. I personally find the latter course more fun and more satisfying; but to get away with it, you have to have a pretty fair understanding of what contemporary science says, and you have to understand and accept the implications of what you're doing. I'll say more about this in chapter eleven.

WHY HASN'T IT HAPPENED?
THE FERMI PARADOX REVISITED

In chapter four I briefly mentioned the Fermi paradox: The apparent contradiction between the expectation that life should be common and interstellar communication and travel feasible (though not easy), and the observation that we have no convincing evidence that anyone else has visited Earth. Let's now take a closer look at the Drake (or Drake-Sagan) equation, which estimates the number of civilizations in the Galaxy with whom we might be able to communicate (whether by radio or face-to-face) as

$$N = R_*Pn_ef_lf_if_cL.$$

Here R_* is the average rate of star formation over the lifetime of the Galaxy (about one star per year). P is the fraction of stars with planets in stable orbits; n_e the average number of planets per system with conditions suitable for life; f_l the fraction of such suitable planets that actually have life; f_i the fraction of life-bearing planets that have intelligent life with manipulative abilities; f_c the fraction of intelligent species that develop technological civilizations; and L is the average lifespan of a technological civilization. The essence of our argument in chapter four was that P and f_l seem likely to be fairly close to 1 (their maximum possible value), n_e also seems likely to be about 1 (given planets, it's likely that at least one of them is in a situation conducive to life, but less likely that more than one are), and we weren't yet in a position to say much about f_l, f_i, f_c or L.

We're now in a slightly better position, since we've looked at some of the considerations likely to influence each of those factors; but we still can't say anything very definite about them. As Donald Kingsbury has pointed out, you can't make valid statistical inferences from a single data point. We have only had the opportunity to observe one planet that has spawned a technological civilization, and we (fortunately) don't yet know how long that one will last. So we can, at best, make educated guesses about how often it happens or how long most of them survive. Not surprisingly, the guesses made by scientists looking at the problem have varied widely; but a typical result is an estimate that our Galaxy might contain about a million stars holding technological civilizations.

Typically, such stars would be separated by a few hundred light-years. Since research in the last couple of decades also suggests that starships, at least "slow" ones, are possible, planetary systems with advanced civilizations could be much more common than the preceding argument suggests. The Drake equation attempts to estimate how many stars might have native civilizations; but it now appears that once one of those reaches a certain point, it can establish colonies on others. Those can eventually repeat the process, and even one species inclined to do so could pretty well fill the galaxy in mere millions of years. That sounds like a lot to us, but it's not much in astronomical or even geological terms, and perhaps not in terms of the life expectancy of a successful civilization. We have no reason to assume there are no races that much older than us (though it is conceivable; somebody has to be first!).

So where is everybody? Our attempts at detecting alien radio signals have so far come up dry, even though the scenario just described suggests that we could easily have lots of neighbors.

Nobody has found any clear and generally convincing evidence of alien visitation on Earth or elsewhere in the Solar System (though there are a few items that deserve a closer examination than they've received so far, such as the "humanoid face" on Mars described by Richard C. Hoagland). If intelligent civilizations are common, and capable of spreading through the Galaxy, it seems just a bit odd if none of them have passed this way.

Curiosity about this oddity has led to a great deal of speculation on possible reasons for our apparent solitude. The ideas range from the notion that some as yet unknown requirement for the creation of life makes it more difficult and rarer than we've guessed, to the idea that we're the first to get this far in this part of the Galaxy. Maybe the aliens are here, observing us but deliberately keeping out of sight, for any of several possible reasons. Or maybe when beings learn enough to be able to live long lives, they become afraid to take the risks that exploration and colonization would entail. (There's evidence that some humans are doing that right now!)

Far more explanations have been put forth than I can describe here. David Brin did an excellent review of the whole subject in his 1983 article "Xenology: The New Science of Asking, 'Who's Out There?' " In that article he traced the evolution of thought about this problem and described a wide range of possible explanations for "The Great Silence." He also invited readers to suggest their ideas, and published some of those in a follow-up article ("Just How Dangerous *Is* the Galaxy?") two years later. By then the explanations had proliferated so much that he gave a full-page chart classifying them succinctly, plus more detailed descriptions of two dozen ideas grouped under the headings "Solitude," "Graduation," "Timidity," "Quarantine," "Macrolife," "Dangerous Natural Forces," "Dangerous 'Unnatural' Forces" and "A Grasp at Optimism."

None of these explanations, of course, is assumed to be the whole explanation. It's quite possible that the Galaxy contains lots of civilizations, but we've seen no evidence of this one for that reason, that one for another reason, a third for still another, and so on, with the net result that we've seen no evidence of any of them.

You may find that such discussions suggest story ideas to you; but for many stories, the question of how abundant life and intelligence and civilization are is at most a background issue. It will clearly be important if your story centers on one of the possible explanations for the Fermi paradox, or if it postulates an interstellar empire or takes its characters to many stellar systems (in which case you will need to consider who, if anybody, was already there). But if your goal is just to tell a story about a particular interaction between humans and one set of aliens, you may not be very concerned about how many other sets there might be or why we haven't heard from them. For such a story it may be enough to know that at least one other species can exist and can come into contact with us. Most stories will be about interactions that do occur, not those that don't.

KINDS OF INTERACTIONS

So what kinds of interactions might occur between humans and aliens (or between different kinds of aliens)? I can only survey a few of the possibilities that others have thought of, and hope that will stimulate you to think of new ones. Would-be writers have sometimes asked me, "What topics are hot now?" My answer is that they should be guided by a different question; I'm not interested in repetitions of what others have already done, but in what *you* can do that turns my mind in a direction it hadn't thought of before.

Human-alien interactions can involve individuals, cultures or both. They can be biological, cultural or both. I offer my samples in no particular order; this is not, after all, a one-dimensional continuum.

Individual Interactions

These interactions, with the feeling of intimacy that the word implies, may occur as quiet little stories involving just a couple of beings, or as a detail in something of much larger scope. (Indeed, such details are needed in works of large scope, to help make the whole thing "real" at a level individual readers can relate to personally.)

Good examples of "quiet little stories" are Clifford D. Simak's "A Death in the House," in which a farmer takes a dying alien into his home; and Mark Rich's "Across the Sky," in which a human girl and a lonely alien on a park bench share parts of their very different ways of growing up (she loses a tooth, he loses part of his memory).

My *Sins of the Fathers* and *Lifeboat Earth* involve action on an enormous scale: a whole galaxy rendered uninhabitable; one species rescuing another by moving its whole planet to a different galaxy, with wholesale extinctions and massive guilt an inevitable part of the price for that much survival. But one of my personal favorite parts is this one-paragraph vignette in *Sins* in which Sandy, the only human who makes much effort to get to know the Kyyra ambassador Beldan personally,

> . . . showed Beldan her oboe, as one of the rough human counterparts to his music-pipe. He watched and listened attentively as she warmed up with a few quick scales and arpeggios and then started one of the oboe solos from the slow movement of the Mahler symphony he had heard. Halfway through it, he suddenly took out his pipe and began playing along, improvising a part that was nothing Sandy had ever heard but that blended uncannily. And where the Mahler part sank back into the orchestra, she found herself improvising too, to avoid stopping. For over a minute the two of them played on, listening to each other and weaving a counterpoint that, at least to Sandy, made good musical sense. Then, partly because she was afraid she couldn't sustain it any longer, she led her part to an ending, and Beldan followed. They stopped together. For another minute Sandy sat almost breathless with exhilaration at what she thought they had done—but afraid to ask. Finally Beldan said, "That was very good," and she knew she was right.

Of course, not all individual interactions are quiet, special shared moments. In A.E. van Vogt's "Cooperate—or Else!," and later in Barry B. Longyear's "Enemy Mine," it's a matter of life or death. In each case a human and an alien from warring cultures must cooperate to survive when stranded together on a hostile world.

Also in each case—and to varying degrees in my other examples—the interaction between individuals sheds light on the differences between their cultures. In the van Vogt and Longyear examples, the individual interaction is literally a part of a cultural interaction, but most individual human-alien interactions in stories will to some extent and in some way reflect in microcosm a relationship between the individuals' cultures.

Observation

Many science fiction stories overtly involve cultural interactions, which span a wide spectrum. Many deal with *observation* of one culture by another, with the observing group trying not to be noticed by the observed. Of course, it seldom works out that way; the story begins when they are observed despite their best efforts.

Chet and Tina Barlin, in my *Newton and the Quasi-Apple*, make a career of observing alien cultures. They use devices like invisible landing craft, long-distance microphones and compact telescopes to avoid direct contact with their subjects because the government that employs them has a strict policy against interference. Sometimes, though, interference seems necessary—and, of course, has consequences beyond the easily foreseen. In *Newton and the Quasi-Apple* they get permission to help—ever so slightly—a promising culture to survive repeated raids by barbarians. Unfortunately, the tiny advantage they introduce threatens to nip a major scientific breakthrough in the bud.

Chet and Tina's government, at the time of *Newton*, follows what *Star Trek* calls the "Prime Directive": a policy of avoiding interference with less developed cultures. In a recent editorial called "Interference," I reexamined the question of why a civilization might choose to follow or reject such a policy. A whole range of attitudes toward the question is possible, and there is little justification for *a priori* assumptions about how "hands-off" or aggressive either our own descendants or any alien culture might be. The most likely general and long-term scenario, I suspect, is that any culture's philosophy will fluctuate between extremes. The same government that wanted my Barlins to keep hands off had earlier (e.g., in "War of Independence") pursued a "Manifest Destiny" policy, colonizing everything they could get their hands on, with little regard for prior occupants.

Conquest and Colonization

This leads us to another broad category of interactions—invasion, defense, war and colonization. One of the best-known early works of science fiction was H.G. Wells's *War of the Worlds*, later adapted for an American audience as an Orson Welles radio play that caused widespread panic. The Martians invading Earth appeared as genocidal monsters bent on wiping us out to make room for themselves, and that still sometimes works if you can convince your readers that your aliens are so alien we can't understand what makes them tick. A successful recent example that falls roughly into this category is Joe Haldeman's *The Forever War*. Often, though, today's readers expect all the characters *including aliens* to have understandable and believable motivations.

So if you want alien invaders, you should at least think about why they would go to the trouble. Many of the old pulp conventions don't hold up unless you concoct just the right set of circumstances to make them work. Do they want us as slaves? Maybe; a highly skilled storyteller like Gordon R. Dickson can still make it believable and memorable, as in *Way of the Pilgrim*. To impress readers who've read that, you'll have to do it at least as well—which means you'll have to consider such questions as, "What can we do for them that their own machines can't do better and cheaper?"

Would they want us for food? We'd probably give them indigestion; if we don't, you'll need to explain (or at least be able to) why our biochemistries are that similar. Would they want our real estate? Chlorine-breathers, for example, would have little use for it. To like the kind of property we do, they must be at least fairly similar to us—or they must be prepared to "terraform" it to their own specifications, which is a huge job. (Or to modify *themselves* to fit into a preexisting ecosystem without disturbing it unnecessarily, as in Joan Slonzewski's "Microbe.")

If two cultures *are* enough alike to be interested in occupying the same place, many possibilities for conflict exist. Our own history suggests that a technologically advanced culture is likely to smother a less advanced one merely by coming into contact with it. Much science fiction, such as W.R. Thompson's "Ghost Dance," is haunted by the danger of this either happening to us or being caused by us. Can the danger be avoided, if it's recognized and due precautions taken? Probably it can, but what are proper precautions—and are they always an option? Susan Shwartz, in *Heritage of Flight*, puts her human colonists in a situation where they must choose between their own extinction and genocide: They are stranded on a world with inhabitants who are quite likable as adults, but a literally lethal menace in their larval stage. Other writers, such as Poul Anderson in *The People of the Wind* and W.R. Thompson in his kya series taken as a whole (see chapter ten), show ways humans and aliens might manage to share space, retaining elements of both cultures yet adding others not found in either alone.

Numerous variations on such themes can be imagined. One (so common that a new story must come up with quite an original twist to revive it) is the multispecies galactic federation deliberating on whether to invite our species to membership or exterminate it as a threat to the others. A particularly well-developed and thought-provoking variation is the galactic "superculture" in David Brin's "Uplift" novels, including *Sundiver, Startide Rising* and *The Uplift War*. Here, species on the verge of intelligence are helped over the hump (or "uplifted") by more advanced "patron" races, and in turn later uplift still younger "client" species.

Some stories have created unique interactions between an individual and an alien culture. Kris Neville's "Bettyann" and Laura Frankos's "Hoofer" deal in quite different ways with aliens who have found ways of fitting, at least for a while, into a human culture on Earth (but then, they have the rare ability to look human). In Clifford D. Simak's *Way Station*, a reclusive Wisconsin farmer is actually maintaining a way station for interstellar travelers.

Some human-alien interactions might involve religion, as with the misguided missionaries in Katherine MacLean's "Unhuman Sacrifice." Others may involve vastly different species collaborating on an important project that neither of them could accomplish alone, as in Marc Stiegler's "Petals of Rose."

Some human-alien relationships are patterned on well-known biological relationships, even if they can't actually be biological as we usually understand that term. *The Puppet Masters* in Robert A. Heinlein's novel exemplify a type of parasitism (one organism supporting itself at the expense of another). The alien detective's relationship with its human host in Hal Clement's *Needle* is a type of symbiosis (two organisms in a mutually beneficial interaction, each doing for the other something that it can't do on its own).

Some human-alien interactions will be unique and hard to classify—and some of those may be the most haunting and memorable of all. Consider Ted Reynolds's "Can These Bones Live?," which might be considered the ultimate wish-fulfillment story: Humanity is extinct, but aliens revive a single individual and offer her a single wish—and a test. Or Chad Oliver's "Transfusion," in which a race faces aggression of such a nature and on such a scale that it needs a transfusion of *really* fresh ideas—so it seeds a world to grow a new species to generate them. In F. Alexander Brejcha's "With Other Eyes," a man is forced to see not only himself but everything else through literally alien eyes—and to act as a suicide hotline for an entire species.

Finally, I should mention a few overworked types of interactions that don't seem very likely—while acknowledging that some inspired writer may find a way to turn any one of them into a fresh and memorable story. One of the old pulp conventions, for example, has alien invaders collecting Earth women for much the same purposes as certain human villains. A kinder and gentler (but no less improbable) variant is the romantic liaison between a human and an alien. Either of these might lead in careless fiction to human-alien hybrids, but in reality it would take exceedingly special circumstances to make that happen. Even if similar circumstances caused evolution to converge enough to produce aliens who were virtually identical in external appearance to humans, it's most unlikely that their genetic means to that end would be similar enough to allow interfertility.

A similar argument applies to interstellar infection, such as the "ordinary" Earthly disease that was the ultimate undoing of the Martians in *War of the Worlds*, or *The Andromeda Strain* in Michael Crichton's novel. It could happen, under very special conditions; but in general a microorganism can only infect something that it has evolved to infect. I believe it was Poul Anderson who observed that humans would be more likely to catch alfalfa wilt than most alien diseases. (On the other hand, genetic engineers have found great potential in *recombinant DNA*, that is, combining DNA from unrelated species to produce results not found in nature, such as bacteria that make human insulin. So even if humans and aliens can't have children together or give each other diseases by "natural" means, there may be interesting possibilities in combining their genetic material in a laboratory setting.)

Then there is the "incomprehensible" alien—the being whose ways of living and thinking are so utterly unlike those of humans that no common ground exists and no interaction is possible. This, or something like it, has occasionally been made to work in fiction. Clifford D. Simak's *The Visitors* is perhaps one of the purest examples—huge, mysterious objects that appear on Earth and hang around without ever revealing what they are, where they're from or why they've come. There are traces of the idea in Joe Haldeman's *The Forever War* and Jeffery D. Kooistra's "Sunshine, Genius, and Rust" and "Young Again," in which there's plenty of interaction (warfare) but very little communication.

Too often, though, "incomprehensibly alien" seems more like a cop-out, a convenient excuse for the author to shirk the responsibility of figuring out what sort of interaction might *really* occur. Logic is not a purely arbitrary invention; if an alien being's actions strike us as illogical, it more likely indicates that we don't understand the *premises* on which its actions are logically based. Given enough of the right kind of effort, we should be able to determine what its fundamental drives are. Once we know that, even though we may find it hard to imagine having those drives, we should be able to understand, at least dimly, why just about any being behaves the way it does.

Especially if we want to write stories about them.

CHAPTER 9

Writing About Aliens

Showing Alien Character and Motivations

Writing stories about aliens requires all the skills and techniques demanded by any other kind of story, but also poses some special problems and challenges of its own. Let's look at several of these, beginning with one directly related to the note on which I ended the last chapter.

HUMANS IN FUNNY SUITS

Aliens who have evolved to be successful are unlikely to behave illogically, or at least any more so than humans do. Their behavior will grow logically out of more or less clearly defined motivations—but those motivations will not be quite the same as those of any human. (And never forget that even the motivations of individual humans, especially if they are from different cultures, may be quite different.)

The conflicts that generate aliens' stories, whether they're conflicts between different aliens or between aliens and humans, should grow out of their nature and motivations. In telling any story, it's a good idea to look at each potential turning point from the viewpoint of each character involved and let him, her or whatever make the best move possible from his own point of view. When aliens are involved, you must think out how they would see the situation, rather than making them go puppetlike through motions that you as author find convenient. In Poul Anderson's *The People of the Wind*, everything the Ythrians do is shaped by their background as flying carnivores who live in an essentially three-dimensional world and need lots of energy and space. In Eric Vinicoff and Marcia Martin's "The Weigher," everything depends on a concept of honor evolved by catlike carnivores, which is subtly but significantly different from ours.

ALIENS ARE INDIVIDUALS

Just as it's unreasonable and unjust to assume that all Italians, African-Americans, Asians or WASPs fit a stereotype, you must remember that your aliens are different from each other, as well as from us. Any real planet, even if dominated by a single species, will likely have a multitude of cultures and factions. Each of those will contain an even larger multitude of individuals, each with a unique physique and psychology. How different depends on evolutionary background. On Earth, all cheetahs are very nearly identical, both superficially and genetically, but there must be some very special reason for that. Most geneticists think it suggests that cheetahs once came very close to extinction, and all those now alive are direct descendants of a very few individuals.

Sculpting alien characters into individuals is done in much the same ways as with human characters. You can give them distinctive physical characteristics, habits, attitudes and personal eccentricities such as speech habits or mannerisms. The main difference is that the limits within which individual variations fall are determined by the general characteristics of the alien species and culture rather than those of humans. Nearly all adult humans fall into a fairly narrow range of heights and weights, can eat a wide variety of foods, and enjoy interacting with others of their species. But they can be light or dark-skinned, blonde or brunette or gray or bald, tall or short, portly or thin. Some choose to be vegetarians while others hate vegetables; some are boisterous and gregarious while others are shy and reclusive. Any kind of alien is likely to show similar variety, but within a different range—and the range may be over a variable that doesn't even exist for humans.

Winged beings such as Ythrians, for example, might vary in their tastes for flying in marginal weather. Some might find it exhilarating to fight fierce winds and win, while others might hate to fly unless absolutely necessary except on calm, clear days. The kya students in W.R. Thompson's "Touchdown, Touchdown, Rah! Rah! Rah!" are divided into factions with differing attitudes toward humans. Some individuals don't identify absolutely and unequivocally with either faction; and none of them, as a result of their herbivore background, can accept moderately violent behavior that humans consider unremarkable. A rich variety of characterization of both cultures and individuals within alien species can be found in the novels of C.J. Cherryh.

In bringing both individuals and their cultures to life, details are important—the little things that don't directly make large contributions to plot motion, but help make everything feel real and consistent. Sometimes when you start thinking about them, they suggest still others. In my *Sins of the Fathers*, the Kyyra, in their very first appearance, make a striking visual impression on the humans seeing them, but one of them immediately strikes the observers as older than the rest: "Hard to judge in an alien, perhaps, but old age is a matter of increasing entropy regardless of species, and this one gave that impression—through the slightly olive cast and lesser smoothness of his skin, and in a variety of other ways too subtle for Clark to put his finger on." Soon afterward, and throughout the book, the Kyyra show two characteristic reactions to stress. When unpleasantly surprised, their eyes jerk involuntarily back into their sockets, perhaps a survival of an ancestral reflex to protect the eyes. When troubled by something that's been bothering them and won't go away, they often take out "music-pipes" and improvise snatches of melody. This started out as an analog of the way humans sometimes light up a cigarette when nervous; but then I realized that with their absolutely tonal language they might make "musical puns," playing tunes that suggested different sentences with ironically related meanings.

THE DANGER OF LECTURING

When you're writing about human characters for human readers, you and your readers share a great deal of background knowledge that you can take for granted. You know, for example, how many arms and legs a human has, what a hug or a hot stove feels like, and the pleasures and pains a child experiences in growing up. These things aren't exactly the same for any two individuals—there's a good deal of difference between growing up on an Iowa farm and on the streets of Harlem, and a nod or a belch may mean quite different things in different countries—but there's an underlying base of things that we have sufficiently in common that they don't need to be spelled out to be understood.

When you're writing about aliens, there's much less that you can assume, and much more that you have to convey, explicitly or implicitly. Your reader does not even know at the outset whether your alien characters are ten feet or ten inches tall, whether they have arms or tentacles, or whether they like to eat fermented vegetables or still-squirming meat. So you have to give more attention to how to get background information across without stopping the story in its tracks or alienating the reader. Readers these days are not inclined to sit still through long lectures at the beginning of a story while waiting for something to happen, or in the middle, with action grinding to a halt for somebody to talk. Occasionally a bit of lecturing is unavoidable, and when that happens there are ways to make it as painless as possible; but before using them you should make every effort to find other approaches.

First, consider whether you need to tell a particular bit of information at all. I usually prefer to know as much as I can about my characters and background, and tell only what I have to.

For knowing as much as possible, when an elaborate background has to be constructed, made to fit together into a consistent whole, and kept track of, I've found it helpful to use a type of computer program called "hypertext" (see my articles in the References). If you don't have that, or don't find it congenial, you can use sheets of paper or index cards.

Once you've constructed an elaborate background, there's a great temptation to show it all off. Resist that temptation. Before including any detail in the story, ask yourself, "Does the reader need or want to know this?" If not, leave it out! In general, only include things that are necessary to make the plot intelligible or to make the setting, characters and action sufficiently vivid to form a clear, "real" picture in the reader's mind. The effort that went into creating the rest was not wasted. The fact that what you include in the story is consistent with a larger whole will add much to the story's feeling of solidity.

Things like body shape and mannerisms can often be suggested unobtrusively by having one character looking another over when they meet. More involved cultural background that is important to the story can sometimes be exhibited by arranging for at least one character to visit the culture in question, as when Sandy wangles an invitation aboard the Kyyra starship in *The Sins of the Fathers*. You must be careful, though, to have a suitable justification for the visit, and not to make it a mere "tour of wonders." Sandy learns important things by looking around and asking questions about what she sees and experiences; but her visit doesn't happen until fairly late in the book, and she'd been trying for weeks to get aboard the ship, hoping to see something that would clear up a mystery that had pervaded everything that went before.

Sometimes you can turn that method around and reveal a lot about one culture by plunging one of its members into another, as in W.R. Thompson's "On Tour With Gyez," in which a kya science fiction writer is sent on a book promotion tour on Earth.

When the action takes place entirely within an alien setting, the characters will normally take it for granted, if they live there. You can still evoke a surprisingly vivid picture of it simply by the way you coin words to describe it. Consider, for example, this paragraph from Poul Anderson's *The People of the Wind*:

> Further down a slope lay sheds, barns, and mews. The whole could not be seen at once from the ground, because Ythrian trees grew among the buildings: braidbark, copperwood gaunt lightningrod, jewelleaf which sheened beneath the moon and by day would shimmer iridescent.

Anderson's reader has never seen a braidbark, copperwood or jewelleaf, but gets an instant picture from each one-word name, complete with overtones like suggestions of texture.

When you must lecture, because information really needs to be conveyed and can't be fitted gracefully into dialogue and action, a variety of tricks can be used to disguise that fact, or at least make it more palatable. In *The People of the Wind*, Anderson puts sympathetic characters in the position of needing the information and therefore asking for a lecture, and then lets the reader watch it with them, along with the characters' reactions. If you try this, you must be prepared to make your lecturing intrinsically very interesting, and recognize that even then some readers will be tempted to skip past it.

Another approach is to dole out necessary background in small, plainly labeled bites, as G. David Nordley does in the brief excerpts from relevant documents set in italics at the beginnings of sections of his "Trimus" stories. To my mind one of the most successful approaches is one that occurs repeatedly in almost any Isaac Asimov novel—one character is trying to pry information out of another who's reluctant to give it. Some writers attempt this by having one character feed another questions, most of which real characters in their situation would not need to ask, simply to prompt an answer and thinly disguise a lecture as a dialogue. They miss the crucial ingredient in the Asimov dialogues—an underlying interpersonal conflict that drives the scene from beginning to end and incidentally delivers important information.

VIEWPOINTS

Having a viewpoint character observe things the reader needs to know is certainly convenient for the author, when it's feasible, but it's not always equally easy. It's easiest when you have a human viewpoint character, with whom a reader can identify. In that case the writer, reader and viewpoint character all share that common human background, and can see an alien in terms of how it compares to themselves and that shared knowledge. Sometimes, though, you might prefer not to do that—or might not be able to.

Rick Cook and Peter L. Manly's "Symphony for Skyfall" deals with the efforts of intelligent natives of Jupiter to survive the impacts of fragments of Comet Shoemaker-Levy 9 on their planet. Though the story was written slightly before it happened, that was a real event, and the story was constrained by what could be known about it by Earth-based observers at that time. It was pretty certain, for example, that there would be neither humans present on Jupiter nor radio contact between us and anyone living there. Thus there was no way to have a human character on the scene, and there was plenty of story without one—the survival of an intelligent race was literally at stake. Thus the authors had to tell their story from an alien viewpoint.

That's one of the most difficult challenges in all of science fiction. The writer has to tell a story, and make a reader care about it, through characters with whom neither of them shares any background. Thus it's necessary to set the scene, establish what kinds of beings these are, and create a vivid picture of what's happening, all at once. The road is filled with pitfalls. If you make your aliens too much like us, they'll be easy to identify with, but nobody will take them seriously as aliens—they'll be "humans in funny suits." If you make them fully as alien as they're likely to be, and insist on taking the pure, high road of not using any Earthly names for things that don't exist on Earth, you'll wind up with a story that's authentically alien but totally unintelligible. An occasional coined word, or untranslated word from an alien language, gives flavor and color; too many of them, and you convey no information.

In "Symphony for Skyfall," Cook and Manly chose an effective compromise. It's not quite true that our world and theirs share *nothing*—we all have to make a living, and any ecosystem will include predators and prey. So Cook and Manly unabashedly used some English words for analogs of things in the Jovian ecosystem, to convey a quick picture to a human reader, but quickly added enough detail to make the reader fine-tune that picture. The story begins:

> Shark!
>
> Ensign stretched his timpani even tighter and listened again. The clouds swirled around his body, obscuring his own wingtips in the mist of opaque orange and pink. Wind-driven ice crystals stung against his taut membranes. The air pressed in on him thick and oppressive. He wished he were above the clouds and out in the clean sunlight with the rest of his pod. . . .

For one word, you might think you'd been plunged into an Earthly ocean, with a character threatened by a literal shark. The very next sentence makes it clear that you're in a much more alien place. By the end of the paragraph you know the viewpoint character you've latched onto lives in the dense atmosphere of what must be a very large planet. You know that he plays a role more or less analogous to that of whales, but you also know that he is not a whale. The predator-approaching-prey image remains sharp and clear, and your mind is reset to interpret terms like "shark" differently than usual for the duration of this story.

Now consider the same two paragraphs, substituting, "Bliggleblop" for "Shark" and "snyunk" for "pod." If that was all you'd seen, you wouldn't have much of a picture at all. You might still be wondering—if you still cared—just what a "snyunk" was, in what sense Ensign considered it "his," and whether a bliggleblop was somehow threatening or Ensign was getting excited about it for some other reason.

How much alien jargon and how much not-quite-appropriate English jargon to use in such a case is always a judgment call, and somebody will always disagree with the way you make it. (For some other examples of alien viewpoints, you might see Vinicoff and Martin's "The Weigher," Thompson's "On Tour With Gyez," and Allison Tellure's "Skysinger" stories.) Since it's so difficult to hit the right balance between the clear and the exotic with an alien viewpoint, you might prefer, when it is possible, to have at least one human character to serve as an intermediary between alien characters and reader. Of course, such a character can't be merely a passive observer. Even if your original interest in a story lies in a conflict, say, between two intelligences that arose on a single planet, once you let human observers go there they must surely be drawn into the fray, acting and being acted upon. The story will thus become something quite different from what it would have been without them.

LANGUAGE PROBLEMS

I have already hinted at some of the special problems aliens force on a writer in matters of language. The characters themselves will face even more basic ones, and the writer must decide how to deal with them to get the story moving yet keep it believable. Any time two independently evolved species come into contact, you must decide how, if at all, they're going to learn to talk to each other. Assuming that their built-in linguistic apparatus is similar enough that both of them can speak at least one of their languages, they will need time together to learn it. That's likely to be a tedious process that the reader doesn't care to spend much time on, so you may have to gloss over it, and still risk burdening your story with a period of no "real" action.

Science fiction writers have invented a number of more or less plausible ways to shortcut that awkward necessity. One of the most convenient is the *translator*, a "black box" or highly sophisticated computer that automatically translates one language into another. A translator between two known languages is clearly possible; primitive versions are already on the market.

A "universal translator," which analyzes a new language and quickly prepares a program for on-the-spot translation or language instruction, is not inconceivable, but it's a lot harder than most writers seem to realize. A language is not just a code or cypher. It has a distinct structure of its own that may be so different from that of another that translation requires "melting the ideas down and recasting them in a new form." Even a message in a highly sophisticated code developed by U.S. military cryptographers is still English at heart, wearing a disguise that can be penetrated with enough determined effort. The same message translated as accurately as possible into Navajo is so different in fundamental structure that such things were used in World War II as an "unbreakable code."

Furthermore, merely analyzing the structure of a language is not enough—you also have to know how it relates to its subject matter. So science-fictional translators that learn a language simply by analyzing a sample of it are unconvincing. Such a machine would also have to analyze the speakers, and their surroundings and activities, for quite a while. Given the opportunity and ability to do that, and to analyze very complicated correlations, a highly sophisticated artificial intelligence might be able to do it. On the other hand, a highly sophisticated natural intelligence might do it at least as well, which is why my Chet and Tina Barlin spend a lot of time surreptitiously observing their subjects before even considering direct contact.

Sometimes, of course, that process can also be shortened. Many storybook aliens have come to Earth already armed with a fair, if oddly lopsided, understanding of human language and culture obtained by watching old television broadcasts on their way here.

Electronic and/or mechanical intermediaries are likely to prove useful in many human-alien contacts, if only for a reason I already mentioned in chapter seven: the fact that their signal-producing methods may be so different that neither can make the sounds (or light or chemical signals) used by the other. A moderately extreme example of this occurs in my "Pinocchio," in which a computer is equipped with microphones, speakers and a monitor screen to translate dolphin utterances into human meaning. Dolphin sounds cover a much wider frequency range than human speech or hearing, but the differences go even beyond that. As the human who developed the system explains, "The phonation apparatus in [Pinocchio's] blowhole is divided and he can use the two halves singly, jointly or independently.... The first two columns of the [computer] display give a very free verbal translation of what he's saying, or both messages if he says two things at once. Some of the sounds carry connotations to compensate for the lack of an expressive face, and the third column has comments about those." So Pinocchio's first bit of dialogue that my human protagonist hears looks like this on the screen:

GOOD MORNING, MASON.		•	FRIENDLINESS.
	•	•	
	•	•	MODERATE
	•	•	CHEERFULNESS.
	•	•	
	• IS THIS SANDY?	•	CURIOSITY.
	•	•	
	•	•	EAGERNESS.
	•	•	
	•	•	SONAR.

Nothing in the chart is arbitrary; I had clearly in mind exactly what Pinocchio was doing and why each word appeared where it did. Many readers found it and its explanation interesting—once. If I had shown all of Pinocchio's dialogue that way, few readers would have had the patience to read the whole story. So I showed how it really worked once, at the beginning, and then translated later lines into colloquial English conventionally written. (Which, by the way, is usually a good way to handle any sort of accent or dialect. As Gordon R. Dickson once advised me, "You don't want to remind the reader that he's reading!")

Slightly less exotic forms of technological communication aids between beings with incompatible speech methods are already in use right here on Earth. Several laboratories (see my essay on "Self-Fulfilling Prophecies") have been using such methods as keyboards with visual symbols to converse with gorillas and chimpanzees in an invented language. Early efforts to teach apes to talk had very little success, apparently because they're simply not built for human speech. Given a more congenial medium, some individuals have demonstrated an ability to use a vocabulary of several hundred words in meaningful sentences. (See Sue Savage-Rumbaugh and Roger Lewin's *Kanzi: The Ape on the Brink of the Human Mind*.)

Communication between beings with very different ways of

talking does not necessarily require fancy hardware. Some labs have had impressive successes in teaching apes American Sign Language (Ameslan), originally developed for hearing-impaired humans. In my *Tweedlioop*, the communication breakthrough occurs when two children, one human and one alien, cut to the simplest approach that works while their elders dither over what they might do. Neither can make the sounds of the other's language, but both can learn to understand them. So they do.

In "Pinocchio" and many other stories, a computer will sometimes render a word of one language as UNTRANSLATABLE into the other. A colleague recently argued on a convention panel that there are no untranslatable words—any meaning can be gotten across, even if it takes ten minutes of explanation. I disagreed, but we weren't really as far apart as we sounded. I basically agreed with him in chapter eight, when I doubted that many aliens were likely to be truly and hopelessly incomprehensible. But I don't think a ten-minute explanation of a word can really be considered a translation (and I can easily think of examples that would require much more than ten minutes even to translate from academic English to street English, such as "Bessel function"). Let's just say that most languages will contain words that are not simply or easily translatable into some other languages—words that have no equivalent of comparable length and/or similar connotations.

A particular type of problem word that often comes up in science fiction is the unit of measurement. Writers sometimes like to use phrases like "nine sipaicho" to describe the distance that an alien character has to cover before nightfall, thinking it conveys some of the exotic flavor of alienness. Maybe it does, but it also conveys no information. If "nine sipaicho" is equivalent to "seven kilometers," then seven kilometers is almost always the best translation for an English-speaking reader. (*Astronomical* units in everyday use present a special problem. Will "day" and "year" mean the lengths of time defined by the rotational and orbital periods of Earth, or the rotational and orbital periods of the planet in your story? You must decide, and make clear to the reader what convention you're using.)

There are better ways than meaningless words to convey the feeling of alienness and (better yet) some of the mind-set of your aliens. One is to translate literally idioms that reflect their way of viewing the world. W.R. Thompson's kya, with their herbivorous herd background, rely much more on scent and less on sight than humans, so many of their figures of speech refer to smells where ours might refer to colors or shapes. Gyez asks his guide, "Will I have some time to play tourist? I'd like to take in the scents." A similar trick is to retain some of their characteristic thought structure when they learn a human language. Kya speaking English often begin sentences with a present participle or a phrase built around one. Wishing he could spend more time with human writers, the kya writer Gyez says, "Writing in the same genre, I might pick up some new ideas. . . ."

Such devices must be used with care. I once tried to tell a story about members of a species with three sexes and well-differentiated sex roles in their society. It seemed obvious to me that each sex needed to have its own set of pronouns, so I used *he/him* and *she/her* for two sexes and *le/lim* for the third. Unfortunately, most people got so hung up on the third pronoun that they couldn't read the story until I grudgingly changed it to use a single English pronoun for the two least dissimilar alien sexes. Pronouns seem to represent a deeper level of programming than nouns or verbs, and it's harder to get people to accept a change at that level of their own language (a fact further supported by the observed difficulty of getting a gender-unspecified pronoun generally accepted into English). Allison Tellure seems to have got away with it in "Green-Eyed Lady, Laughing Lady," but only in a limited way and for the duration of a short story.

As Orson Scott Card has pointed out, you also have to be extra careful with *metaphors* in science fiction, because they might be taken and/or meant literally. "He cast his eyes toward the ceiling" means quite different things when you're talking about ordinary humans and when you're talking about someone whose eyes are detachable remote sensors with flight capability!

◆ ◆ ◆

The most general advice I can give is that there is no absolutely general advice. I could spend as many pages on this as I liked, and still could not give you a detailed, exhaustive "how-to." The very essence of science fiction is that you'll be creating situations that no one has had to deal with before—and then inventing ways to deal with them. In "Petals of Rose," Marc Stiegler's human characters had to cooperate with beings who lived so fast and intensely that contact with them was dazzling and exhausting. The story contains an extraordinary number of characters for its length, some of whom might live their entire lives and die in a page or two—yet the author had to make the reader know and care about each one in that brief time.

You may never have to deal with *that* problem, but you may create one just as challenging. Each case is unique and must be handled in the way best suited to it, even if that way has to be invented for the occasion. My hope in this chapter is to give you a better idea of what to watch for as you read other authors' work, to gain a feel for how they solved their problems that will in turn help you solve yours.

CHAPTER 10

Case Studies

So far we have looked at various aspects of creating and writing about aliens, illustrating each with examples from real science fiction. In actual writing, of course, you will seldom be dealing with any of those aspects in isolation. No real species, and no adequately realized fictitious species, is only an adaptation to a particular kind of starlight or atmosphere or gravity, or characterized only by its language or religion or technology. Real species are necessarily the product of everything that went into producing them. The way a star forms shapes the planets that form with it. The way a planet forms shapes the things that live on it. The way a species evolves shapes any civilization it might develop. In writing your own science fiction, you will usually have to think about at least a few of these areas in conjunction with each other, and sometimes you will have to think about all of them. The purpose of this chapter is to give you some examples of how that process has worked in the development of some existing stories—not isolated examples of physical forms or linguistic structures, but the creation of an *integrated* combination of world and alien that clearly belong together.

Since many aspects of the stories I'll be discussing have already been described in earlier chapters, I will not repeat all that here. My object now is simply to give you a brief look at the overall process of creating several stories, as examples of the range of ways it can work and how the pieces fit together and influence each other. As I've said earlier, there is no set formula. How you approach creating a story, and how much effort you put into any particular aspect of it, depends on what you're trying to do with it and how interested you are in this or that. As Hal Clement suggests, "Work out your world and its creatures as long as it remains fun; then write your story, making use of any of the details you have worked out which *help the story*."

Perhaps inevitably, the stories whose backgrounds and developments I know best are my own. Fortunately those include a variety of goals and approaches, and I do know at least a *little* about some stories by others.

A FEW OF MY OWN . . .

Aliens may be very like humans, or very different from us. The very similar ones are probably so rare that it's generally best not to use them unless you have a particular reason to do so—and even then, you must be careful how you use them. One story that needed very humanoid aliens, and a world to fit them, is my . . .

Newton and the Quasi-Apple

Newton grew from an idea that originally had nothing to do with aliens: "quasimaterials," or artificial kinds of "matter" with properties different from those of natural matter. I first attempted to use these in a satirical farce set in near-future academia (I was in graduate school and looking for an assistant professorship at the time), but editor John W. Campbell said the idea was too good to waste on such a trivial story line. I wasn't sure what else to do with it until the following fall, when I had that assistant professorship and for the first time found myself developing my own course and lectures.

It's been said that the best way to learn something is to teach it, and I've found a lot of truth in that. As a physics student, I'd never fully appreciated the magnitude of Isaac Newton's accomplishment in formulating his laws of motion and gravitation. From my twentieth-century perspective, it all seemed so *simple*. It wasn't until the night before I was supposed to tell my students about it that it really hit me what an awesome achievement it was for somebody who knew only what Newton knew in the seventeenth century.

It hit me *hard*. It haunted my subconscious that whole night, and the next morning, when I was giving the lecture I'd thought out the night before, something else happened. Right in the middle of it, something leaped out of my subconscious and demanded, "*Could he still have done it if somebody'd shown him quasimaterials that* didn't *follow his laws?*"

I realized right away that that was the extra ingredient I needed to write a quasimaterial story I could sell John Campbell. I could hardly wait to write it down in my pocket notebook, before I lost it, but I had to finish the lecture first. I wrote it down right outside the door, as soon as class was over, before I even went back to my office.

That incident illustrates something that happens quite often in writing: A story grows, not from a single idea, but from two or more seemingly unrelated ideas colliding and igniting. The note in my pocket notebook was still a long way from being a story, of course. I needed to decide who the characters were, and all the background that went with them. I could have done it as an alternate-Earth story, with aliens or time travelers showing the real Isaac Newton quasimaterials, destroying his faith in his theories, and thereby thwarting the next major step in the development of science. Or I could do it by having future humans visit a world on which a local counterpart of Newton was about to make comparable break-throughs, and inadvertently cause him the same sort of problems.

I chose the latter, partly because it was the first one that occurred to me and partly because it was easier. To use the real Sir Isaac, I would have had to do extensive research on his life and times, because science fiction readers *love* to catch writers in error about real, verifiable facts. That type of story can be fun, but at that point in my life I didn't have time to do that research. It might have taken me a year to do it to my satisfaction; I had an editor interested now and I thought it had been too long since I'd sold him anything. So I wanted to send him a good story soon, before he forgot he was interested.

If I put the whole thing in the future and used an alien Newton-analog, I could make the whole thing up and nobody could catch me in contradiction of historic fact. All I had to do was make it reasonably consistent internally, and I had a head start on that because I already had an outline of a future history in which I'd set other stories. So with that as my human background, I sent the cultural survey team of Chet and Tina Barlin to a world where they would find an excuse to introduce a very few carefully selected examples of quasimaterials, which most of the locals would uncriti-cally accept as "magic."

Except "Newton." He might be troubled by the doubts I men-tioned above, but he'd also have an even bigger problem—espe-cially if he'd already pretty well formulated his laws and felt good about them. The local establishment, feeling threatened by his new ideas, might seize upon the quasimaterials as evidence that his theories were nonsense and ridicule him into oblivion. The Barlins, realizing this had happened, would have to find a way to undo the damage.

Because of the fundamental nature of the story I wanted to tell, I needed unusually humanoid aliens, which made some parts of my job easier. They had to be pretty humanoid because I wanted their history to parallel ours pretty closely, up to the point where I threw in the monkey wrench. To be that humanoid, they had to evolve on an Earthlike planet, complete with a similar axial tilt and consequently similar climate patterns. So I could take much of the physical background as qualitatively similar to what we're used to, with only "cosmetic" changes such as a different kind of autumnal color change and leaf loss, and domestic animals whose edible parts could be plucked off like fruit and regenerated instead of killing the whole animal.

Since I already had a good excuse to use an unusually Earthlike planet, I went so far as to make its intelligent natives so humanoid that humans could pass themselves off as travelers from an unfamiliar part of the same planet instead of admitting they were from the stars. That was highly desirable for story purposes, since it let humans who were not supposed to admit that interact more directly than they otherwise could have. Of course, they weren't completely identical to the natives, so it helped that the locals were used to seeing and accepting a lot of unfamiliar things. The local theocracy—the one under whose auspices Terek (my "Newton") worked took as a fundamental precept that, "Magnificent and infinitely varied are the ways of the Supreme Presence." So, naturally, they wouldn't take kindly to a theory that put limits on the ways of the the Supreme Presence. . . .

The Kyyra

In *Newton* I had special reasons for using a very Earthlike planet with very humanoid inhabitants. Such things may well be out there, but you wouldn't want to make a habit of using them in your stories. There are too many other possibilities, and the ones that much like us must be quite rare.

The Kyyra, in *The Sins of the Fathers* and *Lifeboat Earth*, are fairly humanoid, but nowhere near as much so as the Kemrekl in *Newton*—and they came to us. Like the Kemrekl, their nature was shaped in part by the story I wanted to tell and the role I wanted them to play in it. And, like *Newton*, that story grew from the collision of several ideas, only one of which had anything to do with aliens.

It started with the realization that a faster-than-light ship could overtake light that had already passed Earth and thereby get a second look at an astronomical event that Earth-based astronomers saw before they had good enough instruments to study it well. By itself, that didn't make much of a story, but Ben Bova, who was editing *Analog* then, goaded me to build something on it. I began to see how I might do that when I realized that an FTL ship that set out to get a second look at an "old" astronomical event, could also get an "advance" look at an event from which no light had yet reached us. In particular, I remembered thinking, when reading about the galactic core explosions sometimes seen in other galaxies, that one could have occurred in our Galaxy any time in the last 30,000 years—and we wouldn't know about it until the first light reached us.

Eventually I saw that that could combine naturally with one more entry in my unused idea file: "Suppose the Earth were about to become uninhabitable and aliens offered to rescue us, but refused to discuss the reasons for their offer. Should we accept their help?"

That's the kind of question that's clearly the germ of a story. To answer it, I had to think about the answers to a whole complex of subsidiary questions, of which the most important for our present purposes was, "What kind of aliens were they and what were their reasons for offering to help?"

Giving them a plausible motive was quite a challenge. They had to come from closer to the galactic center than us, to know about it before us and already be fleeing to another galaxy. But why should they be looking for other victims and taking time and trouble to help them escape, too? Admittedly aliens might have different priorities than humans, but pure unmitigated altruism would be, at best, hard for most human readers to swallow. Fortunately, somewhere my subconscious reminded me of two things: That a much more advanced civilization might be capable of manipulating whole stars, and that some astronomers had suggested that in a region where stars are packed tightly together, a supernova might set off a chain reaction of other supernovas.

And guilt can be a powerful motivator, easily recognized and understood by human readers. Not that it will work the same way in all intelligent species, but a feeling of responsibility for actions and their consequences will often be a species survival trait. . . .

So suppose the Kyyra started the core explosion, and therefore felt obligated to try to help any innocent victims they found on the way out. I already knew they had to be much older and more technologically advanced than us, since the basic premise depended on their being able to move whole planets, populations and all, across intergalactic distances at FTL speeds. Given that, it was relatively easy to accept that they routinely practiced industry on a stellar scale—things like setting off supernovas to make heavy elements. If they lived close to the core, they might try it in a region where stars were a little too densely packed for that to be safe.

And it seemed perfectly natural that, while they might feel obliged to offer help, they wouldn't want to talk about it. "Hi, neighbor. I live down the pike a piece and I just blew up your galaxy. . . ."

I was beginning to see how the big picture fit together. I knew what had happened, why they were offering to help, and why they didn't want to discuss it. I knew they were way beyond us, in at least some ways—but I still needed to know who they were, to make them real enough for humans to care about and react to.

So I tried to imagine in some detail what a much older humanoid culture might be like, and how it got that way. I wound up exploring the broad outlines of several thousand years of their history and inventing some new physics, with quite specific properties and limitations, for them to use in their FTL planet-moving. I didn't know a lot of details about their planet of origin; neither did they, since it was so far in their past and they had since spread to so many others and changed them so much. It seemed quite likely that they might have followed a trend that many humans sometimes seem bent on—filling their entire planet with themselves at the expense of almost everything else. A more or less natural planet, like Earth, still harboring a multitude of naturally occurring life-forms, might be to them a completely strange, beautiful yet terrifying thing. To enable that many of them to live together, my subconscious dredged up another idea I had once tried unsuccessfully to use by itself: a massive computer, combining functions and attributes of God and government, that continually monitors and adjusts individual minds to live in harmony.

For the humans to whom the Kyyra brought bad tidings, the urge to survive an overwhelming catastrophe had to battle with fear of trusting obviously powerful beings who are very secretive about their motives. So the human need to make a decision on the Kyyra offer was inextricably entwined with the desire to solve the mystery of *why.*

To make humans even consider their offer seriously, the Kyyra had to make a particular kind of impression on those who saw them. If they had been wimpy, ugly little guys who didn't seem to know what they were doing, there wouldn't have been much conflict—few people would have even given much thought to accepting their offer. So I made them an imposing presence: statuesque, clad in resplendent robes, giving every impression of being older, wiser and very much in control. The only problem was that they wouldn't say what was in it for them. . . .

The key to learning was a single human, Sandy, with a history of establishing easy rapport with both people and animals, who befriended the Kyyra ambassador, Beldan. She began to see the more vulnerable side of him and his species and eventually got to visit their orbiting ship. There she found enough extra clues to figure out what was going on. Here, too, little pieces fit together in a multitude of ways. For example, in their clothing and shipboard furnishings, the Kyyra made casual use of what humans consider precious metals, made possible by their industrial use of supernovas.

Pinocchio

Once the decision was made (in a way I won't divulge) and the Earth was on its way, I needed one more alien—the dolphin Pinocchio. *Lifeboat Earth* is an episodic story (the five major sections first appeared as independent novelettes in *Analog*) spanning several decades. Even with Kyyra technology, so far beyond ours that it looked like magic, moving Earth to the galaxy M31 was an unprecedentedly traumatic experience. *Homo sapiens* would survive, but many individuals and many other species would not. Life during the journey would be grim and bleak, and even some who would live out normal lifespans would not live to see its end.

People can't get their emotional teeth into a tragedy that big. To make them feel how grim it is, you have to narrow the focus and show them how it affects an individual life. You have to let them watch it hurt somebody they care about—which means first you have to make them care, and then you have to let the hurt happen.

One of the most tragic aspects of Earth's flight from the galaxy was the extinction of other species, so I wanted to tell a story about one of the last members of one of those species. There would be many such losses, but the ones humans would feel most deeply would be those of obviously intelligent species toward which people felt sympathetic—especially if they could speak for themselves. Bottlenose dolphins seemed ideal, since some research suggested they could speak for themselves, and most humans found them unusually likable. So I immersed myself in that research and did some observing of my own. I figured out what sort of culture and personalities they might have, based on the research to date, and how the Earth-moving experience might look to them. Then I set Sandy to the task of trying to talk one of the last survivors out of letting himself be the last.

It was a unique alien-building experience, which several others (e.g., Mark Jarvis in "Collaboration") have also done in their own ways. As in my other examples, I needed an alien to play a certain kind of role in a story. But since this was a real alien about which a considerable amount was known, I couldn't create it from whole cloth. I had to start with the known facts and build on them. My total picture is fictitious, but includes many real elements. Yet, from a human standpoint, it is a truly *alien* intelligence.

. . . AND A FEW BY OTHERS

My examples so far have started with a concept of the general shape of a story, and developed aliens appropriate to it. As the aliens took concrete form, of course, their nature dictated many of the details of the story; good characters of any kind are unwilling to be mere puppets for a preconceived plot. But in all these cases the general concept came first, and the aliens were created to fit it.

That's not, of course, the only way it can happen. Another category of approaches is what I might call the "Because It's There" method, in which the author first figures out that a particular kind of interesting alien or world can exist, explores its characteristics, and then sees what kinds of story it suggests.

Mission of Gravity

Hal Clement is one of the most avid and skilled practitioners of this approach. In *Mission of Gravity*, for example, he recognized some of the properties an extremely massive planet might have, such as very high surface gravity and a very rapid spin rate, leading to a flattened shape and an extreme variation in apparent gravity from equator to poles. Clement had the ability and interest to work these things out in quantitative detail for a planet named Mesklin, so he did. Once armed with that knowledge, he was in a position to figure out what sorts of things could live there, how they might evolve, and what kinds of problems both they and human explorers might face. From there it was natural for his focus to narrow to individual Mesklinites and visitors and specific problems, and let those generate a story. Fortunately for those who would like to see something of the process and how the pieces fit together, he also put quite a bit of that into the fact article "Whirligig World," and I can summarize some of the highlights here.

His inspiration was not purely abstract, but grew out of real astronomical research published by K. Aa. Strand on 61 Cygni, a binary star system eleven light-years from Earth. These were the first observations suggesting that a star other than the Sun had a "planetary" companion. It couldn't be seen from Earth, but its presence and some of its gross characteristics could be deduced from perturbations in the orbits of the other components. At a time when other solar systems were almost purely conjectural, Clement was naturally fascinated by the possibility that here, finally, was direct evidence for another abode for life. He set about considering what it might be like and what, if anything, might live there.

The unseen companion of 61 Cygni A—Mesklin—appeared to be more massive than any of our planets. With about sixteen times the mass of Jupiter, its core must be so compressed that its diameter would actually be a bit less than that of Uranus. It's a bordlerline case—it could be a very faint star (a brown dwarf) or a superjovian planet. Clement chose to regard it as more planet than star, which made it easier to set action there—but still not easy.

With so much mass in such a small package, its surface gravity would be some three hundred times that of Earth. That would be a very serious problem for any humans who wanted to explore it, and Clement wanted to put humans there. As a scientist himself, he knew that the first thing humans would want to do with such a world would be to learn all they could about it; and human characters make it easier for a human reader to get into a story. But Clement didn't want to depend on "magic," such as "gravity shields," to make that possible.

Fortunately known science provided another way—and using

it suggested many elements of the story. It was highly probable (remember our discussions of star and planet formation) that Mesklin would be spinning quite rapidly. Even if it remained spherical, that would mean that the "effective gravity" felt by someone standing on the equator would be less than that at the poles, because the actual gravity would be partly offset by "centrifugal force" at the equator. Moreover, it wouldn't be spherical, because such spinning would also tend to flatten the planet along its polar axis. This would make the difference in effective gravity between equator and poles even larger, since the actual gravity would be stronger at the poles. Clement developed a model of Mesklin including specific numbers for size, rotation rate and related quantities. The most important of these for story purposes are the effective surface gravity, ranging from 3g at the equator (g = gravitational acceleration on Earth) to 700g at the poles.

That made it marginally possible to send the humans to the equator, though it would still be so uncomfortable that they would only go personally as a last resort. They started with an unmanned research probe to the high-gravity south pole—but it refused to respond to the command to come home. Some of its data was sent back by telemetry, but for much of it the researchers needed to recover the probe itself.

There's the beginning of a story situation—a large investment in an important research project, and much of the valuable data trapped where the researchers can't get at it. The driving problem is: How can they salvage as much as possible? They do go personally, building a station on the relatively low-g equator, to do what they can. They can't go to the higher latitudes, but they meet a native who can.

To create plausible Mesklinites who could try to rescue the humans' lost probe, Clement had to consider both the biochemical and physical requirements imposed by the environment. For the former, he got some help from biochemist Isaac Asimov, the two of them brainstorming the biochemical outlines of a system that could produce hydrogen-breathing animals. Because of the high gravity, falling would be extremely dangerous, so animals living there would be built of sturdy material, small and low to the ground. Thus Mesklinite hero Barlennan looks rather like a centipede, with other features such as those I've mentioned in earlier chapters.

Barlennan is described by Clement as "captain and owner of a tramp ship, half trader and (*probably*) half pirate." The story is his quest to recover the information locked in the humans' probe, which requires Barlennan and his crew to travel farther and farther into the high-gravity high latitudes, in the process encountering various Mesklinite cultures and physical problems posed by the increasingly hostile environment.

Much of the action generates itself. Once the author sees a problem his characters are likely to encounter, they must find a way to deal with it. Much of the author's work consisted of "finding things that are taken for granted on our world and would not be true on this one." Those include such things as the impossibility of throwing, jumping or flying, at least in the upper latitudes. On Mesklin, the fear of heights and falling runs deep and pervades everything, for a very good reason. A sixty-foot cliff encountered at one point in the story amounts to an insurmountable obstacle; and one native culture has good engineers, but their greatest accomplishments are walls three inches high.

The People of the Wind

If *Mission of Gravity* is an example of a story in which the setting came first and led then to a set of aliens and a story involving them, Poul Anderson's *The People of the Wind* exemplifies a variation in which the aliens came first and world and story grew around them. Certain elements of the story contain strong hints at its origins. I suspect it began with looking at the common assumption that winged flight and intelligence are incompatible—that intelligence requires brain and body to be too big, while flight requires them to be too small—and questioning it. The question "How could a winged creature be intelligent?" leads (as usual) to a series of subsidiary questions. What kind of a planet would make it easier? What features of body design would help? How might those evolve? What sorts of behavior would evolve along with them? How might those turn into civilization?

The People of the Wind contains unusually explicit discussions of how the answers to those questions developed, influenced each other and led ultimately to the growth of a distinctive, memorable and very alien civilization. The story is largely character-driven, but the characters—like human characters—grow out of their species' evolutionary background and their individual circumstances.

Perhaps at least in part because the Ythrian culture is so alien, the author chose to have it share a planet with humans, a new composite culture growing out of the interaction between the two. Ben Bova has observed that a useful way to generate a story is to rub two characters together and watch what happens. The same is true of cultures. The humans in *The People of the Wind* not only provide a "reader-friendly" window into Ythrian society, but the interplay of the two species sheds light on both and adds depth to the story.

The Ythrians first appear in the short story "Wings of Victory," about humans' first encounter with them, in their native world. The humans are slow to recognize them as intelligent because they're so sure, on theoretical grounds, that flyers can't be intelligent. The relatively low gravity on Ythri makes it a little easier, but the real key to making flight possible for a body big enough to support intelligence is a "supercharger." That's a mechanism by which wing motion can pump pressurized oxygen over surfaces where it can be absorbed directly into the bloodstream, supplementing that supplied by the lungs.

Anderson, justly renowned for his care in creating fully realized, multidimensional worlds, not only envisioned the mechanical solution, but worked out a detailed evolutionary history for the Ythrians. Their ancestors were analogous to our amphibians; the supercharger evolved from gills, while grasping talons became "hands." The Ythrians could walk when they had to, on claws at the bends in their wings; but the air was their true home. The large energy requirements for flight, along with their breeding methods, have shaped virtually everything about their cultures. They must, for example, live in small groups with large territories; and their political institutions are looser and more individualistic than those of humans.

Anderson had already set many stories, the "Polesotechnic League" series, in a broad future history, and that provided a natural setup for the more extensive human interaction he wanted in *The People of the Wind* (which takes place centuries after "Wings of Victory"). Influenced by their early contacts with humans, Ythrians have also become spacefaring, though on a more modest scale. At a time of impending collapse of the Polesotechnic League, a group of humans move into an Ythrian-dominated region of space, and they and some Ythrians set up a joint colony on the planet Avalon.

The Polesotechnic League was succeeded by a much stronger

Terran Empire, which eventually threatens the Ythrians—and the joint colony on Avalon. But that is no longer just a planet with humans here and Ythrians there; the two cultures have influenced each other to the extent that they are becoming a single hybrid culture. Naturally not everyone welcomes this. Elders of each species are concerned about the increasing tendency of their young to adopt ways and friends of the other.

The central story line of *People* is the war—Avalon against the encroaching Empire. But against that background Anderson weaves a rich tapestry of subplots involving individual interactions—human-human, Ythrian-Ythrian and human-Ythrian. And the human reader gets a very "inside" feel for what it is to be Ythrian, even unto a long and evocative poem distilling much of the essence of the Ythrian way of life.

The Kya

The principle of letting the interplay of two cultures or species illuminate both has been exploited, in a wide variety of ways, in many stories involving aliens and humans. In W.R. Thompson's kya series, humans and the kya, with their culture shaped by herbivorous herd-living ancestors, interact in a different set of ways in each story. There are quite a few of those stories now, but surprisingly enough, the author's original plan was for a single story, and the kya were not its primary focus.

The plot of the first story, "Maverick," hinged on a different, ancient and *extremely* alien, group of aliens called the Nomads. Evolved in interstellar space, they had the disconcerting habit of imposing their will on other species and occasionally exterminating an entire planetful of beings who displeased them. Naturally humans felt a need to learn as much as they could about this potential threat, but virtually nothing was known about them except that they had left vaults on several planets containing what appeared to be extensive information—evidently intended to be found, but as yet undeciphered.

One of the nomad vaults was on the planet Kya. To get access to it, humans needed the cooperation of Kya's intelligent natives, the kya. The basic idea of the first story was simply that, because of the Nomad threat, human scientists had to deal with another species (the kya) and had trouble doing so because of their cultural differences. To make that kind of story work, the kya had to be similar enough to make mutual understanding seem easy, but just different enough to cause trouble.

With those constraints, Thompson (to whom I am grateful for sharing his memories of the process) set about creating the beings with whom his scientists had to deal. Their planet had to be fairly Earthlike, so neither species would have to spend all its time in spacesuits. Their biology had to be just different enough so humans and kya couldn't catch each other's diseases, which would create complications that would divert the story from its main thrust. But they had to be alien, with basic motivations different from ours, and a logical way to ensure that was to let them evolve from a different kind of ancestors.

Humans evolved from tribal apes, which has shaped our behavior and social institutions all the way up to the present. What might the kya evolve from, and how would their origins shape their societies? Thompson took his inspiration from watching two types of Earthly animals. Deer were the primary influence; watching a herd of them got him thinking about how typical herd behaviors might transform into civilization. In what may seem an odd juxtaposition, cats also made an important contribution. Their behavior is strongly influenced by an acute sense of smell. If intelligent beings had one, how would it affect their worldview and ways?

So Thompson started thinking, partly on paper, about what kind of society might develop among intelligent, herd-dwelling herbivores with a powerful sense of smell. It seemed likely that their social structures would be "tighter" than ours, with more tendency to act cooperatively and look out for their fellows' welfare, and less inclination to follow leaders who were not clearly acting in the herd's best interests.

Why would they evolve intelligence in the first place? It's often assumed that herbivores wouldn't, since, as the saying goes, it doesn't take many smarts to subdue a blade of grass. But that may be an oversimplification. Curiosity might evolve if the quality of grazing land varies considerably from place to place. And while catching grass doesn't require much cleverness, evading predators might, if the predators are such that such typical herbivore defenses as running away and reproducing in large numbers aren't enough.

How about the scent? Among cats and other animals that use it more than we do, it pervades all aspects of life—cats greet others by sniffing, and leave scents to mark objects and individuals as theirs. So, too, do the kya use a deep sniff as a polite greeting, and many of their figures of speech are based on scent.

Such is the evolutionary background of the kya. Thinking about its details and ramifications led to an even more vivid picture of the kya culture and how its members might react in various situations. Some of those details, such as the mutually puzzling behavior of humans and kya toward oddly acting individuals, helped generate the plot of "Maverick."

But note carefully that the thinking in the culture-building stage was not directed primarily at, "What happens in 'Maverick?'," but rather at, "Who are the kya, how do they think and live, and how did they get that way?" When that kind of thinking gets going well, it typically generates many interesting ideas that have no place in the story you're working on, but suggest others. The Nomad problem that was the original driving force for "Maverick" is pretty well wrapped up in the second story, "Outlaw"; but the kya are still generating new stories based on some of the other ideas that came up in creating them. The kya game of bagdrag, for example (see also chapter six), was mentioned in passing in "Maverick," but became a prime focus of the later story "Touchdown, Touchdown, Rah, Rah, Rah!"

It's not really surprising that it is the kya, not the Nomads, who keep generating new stories. The Nomads are too alien for humans to relate to for very long; the kya are indeed "similar enough . . . but just different enough."

Trimus

In G. David Nordley's "Trimus" stories, it's not obvious to the reader which came first—the unique planet Trimus, the deliberate attempt to create a society in which three very different species share it equally or the species themselves. All are so interrelated, and developed with such depth and subtlety, that the author could have started anywhere in the complex and must have gone through a great deal of back-and-forth to make it all fit together.

As it happens, I do know where it started and how it grew, because Mr. Nordley told me and kindly let me see some of his notes. And the answer is: none of the above. As so often happens in writing, a good story (or series) results not from the orderly development of a single germ of idea, but from the collision and interaction of two or more ideas. (Lesson to writers: Always be alert for sparks when two of your ideas get close together!)

Trimus actually started with the "Contact" conferences and newsletters (see References) and Nordley's thinking about the possibility that whales are intelligent. What, he wondered, would it be like to be an intelligent whale—and be harpooned? He began thinking about the possibility of a detective story involving a whale-like alien, probably the victim of a harpooning—but with an unusual twist. Instead of the old cliché of "monster" and/or victim discovered by humans, why not let the whale-like alien be the detective, and an authority figure?

An authority figure in what? Another part of Nordley's mind had been working in parallel on a line of thought that seemed independent: What would conditions be like on a planet that was really a tide-locked satellite of a brown dwarf, orbiting a larger and more "normal" star? (That would be necessary because the brown dwarf alone wouldn't be luminous enough to support life.) Such a world would have three distinct climatic zones that could support three kinds of life, each with a preferred zone but capable of visiting and interacting with others on their home turf. So Nordley conceived the idea of setting up an experiment in coexistence—a little like Anderson's Avalon, but even more so.

That, if the astronomical parameters were right, would provide an opportunity to have humans on the scene, which would help pull human readers into the story. And since Nordley's world, Trimus, offered three distinct zones, he might as well take full advantage of it by adding a third species to the mix.

The fact that humans were to be one of the species imposed some limitations on the astronomical background. Well-versed in the art of world-building, Nordley developed a detailed picture of Trimus and the solar system of which it is a part, choosing the parameters so that one portion of Trimus would be suitable for humans. If you read the stories (as I recommend), you'll easily recognize the Do'utians as the "whale-like aliens" in the original concept, though they've picked up some decidedly un-whale-like characteristics such as a repeatedly branched tongue that serves as a versatile manipulator. They're also amphibious rather than strictly aquatic. Nordley worked out much of their evolutionary and historical background on a world that would make them suited to another of Trimus's zones.

That left the third zone, which would be congenial to a race of flyers, the Kleth. To understand the Kleth, it was necessary to similarly work out their evolutionary background and the nature of their planet of origin. For each of the three species, filling in the whole picture required attention to such aspects of their societies as reproduction and language.

Each species included several different cultural groups within itself, and the ones who settled on Trimus tended to select themselves from particular subcultures. The goal on Trimus was to let each species retain its own identity and character, while cooperating with the others as parts of an integrated society. Making that possible required such things as agreeing on a measurement system and a language that could be used by all three species. Making that possible nudged the author's choices in certain directions.

Do'utian language, for example, is a little like the one I concocted for "Pinocchio," using a broad sonic spectrum and sonic images. Kleth language is more like some human languages. They have a slightly lower but similar vocal range, and their language structure is highly symbolic, tonal, efficient and therefore terse. (They also have the ability to use their wings as sonic reflectors to hear over very large distances.) All of these characteristics are consistent with the anatomies and evolutionary backgrounds of the two species, but they didn't have to be exactly this way. Some of the details were chosen for literary convenience. The language skills of both Do'utians and Kleth include the ability to pronounce English, which, since it is the only one of the three languages usable by all three species, became the *lingua franca* of Trimus.

As with the kya, the original intent of all this background development was to provide a suitable setting for a single story. But the background generated so many interesting spin-off ideas that the temptation to use some of them in more stories was irresistible—especially when the first story was enthusiastically received by its readers.

HOW SHOULD YOU BEGIN?

There's no set formula for creating aliens and telling a story about them. It does seem that there are two basic approaches, depending on where the author's primary interest lies—or perhaps simply which aspect of a certain background occurred to him or her first. Sometimes the process starts with a general idea of the plot, and worlds and beings must be created to make it possible. Sometimes the world or the being is conceived first, and then beings must be developed to inhabit the world, or a world imagined to produce and accommodate the beings—and the story grows out of their natures.

In practice, it's probably quite rare for the development of any real story to follow either of those schemes in a pure, straightforward and simple way. Many writers will sometimes use one kind of starting point and sometimes the other. Once the process has begun, every decision about a new aspect of a story is likely to lead to rethinking and modification of other aspects that you thought you had nailed down. It's best not to become too attached to your original vision; sometimes its only value is to initiate a train of thought that ultimately goes somewhere else entirely. You shouldn't let it run out of control, but you should remain open to any new possibilities that suggest themselves. What matters is the end result: the published story that your readers see. You want that to be as good as it can be, so whatever method makes that happen is a *right* method.

CHAPTER 11

Farther Out

Life Not As We Know It

Most of this book has dealt with creating and writing about aliens and alien societies based more or less closely on known science, and in particular on ones that are at least enough like us to have developed on planets. That covers a vast range of possibilities, but not as broad a range as science fiction, as a whole, should explore. In this final chapter, let's look at some ways science fiction can go beyond that and still be science fiction.

BEYOND PLANETS AND CHEMISTRY

Most of what we have considered so far has implicitly assumed that the life-forms in question evolved on planets in more or less circular orbits around single main-sequence stars and were based on some sort of carbon-based chemistry. In other words, both they and their worlds were at some fundamental level at least recognizably similar to us and ours. That still allowed for plenty of variation. For example, their sun might be younger and bluer or older and redder than ours; their planet might have more or less axial tilt and weaker or stronger gravity; they might breathe hydrogen to reduce carbon compounds instead of oxygen to oxidize them. But at least they had a sun and seasons and gravity, and they got the energy to keep themselves alive by doing some kind of chemistry on carbon compounds. Creating worlds and aliens within those broad parameters is a relatively straightforward matter of following the guidelines laid down in chapters three through five.

I've hinted from time to time at the possibility of environments and life-forms much more fundamentally different from us. A first step in that direction is the planetary system which is more elaborate than a group of planets in essentially independent orbits around a single star, such as the contact binary system in Jerry Oltion and Lee Goodloe's "Contact."

A more extreme example is Dr. Robert L. Forward's *Rocheworld*. Rocheworld is a "planet" of the nearby red dwarf Barnard's Star, but its structure is very different from what we usually understand by "planet." It consists of two smallish planetoids so close together that tidal forces have distorted them into egg-like shapes and locked them into synchronous rotation, the same sides constantly facing each other. Their solid surfaces don't quite touch, but their closest parts are only eighty kilometers apart and they share an atmosphere of methane, ammonia and water vapor. One is "high and dry"; the other has captured all the system's liquid water and formed an ocean of ammonia and water that rises in a steep liquid "mountain" one hundred fifty kilometers high. That ocean is home to a distinctly alien intelligence.

Rocheworld's life is chemical-based, and the two-components-with-one-atmosphere can be considered a planet, of sorts—but it's so different from any "normal" planet that its details are by no means a simple or obvious variation on a standard theme. Figuring out how close they can be without completely destroying each other, and how the atmosphere and water would be distributed, required extensive original calculations. Forward, a highly skilled and imaginative physicist as well as a writer, could do that. If you want to write about something comparably unusual and original, you'll need to be prepared either to do the calculations yourself, or to find someone able and willing to do them for you. For an astronomical configuration so far from the ordinary and familiar, mere guesses are likely to be wildly wrong.

Dragon's Egg, also by Dr. Forward, is even more exotic, literally going beyond *both* planets and chemistry. The intelligent Cheela live on the surface of a neutron star, with half the mass of the sun, a diameter of only twenty kilometers, a surface gravity sixty-seven billion times that of Earth, and a magnetic field nearly a trillion times as strong (which has a dominant influence on how everything works there). Matter that dense doesn't even exist as atoms, so the very concept of "chemistry" does not apply. The majority of it consists of neutrons formed by "squashing the electrons into the protons"; the physical state of this "neutronium" is different at different depths, and other elementary particles occur in much smaller quantities. Chemistry involves electromagnetic interactions of the electron clouds, which are the outer parts of atoms; the most nearly analogous interactions on Dragon's Egg involve the much stronger nuclear forces.

Dragon's Egg has a fully developed ecosystem, in which the Cheela are the dominant animal. They have about the same mass and complexity as humans, but the stuff they are made of is so dense that they are only about five millimeters in diameter and a half millimeter high (or thick). They're built more or less like flattened amoebas because in a gravitational field that strong, you cannot risk falling. As a consequence of general relativistic effects in the intense gravity, time on Dragon's Egg is greatly accelerated compared to ours. In the novel, first (remote) human contact with the Cheela occurs when they are still savages, but six (Earth) years later they have developed beyond humans.

None of these details, which I can barely hint at here, was chosen on a mere whim. They are all interrelated, determined by the starting assumptions and the same laws of physics that apply everywhere—but applied in a highly unfamiliar context. Forward described some of the thinking that went into it in his article "A Taste of Dragon's Egg," explaining how the properties of the world and its inhabitants were determined and how they managed to interact with humans. Still more detail can be found in the novel itself.

One of the things that makes *Dragon's Egg* special is that the author worked the background out with as much rigor and detail as possible, given the present state of physical knowledge. Conceivably someone else might have attempted a story on the same theme without such rigor, and many readers would have been none the wiser. But some would have noticed, and the story would likely have been so full of error as to be more fantasy than science fiction.

There are, of course, successful stories based on less rigorous speculation about extremely exotic life-forms. In many cases this can be justified on the grounds that a possibility can be glimpsed in a general way, but less detailed theory is available to predict exactly how it might work out. Timothy Zahn concocted a deep-space ecosystem in his "space horse" stories. "Artificial life" in "cyberspace" can be as diverse as Joseph H. Delaney and Marc Stiegler's *Valentina* (an intelligent, self-aware and highly personable computer program) and the more profoundly alien entities suggested in Mark Lesney's article. Still other possibilities include the enormous intelligent nebula in Fred Hoyle's *The Black Cloud*, the silicon-based planetary intelligence in Joseph Green's *Conscience Interplanetary*, and the organized electromagnetic waves that forced humans to give up electricity in Fredric Brown's "The Waveries."

In general, the further your speculations go from the kinds of science found in standard books and software packages, the more you must be prepared to take one of two courses: *Research* or *obfuscate*. Scientific journals will often suggest such ideas and give you enough detail to pursue their implications, though doing that may still require you to do esoteric calculations of your own. This is surely to be preferred if you're up to it, since it gives an added layer of resonance and "critic-proofing" to your story. If you're unable or unwilling to do that, you may still be able to tell such a story well enough to satisfy at least some readers by being artfully vague, giving as few numerical details as possible to minimize opportunity for readers to catch you in errors. This is still risky, though. If the science you're trying to use is reasonably well established and you don't understand it, your imaginings may be not only quantitatively, but qualitatively—and perhaps grossly—wrong.

BEYOND KNOWN SCIENCE

As some of the last examples may suggest, the category of stories based on far-out but real science merges gradually into another: stories based in part on new, or invented, science. Please note that this is not automatically the same as wrong science. Faster-than-light travel in which an object can be accelerated to any desired speed simply by giving it the amount of kinetic energy calculated from Newton's equations (the dotted line in figure 11-1) is wrong science. We know it doesn't work that way because even at speeds well below that of light, we have experimental data showing that as you go faster and faster, you need more and more energy to produce even a little additional speed, as described by Einstein's theory of relativity (the solid line in figure 11-1). The fact that the curve becomes ever steeper as the speed approaches that of light, never quite reaching it, is commonly taken as proof that material objects can never reach or exceed the speed of light.

However, there's an important assumption hidden in that proof. It assumes that the relativistic equation defining the solid curve in figure 11-1, based on experimental data for objects up to a point

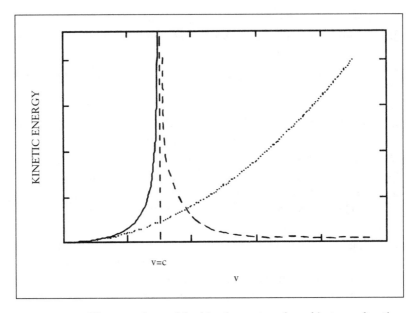

FIGURE 11-1 Three versions of the kinetic energy of an object as a function of speed: classical, relativistic and one of many possible extrapolations. Science invented for science fiction must agree with established science *in regions confirmed by experiment.*

very near the speed of light, continues to hold for all objects at all speeds. But we have no data beyond that point, and at some point beyond it the curve could go off in some quite unexpected direction. It could, for example, suddenly turn down, cross the apparent asymptote (limit) $v = c$, and descend sharply on the other side, as in the dashed curve in figure 11-1. This would have many profound implications, the most important of which is that you could achieve very high FTL speeds with relatively little energy, if you could find a way to jump from one side of the "kinetic barrier" to the other. An analogy with quantum mechanics (a phenomenon called "tunneling") qualitatively suggests a way that could conceivably happen, so I have felt no compunction about using variations on this type of FTL in several stories (including *The Sins of the Fathers* and *Lifeboat Earth*).

Present knowledge provides no reason to believe that the world will turn out to work that way—but neither does it provide any rigorous proof that it can't. I use a "negative impossibility" criterion—anything that can't be rigorously proved impossible with present knowledge is fair game for science fiction.

That does not mean you can ignore present knowledge. The general rule you must keep in mind is what physicists sometimes call the *correspondence principle*: Any new theory must give the same answers as the old *in regions of experience where the old theory has been confirmed by experiment.* Thus, for example, in figure 11-1, the dotted classical curve is indistinguishable from the solid relativistic curve for speeds well below c, and the relativistic curve is indistinguishable from the science-fictional one up to some speed very slightly below c.

How likely is it that future research will turn up such surprises? We have no way of knowing—but we do know that it has happened repeatedly in the past. We have no reason to assume we've had our last major surprises. Relativity and quantum mechanics are two examples of major revisions in physics in this century alone; plate tectonics and the genetic code of DNA are comparable examples from geology and biology.

Remember the correspondence principle—Einstein didn't prove Newton wrong, but merely too limited. Classical physics is a special case of relativistic physics. However, a radically new theory is likely to be understood in terms of a radically new model of how the universe is built. The relativistic picture of the universe is quite different from the classical, and if the dashed curve of figure 11-1 turned out to be right, we would probably need a new model, as different from the current relativistic one as that is from the classical.

This could happen in different ways. In Jeffery D. Kooistra's "Sunshine, Genius, and Rust" and "Young Again," a brilliant theoretical physicist named Dykstra constructs a new theory with testable implications that greatly extend the scope of practical physics. In my *Lifeboat Earth* series, practice came first. Experimentalists stumbled onto ways of doing things that couldn't be predicted by old theories, and the struggle of theorists to formulate a new model to explain them became part of the story background.

Many science-fictional speculations can be thought of as belonging to one of two broad categories. *Extrapolation* means new consequences of well-established science, such as a new way of getting a payload to orbit cheaply or a possible ecosystem based on a known set of chemical reactions working together in a way no one has thought of before. *Innovation* means postulating a brand new scientific principle or kind of science, such as Dykstra physics or the quasimaterials in my *Newton and the Quasi-Apple*. Since past science and technology have involved both kinds of advances, and will probably continue to do so in the future, science fiction should include both as well. Not necessarily in the same story; but for imagining how the future might be, it is important to imagine both new consequences of what we already know, and what sorts of surprises we might have to deal with.

One special case, not clearly either extrapolation or innovation, is the broad area of parapsychological ("psi") phenomena such as telepathy, telekinesis and clairvoyance. Present theory provides little or no basis for understanding them, and their very existence or possibility is controversial. Some scientists think there is enough anecdotal and experimental evidence for their existence to warrant, at least, serious research. Others dismiss them as pure folklore, reject the laboratory results obtained so far, and deny that there's anything there to study.

For science-fictional purposes, I'd say psi effects can meet my "negative impossibility" test and be used legitimately in science fiction, provided that you work out a consistent set of assumptions about how they operate, and don't contradict scientific knowledge that is firmly established. An effective science-fictional use of psi abilities by aliens can be found in the dragons in Anne McCaffrey's *Dragonflight*. However, I should caution you that the psi area was heavily overworked in past years. Readers now tend to be a bit tired of it and resistant to new variations on the theme—unless you can be *very* original and convincing.

CONCLUSION

Early in this book I mentioned that there's something extra special about a story that's not only fantastic but possible. In general, a reader will be more easily convinced of a story's possibility if it's based on something already known than if it depends on something that could be but has not yet shown any evidence of itself. So if you can achieve what you need with known science, it's usually best to do so. There will be times when that isn't possible, and you have to resort to invented science. In *The Sins of the Fathers*, I didn't have to invent galactic core explosions; they'd been observed many times, and a possible mechanism for them had been suggested that

I could use in my story. However, faster-than-light travel was the only way we could have either advance knowledge or any chance of escape—so I had to use it. To use it effectively, I had to decide on a specific model for it, and work within the logical implications of that model—which, as it happened, suggested important parts of the story.

Sometimes you really need new science, and a science fiction that never used any would be incomplete and wrong. But introduce it only when you've found no more conservative way to do what you want—and bear in mind that even the conservative possibilities are more than you think. I've thrown out a number of free story ideas throughout this book, and it's easy to think of more. For example, in chapter five, I described two general types of "intelligence"; can you imagine a third? What would a burrowing civilization be like—say, if prairie dogs inherited the Earth? You've undoubtedly had the experience of being in a stimulating conversation and hearing something that suggested three other lines you'd like to pursue. Being human, you had to pick one; can you imagine a kind of alien that wouldn't have to pick, but could carry on "branching conversations"?

Writing about aliens can be fun, rewarding and challenging. Perhaps the biggest challenge is to make your aliens really *alien* yet also "real" and believable. A good starting point for anyone wanting to do that is to learn all you can about what exists on this planet, be it geology or biology or culture or language—and then go beyond it. That will do at least two things for you. It will stretch your mental horizons, perhaps far enough to ensure that your novelties aren't hopelessly unimaginative even compared to present reality. And it will very likely suggest many ideas that could lead to good stories.

Take one or more of those ideas and pursue their implications as far as you can, using real science insofar as possible and invented science when you must. Get to know your aliens and their world, watch what they do, and then tell their story. With a little luck and a respectable amount of work, you may come up with something not only alien, but believable and memorable.

A Xenologist's Bookshelf:
References, Including
Journals and Software

The following lists include all the references cited in the text, plus some others of general use to writers about aliens. In most cases the significance of an item listed will be evident from the reference(s) to it in the text. Occasionally I will add a comment in italics.

For convenience, I've divided my listings into four broad categories: Nonfiction, Fiction, Software and Miscellaneous Resources. Nonfiction includes both books and articles, alphabetized according to the first author's last name. In most cases I've listed the original publisher, but many books and stories have been reissued many times, sometimes by different publishers; so if you can't find the version listed here, check anthology indexes and *Books in Print*. I have not personally tested all the software listed, but all has been reported to me as useful by people whose opinions I value. "Miscellaneous Resources" includes everything that doesn't fit in the other categories, such as journals and conferences.

Since many items are mentioned in more than one chapter, I've used a single alphabetical listing for the entire book rather than separate listings for the individual chapters. I've also used some well-known short forms of long names, such as *Analog* for *Analog Science Fiction and Fact*.

A library is a good place to start looking for any of the references; but some may be hard to find. Many cities have bookstores specializing in used books and magazines. *Analog* (1540 Broadway, New York, NY 10036) can supply a list of dealers in used science fiction books and magazines if you send a stamped, self-addressed, legal-size envelope with your request.

NONFICTION

Anderson, Poul. "The Creation of Imaginary Worlds," in Reginald Bretnor
(ed.), *Science Fiction, Today and Tomorrow*.

————. "How to Build a Planet," *The S.F.W.A. Handbook,* 1976.

————. *Is There Life On Other Worlds?.* New York: Collier, 1963.

Angier, Natalie. "Cotton-Top Tamarins: Cooperative, Pacifist and Close to Extinct," *New York Times,* September 13, 1994.

Arnold, Roger and Donald Kingsbury. "The Spaceport," *Analog,* November and December 1979.

Asimov, Isaac. "Planets Have an Air About Them," *Astounding,* March 1957.

Ballard, Robert D. and J. Frederick Grassle. "Incredible World of the Deep-Sea Oases," *National Geographic,* November 1979.

Barlowe, Wayne Douglas, Beth Meacham, and Ian Summers. *Barlowe's Guide to Extraterrestrials.* New York: Workman, 1979. (*A good source of capsule descriptions, pictures and references to fiction containing memorable aliens. A good illustrative companion to this book in general and chapter five in particular.*)

Barnes, John. "How to Build a Future," *Analog,* March 1990.

Benedict, Ruth. *Patterns of Culture.* Boston: Houghton Mifflin, 1934; Mentor, 1959.

Bickerton, Derek. "Creole Languages," *Scientific American,* July 1983.

Bretnor, Reginald, (ed.). *The Craft of Science Fiction.* New York: Harper & Row, 1976.

————. (ed.), *Science Fiction, Today and Tomorrow.* New York: Harper & Row, 1974.

Brin, David. "Xenology: The New Science of Asking, 'Who's Out There?'," *Analog,* May 1983.

————. "Just How Dangerous Is the Galaxy?," *Analog,* July 1985.

Bronowski, J. *The Ascent of Man.* New York: Little, Brown & Co., 1973.

Clement, Hal. "The Creation of Imaginary Beings," in Reginald Bretnor (ed.), *Science Fiction, Today and Tomorrow.* New York: Harper & Row, 1974.

————. "Whirligig World," *Astounding,* June 1953.

Cramer, John G. "More About Wormholes—To the Stars in No Time [The Alternate View]," *Analog,* May 1990.

————. "The Quantum Physics of Teleportation [The Alternate View]," *Analog,* December 1993.

————. "Wormholes and Time Machines [The Alternate View]," *Analog,* June 1989.

Cuellar, O. "Animal Parthenogenesis," *Science,* August 26, 1977.

de Camp, L. Sprague. "The Ape-Man Within Us," *Analog,* June 1989.

————. "Design for Life," *Astounding,* May and June 1939.

————. "There Ain't No Such!," *Astounding,* November and December 1939. (*An interesting survey of the wide range of animals that can exist under Earthly conditions.*)

Diamond, Jared. "Zebras and the Anna Karenina Principle," *Natural History*, September 1994.

Dole, Stephen H. *Habitable Planets for Man (2nd Edition)*. New York: American Elsevier, 1970.

Donaldson, Thomas. "The Holes of Space-Time," *Analog*, July 1993.

Drexler, K. Eric. *Engines of Creation*. New York: Anchor Press/Doubleday, 1986. (*For a shorter introduction, see Peterson and Drexler, below.*)

Eulach, V.A. "Those Impossible Autotrophic Men," *Astounding*, October 1956.

Fogg, Martyn J. "On Beanpoles and Drum-Men," *Analog*, December 13, 1988.

Forward, Robert L., Dr. "Faster Than Light," *Analog*, March 1995.

————. "A Taste of Dragon's Egg," *Analog*, April 1980.

Fromkin, Victoria and Robert Rodman. *An Introduction to Language (2nd Edition)*. Austin: Holt, Rinehart and Winston, 1978.

Gazzaniga, M.S. "The Split Brain in Man," *Scientific American*, August 1967.

Gillett, Stephen L., Ph.D. "Fire, Brimstone—and Maybe Life?," *Analog*, July 1990.

————. "On Building an Earthlike Planet," *Analog*, July 1989.

————. "Those Halogen Breathers," *Analog*, October 1984.

————. "Titan As the Abode of Life," *Analog*, November 1992.

————. *World-Building*. Cincinnati: Writer's Digest Books, 1995. (*Part of this series.*)

Gould, Stephen Jay. "Lucy on the Earth in Stasis," *Natural History*, September 1994.

Griffiths, Anthony J.F., et al. *An Introduction to Genetic Analysis 5th Edition*. New York: Freeman, 1993.

Grun, Bernard, and Werner Stein. *The Timetables of History*. New York: Simon and Schuster, 1982.

Hoagland, Richard C. "The Curious Case of the Humanoid Face . . . on Mars," *Analog*, November 1986.

Holmes, Eric, Dr. "The Split Brain," *Analog*, August 1974.

Jacobs, William P. "Caulerpa," *Scientific American*, December 1994.

Kepner, Terry. *Proximity Zero*. Peterborough, NH: The Bob Liddil Group, 1994. (*A handbook containing maps and the kinds of data a science fiction writer needs for all stars within forty light-years of Earth. At this writing, it could be ordered through bookstores.*)

Lesney, Mark S., Ph.D. "Cybernetic Science: The Biology of Artificial Intelligence and Artificial Life," *Analog*, December 1994.

Ley, Willy. "Botanical Invasion," *Astounding*, February 1940. (*A botanical companion to de Camp's "There Ain't No Such!"*)

MacLean, Katherine. "Alien Minds and Nonhuman Intelligences," in Reginald

Bretnor (ed.), *The Craft of Science Fiction*. New York: Harper & Row, 1976.

Mallove, Eugene F. and Gregory L. Matloff. *The Starflight Handbook*. New York: Wiley, 1989.

National Geographic Society. *The Marvels of Animal Behavior*. Washington, D.C.: National Geographic Society, 1972.

Ochoa, George and Jeffrey Osier. *The Writer's Guide to Creating a Science Fiction Universe*. Cincinnati: Writer's Digest Books, 1993.

Peterson, Chris and K. Eric Drexler. "Nanotechnology." *Analog*, Mid-December 1987.

Pournelle, Jerry. "The Construction of Believable Societies," in Reginald Bretnor (ed.), *The Craft of Science Fiction*.

Rothman, Tony and G.F.R. Ellis. "The Garden of Cosmological Delights," *Analog*, May 1985.

Sagan, Carl. *The Dragons of Eden: Speculations on the Evolution of Human Intelligence*. New York: Random House, 1977.

Sagan, Carl, et al. *Murmurs from Earth: The Voyager Record*. New York: Random House, 1978.

Salomon, Warren. "The Economics of Interstellar Commerce," *Analog*, May 1989.

Savage-Rumbaugh, Sue and Roger Lewin. *Kanzi: The Ape at the Brink of the Human Mind*. New York: Wiley, 1994.

Schmidt, Stanley. "Hypertext: A Powerful New Tool for Writers," *Writer's Digest*, February 1990.

————. "Hypertext as a Writing Tool," SFWA Bulletin, Summer 1992.

————. "Interference," *Analog*, August 1994.

————. "Self-Fulfilling Prophecies," *Analog*, December 1980.

Shklovskii, I.S. and Carl Sagan. *Intelligent Life in the Universe*. Merrifield, VA: Holden-Day, 1966.

Smith, Elske V.P. and Kenneth C. Jacobs. *Introductory Astronomy and Astrophysics*. Philadelphia: Saunders, 1973.

Taylor, Edwin F. and John Archibald Wheeler. *Spacetime Physics*. New York: Freeman, 1963, 1966.

Warren, J.W. "Physiology of the Giraffe," *Scientific American*, November 1974.

Wells, H.G. *Outline of History (Revised and Updated)*. New York: Doubleday, 1971.

Zubrin, Robert M. "Nuclear Rocketry Using Indigenous Propellants: The Key to the Solar System," *Analog*, March 1990.

————. "The Magnetic Sail," *Analog*, May 1992.

Zubrin, Robert M., and David A. Baker. "Mars Direct: A Proposal for the Rapid Exploration and Colonization of the Red Planet," *Analog*, July 1991.

FICTION

Allen, Roger MacBride. "Phreak Encounter," *Analog*, May 1986.

Anderson, Kevin J. and Doug Beason. *Assemblers of Infinity*. New York: Bantam, 1993.

Anderson, Poul. *Ensign Flandry*. Radnor, PA: Chilton, 1966.

———. "Peek! I See You," *Analog*, February 1968.

———. *Fire Time*. New York: Ballantine, 1974.

———. *The People of the Wind*. New York: Signet, 1973; see also its prequel, "Wings of Victory," *Analog*, April 1972.

———. "Starfog," *Analog*, August 1967.

———. "Supernova," *Analog*, January 1967.

———. "Trader Team." *Analog*, July-August 1965.

Anthony, Piers. *Cluster*. New York: Avon, 1977.

Ash, Paul. "Big Sword," *Astounding*, October 1958.

Asimov, Isaac. *The Gods Themselves*. New York: Doubleday, 1972.

———. "Paté de Foie Gras," *Astounding*, September 1956.

Bennett, Gregory. "Tinker's Spectacles," *Analog*, June 1993.

Bohnhoff, Maya Kaathryn. "The Secret Life of Gods," *Analog*, September 1995.

Brejcha, F. Alexander. "Looking Through the Personals," *Analog*, October 1994.

———. "With Other Eyes," *Analog*, November 1995.

Brin, David. "The Crystal Spheres," *Analog*, January 1984.

———. "Uplift" novels, including *Sundiver* (New York: Bantam, 1980), *Startide Rising* (New York: Bantam, 1983), and *The Uplift War* (West Bloomfield, MI: Phantasia Press, 1987).

Brown, Fredric. "The Waveries," *Astounding*, January 1945.

Buckley, Bob. "World in the Clouds," *Analog*, March-May 1980.

Burns, Stephen L. "Showdown at Hell Creek," *Analog*, Mid-December 1993.

Campbell, John W., Jr. (originally under pseudonym Don A. Stuart). "Who Goes There?," *Astounding*, August 1938.

Cherryh, C.J. "Chanur" stories, including *The Pride of Chanur* (New York: DAW, 1982) and *Chanur's Venture* (West Bloomfield, MI: Phantasia Press, 1984).

Clarke, Arthur C. *Childhood's End*. New York: Ballantine, 1953.

———. "A Meeting with Medusa," *Playboy*, December 1971; also in *The Sentinel*. New York: Berkley, 1983.

———. *Rendezvous with Rama*. San Diego: Harcourt Brace, 1973.

———. "The Sentinel," in *The Sentinel*. New York: Berkley, 1983.

———. *2010: Odyssey Two*. New York: Ballantine, 1982.

Clement, Hal. *Iceworld*. New York: Gnome Press, 1953.

————. *Mission of Gravity*. New York: Doubleday, 1954.

————. *Needle*. New York: Doubleday, 1950.

————. "Uncommon Sense," *Astounding*, September 1945.

Cook, Rick and Peter L. Manly. "Symphony for Skyfall," *Analog*, July 1994.

Crichton, Michael. *The Andromeda Strain*. New York: Knopf, 1969.

Delaney, Joseph H. and Marc Stiegler. *Valentina*. Riverdale, NY: Baen, 1984.

Dickson, Gordon R. *Way of the Pilgrim*. Tacoma, WA: Ace, 1987.

Dyson, Marianne J. "The Critical Factor," *Analog*, February 1992.

Ecklar, Julia. "Noah's Ark" stories, collected as *ReGenesis*. Tacoma, WA: Ace, 1995.

Flynn, Michael F. "Eifelheim," *Analog* November 1986.

Forward, Robert L., Dr. *Dragon's Egg*. New York: Ballantine, 1980.

————. "Rocheworld," *Analog*, December 1982-February 1983; as *The Flight of the Dragonfly*. New York: Pocket Books, 1984.

Frankos, Laura. "Hoofer," *Analog*, July 1993.

Green, Joseph. *Conscience Interplanetary*. United Kingdom: Gollancz, 1972; New York: Doubleday, 1973.

Haldeman, Joe. *The Forever War*. New York: St. Martin's, 1974.

Heinlein, Robert A. *The Puppet Masters*. New York: Doubleday, 1951.

————. "Universe," *Astounding*, May 1941.

Hoyle, Fred. *The Black Cloud*. New York: Harper & Row, 1957.

Jarvis, Mark. "Collaboration," *Analog*, October 1, 1982.

Kingsbury, Donald. *Courtship Rite*. New York: Simon and Schuster, 1982.

————. *The Moon Goddess and the Sun*. Riverdale, NY: Baen, 1986.

Knight, Damon. "Rule Golden," in *Rule Golden and Other Stories*. New York: Avon, 1979.

Kooistra, Jeffery D. "Sunshine, Genius, and Rust," *Analog*, May 1993.

————. "Young Again," *Analog*, December 1993.

Laumer, Keith. *Retief's War*. New York: Doubleday, 1966.

Le Guin, Ursula K. *The Dispossessed*. New York: HarperCollins, 1974.

————. *The Left Hand of Darkness*. Tacoma, WA: Ace, 1969.

Leinster, Murray (Will F. Jenkins). "First Contact," *Astounding*, May 1945.

Longyear, Barry B. "Enemy Mine," *Asimov's*, September 1979.

McCaffrey, Anne. *Dragonflight*. New York: Ballantine, 1968.

McDowell, Emmett. "Veiled Island," *Astounding*, January 1946.

MacLean, Katherine. "Unhuman Sacrifice," *Astounding*, November 1958.

Neville, Kris. "Bettyann," in Anthony J. Healey (ed.) *New Tales of Space and Time*. New York: Henry Holt, 1951; novel *Bettyann*. Belmont, CA: Belmont, 1970.

Niven, Larry. "Neutron Star," *If*, October 1966; also in collection *Neutron Star*.

New York: Ballantine, 1968.

———. *Ringworld*. New York: Ballantine, 1970.

Nordley, G. David. "Trimus" stories, including "Poles Apart" (*Analog*, Mid-December 1992), "Network" (February 1994), and "Final Review" (July 1995).

Oliver, Chad. "Transfusion," *Astounding*, June 1959.

Oltion, Jerry and Lee Goodloe. "Contact," *Analog*, November 1991.

Piper, H. Beam. "Omnilingual," *Astounding*, February 1957.

Reynolds, Ted. "Can These Bones Live?," *Analog*, March 1979.

Rich, Mark. "Across the Sky," *Analog*, June 1994.

Rollins, Grey. "Victor" stories, including "To Victor Go the Spoils" (*Analog*, June 1990), "Victor Victorious" (December 1990), and "The Victor" (January 1991).

Saberhagen, Fred. "Berserker" stories, including *Berserker* (New York: Ballantine, 1967), *The Ultimate Enemy* (Tacoma, WA: Ace, 1979), and *Earth Descended* (New York: Tor, 1982).

Sakers, Don. "The Leaves of October," *Analog*, August 1983; as *The Leaves of October*. Riverdale, NY: Baen, 1988.

Schmidt, Stanley. " . . . And Comfort to the Enemy," *Analog*, July 1969.

———. *Lifeboat Earth*. New York: Berkley, 1978.

———. *Newton and the Quasi-Apple*. New York: Doubleday, 1975.

———. "Pinocchio," *Analog*, September 1977; also in *Lifeboat Earth*.

———. "The Prophet," *Analog*, April 1972.

———. *The Sins of the Fathers*. New York: Berkley, 1976.

———. *Tweedlioop*. New York: Tor, 1986.

———. "War of Independence," *Asimov's*, August 1982.

Shwartz, Susan. *Heritage of Flight*. New York: Tor, 1989.

Simak, Clifford D. "A Death in the House," *Galaxy*, October 1959.

———. *The Visitors*. New York: Ballantine 1980.

———. *Way Station*. New York: Doubleday, 1963.

Slonczewski, Joan. "Microbe," *Analog*, August 1995.

———. *Still Forms on Foxfield*. New York: Ballantine, 1980.

Stiegler, Marc. "Petals of Rose," *Analog*, November 9, 1981.

Strock, Ian Randal. "The Ears Have It," *Analog*, December 1993.

Tellure, Allison. "Skysinger" stories, including "Lord of All It Surveys" (*Analog*, June 1977), "Skysinger" (August 1977), and "Green-Eyed Lady, Laughing Lady" (March 1, 1982).

Thompson, W.R. "Kya" stories, including "Maverick" (*Analog*, December 1989)), "Varmint" (Mid-December 1989), "Outlaw" (September-October 1990), "Lost in Translation" (Mid-December 1990), "Desperado" (March

1992), "On Tour With Gyez" (October 1993), "Touchdown, Touchdown, Rah, Rah, Rah!" (September 1995).

Turtledove, Harry. (as Eric G. Iverson), "Bluff," *Analog*, February 1985.

————. "sim" stories, collected in *A Different Flesh*. Chicago: Congdon and Weed 1988, Riverdale, NY: Baen 1984.

Vance, Jack. *Big Planet*. New York: Avalon, 1957.

van Vogt, A.E. "Cooperate—or Else!," *Astounding*, April 1942.

————. "Vault of the Beast," *Astounding*, August 1940.

Vinge, Vernor. *Marooned in Realtime*. New York: Bluejay, 1986.

Vinicoff, Eric and Marcia Martin. "The Weigher," *Analog*, October 1984.

Weinbaum, Stanley G. "The Lotus Eaters," *Astounding*, April 1935.

————. "A Martian Odyssey," *Wonder Stories*, July 1934.

————. "Parasite Planet," *Astounding*, February 1935.

Wells, H.G. *The War of the Worlds*. New York: Harper & Row, 1898.

Zahn, Timothy. "Space Horse" stories, including "Unitive Factor" (*Analog*, May 1982) and "Bête Noire" (March 1984).

SOFTWARE

Computer hardware and software change so fast that I can merely hint at the possibilities by describing a couple of programs that science fiction writers have found useful and directing you to some sources of such things.

PCSPACE, recommended to me by Robert R. Chase, enables you to "see" the night sky from any of 1,200 stars in its database. It's available from Andromeda Software, Inc. (P.O. Box 605, Amherst, NY 14226-0605), which also carries a large variety of scientific, astronomical and graphics software for IBM and compatibles.

Writer Daniel Hatch has developed his own program to "create planets from the protostellar nebula up, a whole solar system at a time." It's written in GWBASIC and can be run on IBM and compatible computers, and comes with an article explaining how it works and how to use it. You can get a copy direct from the author by sending $10 to Daniel Hatch, P.O. Box 3315, Enfield, CT 06083.

The Astronomical Society of the Pacific (a nonprofit organization) periodically issues an updated list of astronomical software for computers of various makes, with a directory of vendors. According to my latest information, which I hope will still be correct when you read this, you can get a catalog by sending your name and address with two first-class stamps to A.S.P., Dept. CSP, 390 Ashton Ave., San Francisco, CA 94112.

MISCELLANEOUS RESOURCES

Since all sciences change rapidly and good science fiction depends on up-to-date information, books aren't enough. The following journals are all good sources of reports on recent developments, and may well also suggest story ideas: *National Geographic, Natural History, Nature, The New Scientist, Science, Science News* and *Scientific American.*

Each October's issue of *Scientific American* is devoted to an in-depth examination of a broad theme by several authors prominent in their fields. The October, 1994 issue, on "Life in the Universe," is of special interest to readers of this book.

The "Science Times" section in Tuesday editions of the *New York Times*, is a good source of preliminary information on very recent developments in many fields.

Many science fiction conventions include panels and workshops on creating worlds and aliens. A particularly good series of conferences devoted entirely to this subject has been conducted by the nonprofit organization CONTACT. For information write to CONTACT, Box 506, Capitola, CA 95010 (or e-mail <terrel@cruzio. com>.).

A GLOSSARY OF SELECTED TERMS

This book uses many specialized terms from a variety of fields. Some of them occur only once or twice and are defined when they're introduced; so if you don't find a word or phrase here, try the index. This glossary is intended to provide a ready reference for a few terms of special importance and frequent occurrence. Some of its definitions are of necessity approximate and not fully rigorous, so if you need to know *exactly* what a term means and how to work with it, you should consult a text in the appropriate field to acquire the necessary background.

One general observation on word use within this book: a number of terms, such as "Solar System," "Sun" and "Moon," can apply either to *our* Solar System and its components, or to their analogs in any other system of a star and its accompanying planets. To minimize confusion, I have tried to spell these words with capitals when they apply to our specific examples, and lowercase when the use is general. Thus, for example, "Sun" refers to our Sun, while "sun" means any star in its capacity as the source of heat and light for planets orbiting it. "Moon" is Earth's natural satellite, while "moon" means any satellite of any other planet (including those in our Solar System).

amino acid: Any of a large class of nitrogen-containing acids that are important constituents of organisms.

angular momentum: A property of rotating objects or systems, important because it is conserved (remains constant) when the system is not acted on by external forces (or, more precisely, torques). For a point mass m revolving at speed v in a circle of radius r, angular momentum = mvr. A more complicated system can be viewed as a collection of such masses and its total angular momentum computed by adding up all the separate angular momenta; however, complete specification of angular momentum involves both a magnitude and a direction—i.e., it is a *vector*. For details, see standard physics texts.

arctic zone: That part of a planet on which the sun is sometimes above or below the horizon for a day or more at a time. Arctic zones are centered on the poles and, on planets of moderate axial tilt, tend to have the lowest temperatures occurring on the planet. However, their most important characteristic is not cold, but *large variations*, both seasonal and daily, in daylight/night ratio and weather conditions. A planet with no axial tilt has no arctic zones, by this definition; one with 90° tilt is all arctic.

astronomical unit: A convenient unit for distances within a solar system, equal to the average radius (or, more properly, the semimajor axis) of Earth's orbit.

axial tilt: The angle by which a planet's axis of rotation is tilted from the perpendicular to the plane of its orbit.

binary star (also called *double star*): A pair of stars revolving around their common center of mass.

black hole: A "hole in space" resulting from the collapse of a massive old star to a radius so small that not even light can escape its gravity.

brown dwarf: A "borderline object," or very massive planet or small and feeble star, heated by gravitational contraction and radioactive decay, but not enough to initiate thermonuclear fusion reactions.

carbohydrate: An important class of organic compounds including sugars and starches, made up of carbon, hydrogen and oxygen.

cell: A more or less self-contained, usually microscopic unit that is the basic building block of organisms, at least on Earth—i.e., each organism consists of one cell or an association of many.

center of mass: For astronomical purposes, the point about which the members of a system revolving under their mutual gravitational attraction revolve. For two equal masses, the C.M. is midway between them. For unequal masses, it is closer to the larger mass. If one mass is *much* larger than the other, as in the case of the Sun and Earth, the common C.M. is so close to the center of the larger mass that the smaller is often said, with approximate truth, to revolve around the larger.

centrifugal force: The apparent outward force felt by a revolving object. "Actually," i.e., from the viewpoint of an outside observer, centrifugal force is an illusion caused by the tendency of any object to continue traveling in a straight line—which, for a revolving object, means fly off on a tangent—unless acted on by a force.

centripetal force: The force toward the center that must be applied to a moving object to bend its path into a circle. Note that the centripetal force is not a *result* of circular motion, but its *cause.* Thus the gravitational attraction of the Sun for the Earth *is* the centripetal force that keeps it in orbit.

chromosome: One of the threadlike bodies within a cell that carries genetic information.

conservation law: A physical law stating that a particular quantity characteristic of a system remains constant no matter what internal changes the system undergoes, as long as it is not subjected to external forces. Important conserved quantities include energy, momentum and angular momentum.

convergent evolution: The independent evolution of similar forms in different but similar environments.

COTI: Acronym for Contact with Extraterrestrial Intelligence.

DNA: Deoxyribonucleic acid, the nucleic acid, structurally a double helix, in whose details genetic information is coded in all Earthly organisms.

echolocation: Locating and identifying objects by analyzing echos of sound waves directed toward them, as by bats, dolphins and human-built sonar equipment.

ecology: The interactions and relationships among organisms and between them and their environment. Also sometimes used to mean the system consisting of an environment and the interacting organisms that inhabit it, though a better term for that is *ecosystem.*

electromagnetic radiation: Waves consisting of oscillating electric and magnetic fields, including X-rays, light and radio waves. All types travel at approximately 3×10^8 m/sec in vacuum. For other information on types and characteristics, see figure 3-1.

energy: A physical quantity, roughly defined as capacity to do work, important because it is conserved (remains constant) when a system is not acted on by external forces, and because it is a fundamental requirement of all organisms. Energy can take many forms and be converted from one form to others; for a fuller discussion, see standard textbooks on physics.

escape velocity: The minimum speed that an object launched from some object (such as the surface of a planet) must have to avoid being pulled back to the object by gravity. This definition applies to an object that, once launched, continues only by its own inertia; if it carries and uses a means of propulsion, such as a continuously operating engine, the concept of escape velocity does not apply.

ethology: The study of animal behavior.

eukaryote: A cell containing internal membranes, a well-defined nucleus and chromosomes, and other internal structures; characteristic of most Earthly organisms, including all multicellular forms.

evolution: Broadly, any process of changing form, such as the successive stages of development of an individual human being or star, or the development of new species of plants or animals from old ones. It is *not* equivalent to natural selection or "survival of the fittest," and does not necessarily imply improvement.

extrapolation: Predicting a possible course of events on the basis of established theory by applying it in a region of experience where it has been well tested, or by assuming (which may or may not be true) that it will continue to act the same way in a region where it hasn't been tested.

FTL: Acronym for "faster than light."

hydrocarbon: Any of a class of compounds consisting only of carbon and hydrogen, such as methane (CH_4).

insolation: The amount of energy per unit time per unit area reaching a planet or other object from its sun.

isomers: Molecules having the same chemical formula (i.e., the same numbers of the same kinds of atoms) but different physical structures.

isotopes: Atoms of the same elements but differing in atomic mass—i.e., having the same number of protons but different numbers of neutrons in their nuclei.

jet propulsion: See *rocket propulsion.*

lipid: A class of organic compounds including fats and oils.

magnitude: A logarithmic measure of the brightness of stars or other astronomical objects. *Apparent magnitude* measures apparent brightness, which depends on both intrinsic brightness and viewing distance; *absolute magnitude* measures intrinsic brightness. For details, see the sidebar on page 21.

mass: The amount of matter in an object.

momentum: A physical quantity that is conserved in a system not acted on by external forces, such as a rocket or a pair of colliding objects. Like angular momentum, linear momentum is a *vector,* so both magnitudes and directions must be considered in determining the total momentum of a system.

mutation: A change in genetic code, leading to an inheritable change in characteristics of an organism.

nanotechnology: A kind of technology, now in its infancy, in which macroscopic objects are built up atom by atom by submicroscopic "assemblers."

nebula: A cloud of dust and gas, denser than the average interstellar medium.

neutron star: The last stage of evolution of some massive stars, in which the outer layers have been lost and the remaining core is so compressed by gravity that it consists mostly of neutrons.

nova: An explosion causing a dramatic temporary increase in the brightness of a star; not as drastic as a supernova (*q.v.*), and some stars undergo more than one nova during their lives.

nucleic acid: Any of a class of organic acids important in biochemical processes.

oxidation: The chemical process of moving electrons from an atom or molecule, making it electrically more positive; so-called because oxygen is one of the most common and important oxidizing agents (but not the only one). Since electrons moved *from* one atom or molecule are moved *to* another, a chemical reaction that involves oxidation of one substance necessarily involves reduction (*q.v.*) of another.

parasitism: A relationship between two organisms in which one lives on, and at the expense of, the other.

pheromone: A chemical released by an animal to stimulate a particular kind of behavior in other individuals of the same species.

plate tectonics: A geological theory explaining many of Earth's properties in terms of its surface consisting of several plates floating on a softer mantle and interacting frictionally at the edges.

primary: The largest and dominant member of a system of bodies moving under their mutual gravitational attraction; e.g., the Sun is the primary of the Solar System and Earth the primary of the Earth-Moon system.

prokaryote: A primitive type of cell containing no internal membranes, nucleus or well-defined chromosomes; characteristic of Earthly bacteria and blue-green algae.

protein: Any of a large class of complex combinations of amino acids, which are important constituents of all organisms on Earth.

psi phenomena: Phenomena such as telepathy, telekinesis and clairvoyance, whose existence is suggested by anecdotal evidence but not generally accepted or explained by conventional science; also called *paranormal* or *parapsychological* phenomena.

punctuated equilibrium: A kind of evolution consisting mainly of periods of relative stability, with major changes occurring rapidly and only in response to abrupt and major environmental changes.

quantum mechanics: A form of physics developed in the twentieth century in which both matter and radiation exhibit properties of both particles and waves, and many physical quantities can have only certain discrete values.

recombinant DNA: DNA made in the laboratory by combining DNA from organisms of different species.

reduction: The chemical process of moving electrons to an atom or molecule, making it electrically less positive; one common and important reducing agent is hydrogen. Since electrons moved *from* one atom or molecule are moved *to* another, a chemical reaction that involves reduction of one substance necessarily involves oxidation (*q.v.*) of another.

relativity: A theory developed by Albert Einstein and others in which the speed of light is a universal constant but measurements of space and time depend on the observer.

rocket propulsion: A type of propulsion in which a body is accelerated in one direction by ejecting mass in the opposite direction. In rocket engines, the ejected mass is produced by combustion in a closed chamber into which fuel and an oxidizing agent, both carried on board, are introduced. Jet engines are similar but obtain their oxidant en route by taking air in through the front end.

SETI: Acronym for Search for Extraterrestrial Intelligence.

sonar: Originally an acronym for Sound Navigation Ranging, referring to equipment for underwater echolocation. By extension, any kind of echolocation, whether done in water or by another medium and by machinery or organisms.

spectroscopy: Analysis of sources or absorbers of electromagnetic radiation (such as stars or planetary atmospheres) by separating the light (or other radiation) into its component wavelengths.

stereoisomers: Isomers (*q.v.*) that are mirror images of each other.

supernova: An extremely violent explosion causing the destruction of certain massive stars. The radiation produced would be a threat to life around nearby stars, but supernovae are also important as a source of heavy elements for forming new stars and planets.

surface gravity: The acceleration caused by gravity at the surface of a planet or other body. Often measured in units of *g* or *gees*, the acceleration of gravity at the surface of Earth.

symbiosis: A relationship in which two or more organisms of different types are closely associated and derive mutual benefit.

synchronous rotation: A situation in which a satellite or planet's period of rotation has a simple, stable relationship to its period of revolution around its primary. A body orbiting close to its primary tends to become locked into such a relationship as a result of tidal distortion and braking. Unless otherwise specified, the term usually means the periods of rotation and revolution are *equal*, as in the case of our Moon, which therefore always has the same side facing Earth. However, a similar type of stability can occur with the period of rotation exactly ⅔ that of revolution, as in the case of Mercury in its orbit around the Sun.

temperate zone: A band of latitudes on a planet in which the sun never rises directly overhead or remains above or below the horizon for as long as a full day. On Earth, or any planet with less than 45° tilt, the temperate zones lie between the tropics and arctic zones in each hemisphere.

terraforming: Changing conditions on a planet to resemble those on Earth; by extension, sometimes used to mean artificial modification of any planet to any desired specifications.

tidal forces: Apparent forces caused by the gravitational force on one part of a body being stronger than that on another part; named for their most familiar manifestation, the ocean tides on Earth, which are caused by the Sun and Moon pulling more strongly on the near side than on the far side.

time dilation: A relativistic effect in which travelers moving close to the speed of light experience less passage of time than their stay-at-home counterparts.

time-binding: The transmission of learned information from one generation to later generations.

tropics: That part of a planet on which the sun sometimes rises high enough to pass directly overhead. Arctic zones are centered on the equator and, on planets of moderate axial tilt, tend to have the highest temperatures occurring on the planet. However, their most important characteristic is not heat, but *lack of variation*, both seasonal and daily, in daylight/night ratio and weather conditions. A planet with no axial tilt is entirely tropical, by this definition; one with 90° tilt has no tropical zones.

virtual reality: An extremely convincing illusion of reality created by a computer.

virus: A submicroscopic infective agent variously regarded as the smallest and most primitive kind of organism, or an extremely complicated molecule showing some but not all of the properties of life.

INDEX

More Great Books for Writers!

The Writer's Ultimate Research Guide—Save research time and frustration with the help of this guide. Three hundred fifty-two information-packed pages will point you straight to the knowledge you need to create better, more accurate fiction and nonfiction. Hundreds of listings of books and databases reveal how current the information is, what the content and organization is like and much more! *#10447/$19.99/352 pages*

The Fiction Dictionary—The essential guide to the inside language of fiction. You'll discover genres you've never explored, writing devices you'll want to attempt, fresh characters to populate your stories. *The Fiction Dictionary* dusts off the traditional concept of "dictionary" by giving full, vivid descriptions, and by using lively examples from classic and contemporary fiction . . . turning an authoritative reference into a can't-put-it-down browser. *#48008/$18.99/336 pages*

Description—Discover how to use detailed description to awaken the reader's senses; advance the story using only relevant description; create original word depictions of people, animals, places, weather and much more! *#10451/$15.99/176 pages*

How to Write Like an Expert About Anything—Find out how to use new technology and traditional research methods to get the information you need, envision new markets and write proposals that sell, find and interview experts on any topic and much more! *#10449/$17.99/224 pages*

The Craft of Writing Science Fiction That Sells by Ben Bova—You'll discover how to fascinate audiences (and attract editors) with imaginative, well-told science fiction. Bova shows you how to market your ideas, submit your manuscripts and more! *#10395/$16.95/224 pages*

Voice & Style—Discover how to create character and story voices! You'll learn to write with a spellbinding narrative voice, create original character voices, write dialogue that conveys personality, control tone of voice to create mood and make the story's voices harmonize into a solid style. *#10452/$15.99/176 pages*

The Writer's Guide to Creating a Science Fiction Universe—An easy-to-read guide for writers to put the science back in science-fiction. You'll find contemporary science tailored to the needs of writers plus the "wrong science" you must avoid to be credible in this demanding market. *#10349/$18.95/336 pages*

Science Fiction Writer's Marketplace and Sourcebook—Discover how to write and sell your science fiction and fantasy! Novel excerpts, short stories and advice from pros like Orson Scott Card and Nancy Kress show you how to write a winner! Then, over 100 market listings bring you publishers hungry for your work! You'll get addresses, needs, pay rates, details on SF conventions, on-line services, organizations and more! *#10420/$19.99/464 pages*

How to Write Tales of Horror, Fantasy & Science Fiction—Explore the worlds of the weird, the fantastic and the unknown to create extraordinary speculative fiction! Masters of the craft give you their writing secrets in 27 succinct chapters. *#10245/$14.99/242 pages/paperback*

The Complete Guide to Writing Fiction—This concise guide will help you develop the skills you need to write and sell long and short fiction. You'll get a complete rundown on outlining, narrative writing details, description, pacing and action. *#10158/$18.95/312 pages*

Setting—Expert instruction on using sensual detail, vivid language and keen observation will help you create settings that provide the perfect backdrop to every story. *#10397/$14.99/176 pages*

Conflict, Action & Suspense—Discover how to grab your reader with an action-packed beginning, build the suspense throughout your story and bring it all to a fever pitch through powerful, gripping conflict. *#10396/$14.99/176 pages*

Creating Characters: How to Build Story People—Grab the empathy of your reader with characters so real they'll jump off the page. You'll discover how to make characters come alive with vibrant emotion, quirky personality traits, inspiring heroism, tragic weaknesses and other uniquely human qualities. *#10417/$14.99/192 pages/paperback*

How To Write Science Fiction and Fantasy by Orson Scott Card—You'll discover how to break into this ever-expanding market as you share in vital marketing strategies that made this author a bestseller! *#10181/$13.95/176 pages*

Writing Mysteries—Sue Grafton weaves the experience of today's top mystery authors into a mystery writing "how-to." You'll learn how to create great mystery, including making stories more taut, more immediate and more fraught with tension. *#10286/$18.99/204 pages*

1996 Novel & Short Story Writer's Market—Get the information you need to get your short stories and novels published. You'll discover listings on fiction publishers, plus original articles on fiction writing techniques; detailed subject categories to help you target appropriate publishers; and interviews with writers, publishers and editors! *#10441/$22.99/624 pages*

Writing the Modern Mystery—If you're guilty of plot, character and construction murder, let this guide show you how to write tightly crafted, salable mysteries that will appeal to today's editors and readers. *#10290/$13.99/224 pages/paperback*

Fiction Writer's Workshop—In this interactive workshop, you'll explore each aspect of the art of fiction including point of view, description, revision, voice and more. At the end of each chapter you'll find more than a dozen writing exercises to help you put what you've learned into action. *#48003/$17.99/256 pages*

38 Most Common Fiction Writing Mistakes—Take steps to diagnose and correct the 38 most common fiction writing land mines that can turn dynamite story ideas into slush pile rejects. *#10284/$12.99/118 pages*

Writing the Blockbuster Novel—Let a top-flight agent show you how to weave the essential elements of a blockbuster into your own novels with memorable characters, exotic settings, clashing conflicts and more! *#10393/$18.99/224 pages*

The Writer's Complete Crime Reference Book—Now completely revised and updated! Incredible encyclopedia of hard-to-find facts about the ways of criminals and cops, prosecutors and defenders, victims and juries—everything the crime and mystery writer needs is at your fingertips. *#10371/$19.99/304 pages*

Write Tight—Discover how to say exactly what you want with grace and power, using the right word and the right number of words. Specific instructions and helpful exercises will help you make your writing compact, concise and precise. *#10360/$16.99/192 pages*

Handbook of Short Story Writing, Volume II—Orson Scott Card, Dwight V. Swain, Kit Reed and other noted authors bring you sound advice and timeless techniques for every aspect of the writing process. *#10239/$12.99/252 pages/paperback*

Freeing Your Creativity—Discover how to escape the traps that stifle your creativity. You'll tackle techniques for banishing fears and nourishing ideas so you can get your juices flowing again. *#10430/$14.99/176 pages/paperback*

Mystery Writer's Sourcebook—This updated market guide and resource book takes the mystery out of mystery writing! You'll get in-depth market reports on 120 mystery publishers, 125 agent listings for mystery writers, and techniques from top writers and editors. Two novel excerpts and an award-winning short story are also included for your inspection with comments on why they sold! *#10455/$19.99/475 pages*

The Writer's Digest Guide to Good Writing—In one book, you'll find the best in writing instruction gleaned from the past 75 years of *Writer's Digest* magazine! Phenomonally successful authors like Vonnegut, Steinbeck, Oates, Michener and over a dozen others share their secrets on writing techniques, idea generation, inspiration and getting published. *#10391/$18.99/352 pages*

A Beginner's Guide to Getting Published—This comprehensive collection of articles will calm your worries, energize your work and help you get published! You'll find in-depth, expertly written articles on idea generation, breaking into the business, moving up the ladder and much more! *#10418/$16.99/208 pages*

The Writer's Digest Guide to Manuscript Formats—No matter how good your ideas, an unprofessional format will land your manuscript on the slush pile! You need this easy-to-follow guide on manuscript preparation and presentation—for everything from books and articles to poems and plays. *#10025/$19.99/200 pages*
